1,000,000 Books

are available to read at

Forgotten Books

www.ForgottenBooks.com

Read online
Download PDF
Purchase in print

ISBN 978-1-330-64996-1
PIBN 10087424

This book is a reproduction of an important historical work. Forgotten Books uses state-of-the-art technology to digitally reconstruct the work, preserving the original format whilst repairing imperfections present in the aged copy. In rare cases, an imperfection in the original, such as a blemish or missing page, may be replicated in our edition. We do, however, repair the vast majority of imperfections successfully; any imperfections that remain are intentionally left to preserve the state of such historical works.

Forgotten Books is a registered trademark of FB &c Ltd.
Copyright © 2018 FB &c Ltd.
FB &c Ltd, Dalton House, 60 Windsor Avenue, London, SW19 2RR.
Company number 08720141. Registered in England and Wales.

For support please visit www.forgottenbooks.com

1 MONTH OF FREE READING

at

www.ForgottenBooks.com

By purchasing this book you are eligible for one month membership to ForgottenBooks.com, giving you unlimited access to our entire collection of over 1,000,000 titles via our web site and mobile apps.

To claim your free month visit:
www.forgottenbooks.com/free87424

* Offer is valid for 45 days from date of purchase. Terms and conditions apply.

English
Français
Deutsche
Italiano
Español
Português

www.forgottenbooks.com

Mythology Photography **Fiction** Fishing Christianity **Art** Cooking Essays Buddhism Freemasonry Medicine **Biology** Music **Ancient Egypt** Evolution Carpentry Physics Dance Geology **Mathematics** Fitness Shakespeare **Folklore** Yoga Marketing **Confidence** Immortality Biographies Poetry **Psychology** Witchcraft Electronics Chemistry History **Law** Accounting **Philosophy** Anthropology Alchemy Drama Quantum Mechanics Atheism Sexual Health **Ancient History** **Entrepreneurship** Languages Sport Paleontology Needlework Islam **Metaphysics** Investment Archaeology Parenting Statistics Criminology **Motivational**

THE WORKS OF TACITUS.

WITH

POLITICAL DISCOURSES

UPON THAT

AUTHOR,

By THOMAS GORDON, Esq;

The FOURTH EDITION corrected

VOL. II.

LONDON:
Printed for J. and F. RIVINGTON, L. DAVIS, L. HAWES, W. CLARK and R. COLLINS, W. JOHNSTON, T. LONGMAN, T. CADELL, J. DODSLEY, and RICHARDSON and RICHARDSON.
M.DCC.LXX.

THE

CLUB.

WITH

MORAL DISCOURSES

UPON THAT

TEXT.

BY

THOMAS GORDON, Esq;

LONDON:

MDCCLXX.

THE ANNALS OF TACITUS.

BOOK XI.

The SUMMARY.

The condemnation and death of Valerius Asiaticus, *by the procurement of* Messalina. *The iniquity and venality of the public Pleaders. Their fees ascertained. Civil combustions in Parthia. Secular Plays exhibited at Rome.* Claudius *adds three letters to the Alphabet. A short Dissertation concerning the origin of Letters.* Italus *established King over the Cheruscans.* Corbulo *made Commander in Lower Germany, his severe and excellent discipline.* Curtius Rufus *distinguished with the Triumphal Ornaments. The rise and story of that Roman. Of the institution of the office of Quæstor, and its variations. The Nobility of Gaul admitted to all the rights of Roman Citizens. the number of Patricians augmented.* Messalina *the Empress, her wild lewdness. She openly marries* C. Silius: *is accused to the Emperor, and her adulterers punished. Her execution how procured and effected.*

**** FOR, Messalina, implacable towards Valerius Asiaticus, one twice Consul, whom she believed to have been Poppæa's adulterer, and equally panting after his fine gardens, begun by Lucullus, but by him beautified with signal magnificence, suborned Suillus to accuse both him and her. In the plot was joined Sosibius, Tutor to Britannicus, who, under the mask of zeal, was to warn Claudius, " that mighty wealth in pri-
" vate hands was ever mischievous and threatening
" to Princes. In the assassination of Caligula, Asiati-
" cus had been the principal director, nor feared to
" avow it in a public congregation of the people,
" nor even to claim the glory of the parricide:
" hence his popularity and renown in Rome; in-
" somuch that his purpose of withdrawing and put-
" ting himself at the head of the armies, was al-
" ready a prevailing rumour through all the Pro-
" vinces; for that being born at Vienne, and sup-
" ported there by numerous and powerful families,
" all his own relations, it depended upon his plea-
" sure to excite an insurrection of his countrymen
" the Gauls." This sufficed Claudius, who, in order to seize him, instantly dispatched away Crispinus, Captain of the Prætorian guards, with a body of soldiers, as if a war had been to be crushed. He was found at Baiæ, and hurried to Rome in chains.

Neither was it indulged him to be heard by the Senate; he was privately tried in a chamber in the presence of Messalina. Suilius charged him " with
" corrupting the soldiery, as having by money and
" abominable pleasures engaged them in his inte-
" rest, and prepared them for every the most flagrant
" iniquity; with his adulterous amours with Pop-
" pæa, and with surrendering his person to unnatu-
" ral defilements." This last article overcame his patience, and breaking in upon the accusation,
" Ask

"Ask thy own sons, Suillus, said he; thy sons will satisfy thee that I am a man." As he proceeded in his defence, he forced tears even from Messalina, and in Claudius raised agitations still more powerful. But the Empress leaving the room to dry her eyes, warned Vitellius, "not to suffer the accused to escape." She herself hastened to accomplish the doom of Poppæa, by suborning persons who urged her, through the terrors of imprisonment, to a voluntary end; a catastrophe of which the Emperor was so utterly unapprized, that a few days after, as her husband Scipio was at table with him, he continued asking why he sat down without his wife? till Scipio answered, That she was no more.

Now as Claudius was deliberating about clearing Asiaticus, the hollow Vitellius wept, and recounting their ancient friendship, with the dutiful observance which they had equally paid to Antonia, the Prince's mother; then displaying the good services of Asiaticus to the Commonwealth, particularly his late exploits in Great-Britain, with other arguments which seemed proper to excite mercy; he at last proposed to grant him the free choice of his own death; a sort of clemency of which Claudius declared his approbation. There were some who exhorted him to die gently, by abstinence only; an indulgence which he rejected, but persisting in his wonted exercises, he bathed, and even supped chearfully. He said, he should with more credit have been sacrificed to the dark artifices of Tiberius, or to the fury of Caligula, than thus perish by the devices of a woman, and the prostitute lips of Vitellius; then opened his veins, but first viewed his funeral pile, and directed its removal into another place, lest the smoke should scorch the heads of the trees, and lessen their cool shade. Such was his firmness, even in the arms of death.

The Senate was thereafter summoned, and Suilius proceeded also to accuse the illustrious Roman Knights, sirnamed *Petra*. The real cause of their bane was, that for a place of assignation, they had accommodated Valerius and Poppæa with the use of their house; but to one of them a dream was objected, as if he had beheld Claudius crowned with a chaplet of the ears of corn, their beards downwards, and thence foretold a public famine. Others have related, that the chaplet he beheld was of vine-branches with white leaves, which he construed to portend the death of the Prince at the close of autumn. Whatever he dreamt, this is undoubted, that for a dream both he and his brother were sacrificed. To Crispinus was decreed the Prætorship, and a reward of thirty-seven thousand five hundred crowns, and to Sosibius five-and-twenty thousand, at the motion of Vitellius, who recommended him, as one that assisted Britannicus with good instructions, and Claudius with wholesome councils. Scipio, who was also asked his opinion, said; " Seeing I " entertain of Poppæa's misdeeds the same thoughts, " with all others, believe me to vote as all others " vote;" a delicate temperament between the affections of a husband, and the danger of provoking by his dissent her powerful enemies.

Suilius continued thenceforward an incessant and merciless accuser; and many laboured to emulate his abandoned occupation. For the Emperors, by usurping all the authority of the Magistrates, and the arbitrary dispensation of all the Laws, had opened a field for endless cruelties and depredation; nor of all the commodities of price was aught so saleable, as the faithless spirit of the pleaders; insomuch that Samius, an illustrious Roman Knight, having given Suilius a fee of ten thousand crowns, and finding himself betrayed in the cause, fell upon his sword in the house of his traiterous advocate.

A complaint of this grievance being therefore begun by Caius Silius Consul elect, whose power and overthrow I shall in its place remember, the whole Senate concurred, and demanded, that the Cincian Law might be restored to force; an old Law, which enjoined " that no man should, for pleading " a cause, accept of gift or payment."

Hence they, over whom the infamy was impending, raising a clamour against the motion; Silius, who entertained an animosity against Suillus, persisted with the more asperity, and quoted "the " examples of the ancient Orators, who had esteemed present applause and the praises of posterity, the most illustrious recompence of their eloquence. Otherwise, an accomplishment the most " dignified of all others were debased into sordid " prostitution. Nor, in truth, was the faith of " pleaders to be trusted, where the greatness of gain " was their end. Besides, if no man found his " merchandize in defending suits, there would be " fewer suits to defend; whereas, upon the pre" sent foot, enmities, accusations, mutual hate and " mutual oppressions were promoted and inflamed " to such a degree, that as an inundation of diseases " was the market of Physicians, so the contagion of " the Bar proved the revenue of the Pleaders. They " might remember Caius Asinius and Marcus Messalla, and more lately Arruntius and Eserninus, " men who arrived to the supreme dignities of the " state by a life unblemished, and an eloquence " never exposed to price." This reasoning from the Consul elect found the concurrence of the Senate, and a decree was about to pass, to subject them to the penalties of the Law against extortion; when Suillus, Cossutianus, and the rest, who apprehended not a regulation only, but even their own punishment (for their guilt was manifest) gathered round the Prince, beseeching remission for what was passed;

and after he had, by a motion of his head, signified his assent, they thus proceeded.

" Who was the man of such unbounded vanity as to presume upon an eternity of fame? The practice of pleading was intended only for the present purposes of society, a common refuge for all men, especially that none might for want of pleaders be crushed by the powerful: neither was eloquence itself acquired, or exerted without pains and expence; since they who professed it forsook their own domestic cares, to apply themselves to the business of others. Many followed the profession of war, many that of husbandry, and by both professions a livelihood was gained; and nothing was pursued by any man, but with a view to the advantages it produced. Easily might Asinius and Messalla, enriched by the event of the war between Anthony and Augustus, easily might the Esernini and Arruntii, heirs of wealthy houses, all possess a spirit above the price of pleading: but equally obvious were the examples of Publius Clodius and Caius Curio, for what immense rewards they were wont to plead. For themselves; they were mean Senators, and; as the Commonwealth enjoyed a perfect calm, only aimed at subsisting by the emoluments of peace. Nay, there were those of the commonalty, who strove to shine by the Gown and the Bar; but were the price and encouragement of studying withdrawn, the Studies themselves must perish." Considerations these far from honourable; but to Claudius they appeared of no small force. He therefore settled the utmost measure of fees at two hundred and fifty crowns, and such as exceeded were subjected to the penalties of extortion.

During the same time Mithridates, whom I have mentioned to have reigned in Armenia, and to have been brought in bonds to the tribunal of Cæsar, returned.

turned by the direction of Claudius into his Kingdom, confiding in the power and affiftance of his brother Pharafmenes King of the Iberians, who had fent him advice, " that diffentions prevailed amongft " the Parthians, and that, while the fate of their " own crown was in fufpenfe, foreign conquefts, " as things of lefs moment, muft be neglected." For the many cruelties of Gotarzes, particularly the fudden murder of his brother Artabanus, with that of his wife and fon, and thence the dread of his tyranny to the reft of the nobility, prompted them to call Bardanes to the throne, a Prince of great activity and enterprize, fo much that in two days he travelled three thoufand furlongs, then inftantly invaded, utterly terrified and furprized, and even exterminated Gotarzes. With the fame expedition he feized the neighbouring provinces, all but Seleucia, which alone difowned his fway; fo that, more tranfported with wrath againft the Seleucians, as a people who had likewife revolted from his father, than confulting his prefent intereft, he entangled himfelf in the fiege of a city encompaffed with ftrong walls, replenifhed with ftores, and a river one of its bulwarks. For Gotarzes the while, ftrengthened by forces from the Dahans and Hyrcanians, renewed the war; fo the Bardanes being neceffitated to relinquifh the fiege, retired to the plains of Bactria, and there encamped.

In this combuftion and difunion of the powers in the Eaft, and uncertainty how the fame would terminate, an occafion of poffeffing Armenia was adminiftered to Mithridates, affifted by the Roman foldiers, who demolifhed the ftrong holds, and by the Iberians, who over-ran and wafted the country. For the Armenians made no longer refiftance, after the fate of Demonax their Governor, who had ventured a battle, and was defeated; only fome of the Nobles countenanced Cotys, King of

Armenia the Lefs, who thence became a fhort obftacle, but by letters from the Emperor was awed into acquiefcence. Hence the whole devolved upon Mithridates, who fell however into meafures more violent than befitted a Prince newly eftablifhed. As to the Parthian competitors; in the heat of their preparations for a battle, they all on a fudden ftruck a league, alarmed as they were by a confpiracy of the Parthians againft both, but firft difcovered to Gotarzes, and by him to his brother Bardanes. In the beginning of their interview they were fhy and diffident, at laft ventured to join hands, then fwore upon the altar of the Gods to revenge the treafon of their mutual enemies, and even to refign to each other. But, as Barbanes was held more worthy to retain the Monarchy, Gotarzes, in order to remove with himfelf all ground of jealoufy, retired far into Hyrcania. To Bardanes, upon his return, Seleucia was furrendered in the feventh year of its fiege; fo long had that fingle city fuftained its independency, and baffled the power of Parthia, to the fignal difgrace of the Parthian Monarchy.

He next took poffeffion of the moft potent provinces, and had recovered Armenia, but that Vibius Marfus, Lieutenant of Syria, reftrained him, by threatening him with war. In the mean time, Gotarzes, regretting his conceffion of the Kingdom, and again recalled by the nobility, whofe bondage is ever moft rigorous during peace, formed an army, and was met as far as the river Charinda by Bardanes, who, after an obftinate fight in difputing the paffages, remained conqueror, and thence, by a continued courfe of victories, fubdued all the nations lying between that river and the Gyndes, which parts the Dahans from the Arians. There the torrent of his conquefts was obftructed; for the Parthians, however victorious, refufed profecuting a war fo remote from home. Structures being therefore raifed as

monuments

'monuments of his grandeur and conquests, and to
'signify, that none of the Arsacides before him had
from these nations exacted tribute, he returned,
mighty, in truth, in glory, but thence the more imperious and insupportable to his subjects, who therefore, by guile before concerted, slew him, while, destitute of guards or apprehensions, he was only intent upon the chace, in the flower of his youth, but possessed of such high renown as few of the oldest Kings could have claimed, had he equally studied the love of his people, as he did to awe his enemies. The assassination of Bardanes begot fresh struggles amongst the Parthians, divided as they were about filling the throne. Many adhered to Gotarzes; some proposed Meherdates, the grand-son of Phrahates, and by him given in hostage to the Romans. Gotarzes prevailed, but was no sooner established, but by an abandoned course of cruelties and luxury, he forced the Parthians upon secret recourse to the Roman Emperor, soliciting for Meherdates to occupy the dominions of his ancestors.

Under the same Consuls were celebrated the Secular Games, eight hundred years after the founding of Rome, sixty-four since they had been exhibited by Augustus. The several purposes of these Princes in these games I pass over here, as already largely recounted by me in my History of the Emperor Domitian; for he too presented Secular Games, at which I assisted in person, and the more assiduously, as I was invested with the Quindecemviral Priesthood, and at that time Prætor; a circumstance which from no vain-glory I insert, but because formerly the College of fifteen presided in that festival, and the Magistrates chiefly discharged the offices of the solemnity. Whilst Claudius was beholding the Games in the Circus, and the boys of quality represented on horseback the siege of Troy, amongst them particularly Britanniens the Emperor's son, with Lucius Domitius, who was afterwards adopted into the Claudian family by the name of Nero, and succeeded to the Empire; the affections of the populace appeared more passionate for Domitius, a thing which passed then for a propitious omen, and thence furnished a common tradition, " That in " his infancy two dragons, posted like guards, were " seen about him;" a fable framed in imitation of the miraculous tales current in foreign nations. For Nero himself, a Prince who never abridged his own fame, was wont to declare, that in his chamber was never beheld but one snake only.

In truth, this partiality of the people accrued from the memory of Germanicus, from whom he was the only descendent of the male kind; and the popular commiseration towards his mother Agrippina rose in proportion to the cruel vengeance of Messalina, always her inveterate enemy, and now inflamed with fresh rage; insomuch that, if she did not just then forge crimes and suborn accusers to destroy that lady, it was owing only to a new amour which possessed her with a passion bordering upon fury. She was so vehemently enchanted with the person of Caius Silius, the most beautiful of all the Roman youth; that she obliged him to divorce his wife Junia Silana, a lady of high quality, in order to possess alone the embraces of her adulterer. Nor was Silius unapprized of this crime, nor of the doom which threatened him; but it was destruction without resource, if he withstood Messalina, and glorious rewards were to be the fruits of the compliance. There were some hopes too of blinding Claudius; so that he held the pleasantest counsel the safest, to wait future and distant consequences, and to indulge present prosperity. The Empress, far from pursuing her amour by theft and privacy, frequented his house openly with a numerous train, accompanied him incessantly abroad, loaded him with wealth, covered him with honours;

honours; and, in short, as if the fortune of the Empire had been transferred with the Emperor's wife, at the house of her adulterer were already seen the slaves, freedmen, and equipage of the Prince.

Claudius was a stranger to the disorders of his wife, and then exerting the authority of Censor. He corrected the people by severe edicts for some late instances of their licentiousness, as they had, at the representation of a dramatic piece composed by Publius Pomponius, reviled that Consular in the public Theatre, with several Ladies of illustrious quality. He was likewise the author of a Law to restrain the merciless iniquity of the Usurers, in lending money to young men, to be repaid with increase upon the death of their fathers. The springs that rise in the Simbruine Hills were by him brought to Rome; and to the Roman Alphabet he added new Letters, having learnt, that even those of Greece were not at once devised and completed.

The Ægyptians first of all others represented their sentiments by the figures of animals; and these hieroglyphics carved upon stone, the most ancient monuments of human memory, are still to be seen. That nation boast themselves " the original inventors,
" of Types, and that the Phœnicians having thence
" learnt them, they, who were mighty in commerce
" and the dominion of the seas, carried the same
" into Greece, and assumed the glory of an inven-
" tion which they themselves were taught." For the general tradition is, " that Cadmus arriving
" there in the Phœnician fleet, instructed the Greeks
" in that art, a people as yet rude and uncultivated." Some hold, that " Cecrops the Athenian, or Linus
" of Thebes, and Palamedes the Argive, who lived
" during the times of Troy, devised sixteen
" Letters; and that by others afterwards, especi-
" ally by Simonides, the rest were added." As to Italy, the Etruscans learned them of Damaratus;

the Corinthian, the native Latins of Evander the Arcadian; and the fashion of the Latin Types were the same with those of the ancient Greeks: But we too had few at first, till from time to time the rest were supplied; and now Claudius, by the example of others, added three more, which continned in use during his own reign, and were thenceforth abolished, but are to this day seen in the tables of brass on which are published the decrees of the people, and which hang in the Temples and great squares.

He next made a representation to the Senate concerning the College of Soothsayers; "that they " would not suffer the most ancient discipline of " Italy to be lost through disuse. The Common- " wealth was ever wont, during her times of cala- " mity, to have recourse to those of that science, in " order to retrieve by their counsel the sacred cere- " monies from neglect and corruption, and to cul- " tivate them thereafter with more strict observance. " Thus the nobility of Etruria, whether from their " own zeal, or by appointment of the Roman Se- " nate, had always preserved those mysteries them- " selves, and conveyed the same down to their poste- " rity; a laudable usage, but now faintly observed, " through an universal indifference for all worthy " arts, and more especially through the prevalence " of foreign superstitions. It was true, indeed, that " the Republic at present prospered, but her pro- " sperity was purely to be referred to the benignity of " the Gods; nor during prosperity ought they to " abandon those solemn rites, which in seasons of " difficulty had been ever zealously cultivated." Hence the Senate decree, " That the Pontiffs " should enquire what parts in the mystery of sooth- " saying ought to be retained and confirmed.

The same year, the Cheruscan nation had recourse to Rome for a King. The rage of their own domestic

mestic wars had swept away their principal chiefs; and of the Royal stock only one remained, who resided in the City, his name Italicus, son to Flavius the brother of Arminius, and by his mother grandson to Catumerus Prince of the Cattians. He was himself a handsome person, and in horsemanship and the exercise of arms specially trained, as well according to the manner of his own country as that of ours. The Emperor therefore furnished him with expences and guards, and exhorting him, "to assume with mag-
" nanimity his hereditary grandeur," reminded him withal " that being born at Rome, nor held as a
" hostage there, but living in the full immunity of
" a native Citizen, he was the first who went in
" that character to rule over a strange people."
His accession was indeed, at first, matter of joy to the Germans, and so much the more, for that having had no share in their civil dissensions, he acted with equal courtesy towards them all. Hence his conduct became popular and renowned, as sometimes he studied only affability and moderation, habits that could provoke none; often gave a loose to carrousals and the gratifications of wantonness, such as the Barbarians delight in. So that his name was already famous amongst the adjacent nations, and even amongst nations more remote; when they, who had borne sway in the reign of factions, taking umbrage at his prevailing power, betook themselves to the several neighbouring people, and represented to them, " That the ancient liberty of Germany
" was extirpated, and over the Germans the Roman
" yoke established. Could not, indeed, their whole
" country furnish one native Cheruscan worthy to
" sustain the Sovereignty; but at the head of their
" State they must set the offspring of Flavius, the
" offspring of a traitor, and a spy for the Romans?
" In vain was alledged his kindred to Arminius;
" since even the son of Arminius were to be dreaded

" ed in the fame ftation, if bred in a hoftile foil,
" poifoned with foreign nurture, debafed by foreign
" flavery, inured to foreign manners, and every
" thing foreign. But, for this fon of Flavius, if
" he inherited the fpirit of his father, never had
" man waged war with fiercer enmity againft his
" native country and his own houfehold Gods,
" than the father of this Italiens."

By thefe and the like ftimulations they procured and affembled numerous forces; nor was Italieus followed by fewer, as on his behalf his followers argued, " That he had by no invafion feized the
" throne, but held it by their own invitation; and
" fince in blood he excelled all others, it became
" them to try whether in bravery he would fhew
" himfelf worthy of his grandfather Catumerus.
" Nor was it any ground of fhame to the fon, that
" his father had never violated that faith towards
" the Romans, which with the approbation of the
" Germans he had fworn. But fhamelefly and
" falfly was the found of liberty urged by thofe,
" who, degenerate in their own lives, and deftruc-
" tive by their practices to the public weal, placed
" their only hopes in rending their country by
" civil difcord." The King had the zeal and acclamations of the people, and in a great battle between thefe bofts of Barbarians he acquired the victory. Thenceforward he became tranfported with his good fortune, grew imperious, and was expelled, but again reftored by the forces of the Longobards; and in thefe ftruggles he continued, as well by his fucceffes as misfortunes, to afflict the Cherufcan ftate.

About the fame time the Chaucians, engaged now in no domeftic diffenfions, and animated by the death of Sanquinius Governor of Lower Germany, made incurfions into that Province, before Corbulo arrived to fucceed him. For their leader they had
Gannafcus,

Gannafcus, of the county of the Caninefates, one who had long ferved the Romans amongft their auxiliaries, but deferted, and following the practice of piracy, infefted the neighbouring coafts, and above all terribly ravaged the coafts of Gaul, a nation whom he knew to be rich and unwarlike. But when Corbulo entered the province, where, in this his firft military command, he laid the foundation of his eminent future glory, he difpatched with great diligence the gallies down the Rhine, and the other veffels along the lakes and canals, according to their different fizes and burden. Thus, having funk the enemy's wherries, and put Gannafcus to flight, he took order firft for fettling effectually the ftate of the Province, and then reftored the ancient difcipline amongft the Legions, who were now utter ftrangers to military toils and application, and had been long employed in depredations only. Under Corbulo no man durft ftir from his rank, none, without exprefs orders, durft attack the foe; accoutred with all their arms, they were forced to keep guard and ftand centry; and whatever duties they performed, under all their arms they performed them. It is even reported, "That he punifhed a foldier with death, "for digging in the trenches without his fword, "and another for being there armed only with his "dagger." Inftances, in truth, of feverity without meafure; but whether forged or aggravated, they ftill owed their rife to the rigid fpirit of that Captain: fo that it was manifeft how inexorable in flagrant enormities he muft be, who was thought capable of fuch unrelenting afperity for offences fo fmall.

This terror, however, affected the army and the enemy different ways; by it the Romans increafed in bravery, and the ferocity of the Barbarians was abated. Hence the Frizians, who after their rebellion begun with the defeat of Lucius Apronius, had continued in hoftility, or in uncertain and faith-
lefs

less allegiance, sent us new hostages, and settled themselves in the territory assigned them by Corbulo. Over them he instituted a Senate, Magistrates, and Laws; and, to ensure their subjection, amongst them planted a garrison: he likewise dispatched proper persons to solicit the Chaucians to submission, and at the same time by guile to assail Gannascus. The snare succeeded; neither did the practice of snares towards a deserter, one who had broke his faith, debase the Roman magnanimity; yet, by his assassination, the minds of the Chaucians were enflamed, and by it Corbulo furnished them with matter of rebellion. Thus, his proceedings, though applauded by many, gave umbrage to others. " Why,. " they said, would he be wantonly exciting a peo- " ple to arms ? Upon the Commonwealth must " light all the disasters of the war; but, if success " attended him, then would such a signal Com- " mander prove terrible to the quiet of the State, " and, to a dastardly Prince, insupportable." Hence Claudius became so thoroughly bent against all further irruptions into Germany, that he ordered him to lead back all the Roman forces over the Rhine.

Corbulo was already encamping in the enemy's country, when these orders were delivered him; and though many different apprehensions at once overwhelmed his spirit, his dread of the Emperor, the scorn of the Barbarians, the derision of the Allies; yet, without uttering more than that " happy " were the Roman Captains of old," he ordered the retreat to be sounded. However, to prevent the soldiers from relapsing into a habit of idleness, he employed them in digging a Canal three-and-twenty miles long between the Meuse and the Rhine; by it to open a receptacle for the high tides, and prevent inundations. The Emperor nevertheless allowed him the decorations of Triumph, though he had denied him the prosecution of the war.

Shortly

Shortly after, the fame honour was conferred on Curtius Rufus, who, in the territory of the Mattiacians had opened fome filver mines, a fource of fmall advantage, nor of long continuance; but to the Legions it created eminent labour and damage, as they were forced to cut deep fluices, and toil under the earth at works which even in open air are hard and rigorous. The foldiers, therefore, overcome by thefe hardfhips, and perceiving that the fame drudgeries were exacted from them in feveral Provinces, wrote fecretly to the Emperor, and in the name of the Armies befought him; " that " whomfoever he intended for the Command of " the Legions, he would firft reward them with " the triumphal honours."

Concerning the original of Curtius Rufus, who by fome is reprefented as the fon of a Gladiator, I fhould be forry to publifh a falfe account, and I am alfo tender of recounting that which is true. As foon as he was grown to a man, he followed a Roman Quæftor in Africa; and at the City of Adrumetum, while he walked under the piazza, in the middle of the day, the vifion of a woman above human fize appeared before him, and accofted him with thefe words; " Thou, Rufus, art one who " fhall hereafter come into this Province with Pro- " confular authority." Infpired with hopes from this prefage, he returned to Rome, where, by the largeffes of his friends, and the vigour of his own fpirit, he gained the Quæftorfhip; and ftanding afterwards for the office of Prætor againft the feveral candidates of the Nobility, carried it by the intereft of Tiberius, who, as a fhade to the fordidnefs of his birth, gave him this encomium; " To me Curtius Rufus feems " to be defcended from himfelf." After this, always a fervile flatterer of thofe above him, arrogant to his inferiors, and perverfe to his equals, he lived to a great age, arrived to the Confular power, the honours

honours of Triumph, lastly to the Government of Africa; and, dying there, fulfilled the fatal presage.

About the same time Cneius Novius, a Roman Knight, was discovered armed with a dagger in the throng of those who were paying their court to the Prince; but, upon what motives, was no wise apparent then, nor ever afterwards learnt; for though, when rent by the rack, he at last confessed his own design, his accomplices he never disclosed; whether he would not, or had none, is uncertain. Under the same Consuls it was moved by Publius Dolabella, " that a public entertainment of Gladiators should " be yearly exhibited at the charge of such as ob- " tained the office of Quæstors." An office which in the days of our ancestors was only the price of virtue; and indeed to every Roman, if he confided in his own qualifications, it was free to sue for every Magistracy; nor was want of years held any obstruction, but that some, even in their early youth, might become Consuls and Dictators. As to the Quæstorship, it was as ancient as our Kings, as is manifest from the Law Curiata, revived by Lucius Brutus; and the power of chusing Quæstors continued in the Consuls, till the people would assume the conferring of that honour also. So that Valerius Potitus and Æmilius Mamercus, the first popular Quæstors, were created twenty-three years after the expulsion of the Tarquins, and appointed to attend the armies; upon the multiplication of business, two more were afterwards added, to officiate at Rome. After a long interval, all Italy being now tributary, and large revenues growing from the Provinces, the number was doubled. Sylla next, in order to fill the Senate, upon which he had devolved the authority of adjudging causes, created twenty; and though the Equestrian Order had since recovered the decision of suits, yet the Quæstorship continued still to be, by the rule of merit, gratuitously

touſly granted, till by this motion of Dolabella, it was expoſed, as it were, to ſale by auction.

' In the Conſulſhip of Aulus Vitellius and Lucius Vipſanius, counſels were on foot about ſupplying the vacancies of the Senate; and, as the Nobility of that part of Gaul entitled Comata, had long ſince acquired the diſtinction of Confederates and Citizens of Rome, they now ſued for a common participation of her offices and honours. Hence many and various were the reaſonings of the public upon theſe their pretenſions, and the Prince was beſet with oppolite parties and ſtruggles. He was told, " that
" Italy was not fallen ſo low, but to her own Ca-
" pital ſhe could furniſh a ſupply of Senators. Of
" old her natives only, they who were of the ſame
" blood with the Romans, ſufficed for ſuch re-
" cruits to the Roman State. Nor was there any
" pretence to condemn or amend the inſtitutions of
" the ancient Republic, a Republic which inſpired
" her Citizens with ſuch noble manners, that the
" ſpirit and actions of the old Romans were ſtill
" urged as venerable patterns of virtue and glory
" to us their poſterity.' Was is not ſufficient that
" already the Venetians and Inſubrians had invaded
" the Senate, unleſs a hoſt of foreigners too be
" introduced, like an eſtabliſhment of captivity
" and conqueſt? After this, what dignity would re-
" main to the native Nobility? What means of
" preferment to any poor Senator of Latium? By
" theſe opulent Gauls all public honours would be
" engroſſed, men whoſe fathers and fore-fathers
" were at the head of hoſtile nations, ſlaughtered
" our armies, and at Aleſia beſieged the deified
" Julius; inſtances theſe of later days; but more
" horrible to recount were the ravages of the ancient
" Gauls, who with impious hands demoliſhed the
" great Roman Altar, and defaced the Capitol.
" They might, in truth, enjoy ſtill the title of Ro-
" man

"man Citizens; but, let not the glory of the Fathers,
"let not the lustre of the Magistrates be prostituted,
"and rendered the purchase and spoil of nations."

The Emperor was little affected by these and the like allegations, but, having presently answered those who made them, summoned the Senate, and spoke thus: " The ancestors of my family, and
" the oldest of them, Attus Clausus, who, though
" a Sabine born, were at once adopted a Roman
" Citizen, and enrolled in the number of Patricians,
" furnish me with a lesson, that with parallel mea-
" sures I ought to maintain the Commonwealth,
" by transferring to ourselves all men of signal me-
" rit where-ever found. For I am not ignorant,
" that from Alba we had the Julii, from Camerium
" the Corruncani, and the Porcii from Tusculum.
" But, to avoid the detail of ancient and single
" adoptions, were not the Nobles of Etruria, the
" Nobles of Lucania, nay, those of all Italy, called
" into the body of the Senate? At last our city and
" her privileges became bounded only by the Alps;
" insomuch that, besides the admission of particu-
" lars, whole States and Nations became ingrafted
" into the Roman name. We had then solid peace
" at home, and our arms and reputation flourished
" abroad, when the nations on the other side the
" Po were presented with the rights of Citizens;
" and when, under the guise of planting, out of
" the Legions, Colonies all over the earth, and by
" incorporating with these our Colonies the most
" powerful of the Natives, we thence supported and
" renewed our own exhausted state. Do we regret
" that the Balbi were transplanted to us from Spain,
" or men equally illustrious from the Narbon Gaul;
" they whose descendents remain yet with us, nor
" yield to us in their love of this our common
" country? What proved the bane of the Spartans
" and Athenians, States so potent in arms and con-
" quest,

"quests, but that they held for aliens whomsoever
"they conquered? Much greater was the wisdom
"of Romulus our founder, a Prince who saw se-
"veral people his enemies and his citizens, in one
"and the same day. Even over us Romans fo-
"reigners have been Kings; and, to commit Ma-
"gistracies to the children of freedmen, is no in-
"novation, as many erroneously suppose, but a
"primitive practice of the old Roman people.
"But, it seems, we have had wars with the Gauls.
"What is the consequence? Have the Volscians,
"have the Equians never borne arms against us?
"It is true, our Capital has been taken by the
"Gauls; but by the Tuscans we have been forced
"to give hostages, and by the Samnites to pass
"under a gibbet. However, upon a review of all our
"wars, none will be found more quickly concluded
"than those with the Gauls; and ever since has
"ensued a peace never interrupted, and faithfully
"observed. They are linked with us in private
"manners, in civil and military accomplishments,
"and domestic alliances; and in this conjunction
"with us let them rather introduce amongst us
"their gold and abundance, than enjoy them
"without our participation. All the things, Con-
"script Fathers, which are now held most ancient
"in our State, were once new: the Plebeian Ma-
"gistrates were later than the Patricians; the
"Latin Magistrates later than the Plebeian; those
"of other nations in Italy came after the Latin:
"the present admission of the Gauls will also wax
"old; and what is this day supported by examples,
"will itself hereafter become an example."

By a Decree of the Fathers, which followed this speech, the Eduans first acquired the right of admission into the Senate; the reward this of their ancient confederacy with Rome, and as they only of all the Gauls are entitled the Brethren of the Roman people.

people. About the same time, all the ancient Senators, with such whose fathers had sustained signal offices in the State, were by Claudius assumed into the class of Patricians. For of all the families who by Romulus were named *the older Nobility*, or of those added by Lucius Brutus, and called *the younger*, there were few remaining. Even such whom Cæsar the Dictator by the Cassian Law, and such whom the Emperor Augustus by the Senian Law, had created Patricians, were now extinct. As these reformations made in the State by Claudius, in quality of Censor, were acceptable to the public, he proceeded in them with great alacrity; yet, how to degrade from the Senate those who were of infamous characters, held him some time in suspense; but, as he determined to apply rather a new and tender expedient than to pursue the rigorous example of antiquity, he warned them, "to consult their own qualifications, and "then ask leave to resign their order; a request "easily to be obtained," and then he promised, " to name them as persons removed by abdication, " at the same time that he would pronounce others " judicially expelled; that thus the credit of a " modest and voluntary resignation might soften and " hide the infamy of expulsion by the judgment of "the Censor." For these regulations, the Consul Vipsanius proposed, " that Claudius should be called " the *Father of the Senate*; for that the name of " *Father of his Country* was a common title; and " his extraordinary benefits to the Commonwealth " ought to be distinguished with no ordinary ap- " pellations:" but the Emperor thought the flattery extravagant, and checked the Consul. He then numbered the Citizens, who in that survey amounted to six millions nine hundred thousand. From this time he remained no longer a stranger to his domestic reproach, but was brought to hear and punish the abominations of his wife; whence was to
arise

arife a new paffion, and an inceftuous marriage with his niece.

Meffalina now difdaining her daily adulteries, as too eafy and common, was abandoning herfelf to the gratification of luft never before devifed; when Silius too, by a fatal intoxication, or judging that the dangers hanging over him were only to be averted by dangerous remedies, urged to her, "that all " difguifes muft now be caft off, for they were " gone too far to venture waiting for the death of " the Emperor. To none but the guiltlefs were " unblameable counfels adapted. In glaring guilt " determined intrepidity was the only refource. " They had accomplices at hand, fuch as dreaded " the fame doom; and for himfelf, he was fingle, " childlefs, ready to marry her, and to adopt Bri- " tannicus: to Meffalina fhould ftill remain her " prefent power; and certain fecurity would abide " both, if they prevented Claudius, one fo eafily " circumvented, but fo prone withal to vengeance." Thefe words were but coolly received by Meffalina, from no love to her hufband; but fhe feared that Silius, when he had gained the Sovereignty, would fcorn his old adulterefs; and the treafon, which, to avoid his prefent peril, he now recommended, would then be confidered and repaid according to its genuine value. She, however, coveted the fame of this ftrange matrimony, purely for the enormous meafure of infamy, which, to fuch as are abandoned to debauchery, is the laft improvement of voluptu- oufnefs; neither ftaid fhe longer than till Claudius went to Oftia, to affift at a facrifice there, and then celebrated her new Nuptials with all the ufual folemnities.

I am well aware how fabulous it will appear that fuch blind fecurity fhould poffefs any human heart, much more that a Conful elect fhould, in a city informed of all things, and concealing nothing,
dare

dare to marry the Emperor's wife, at a stated day, witnesses called to sign the contract, with a declaration inserted that by it children were intended; that the Emperor's wife should espouse another husband, in form, hear the solemn words of the Augurs, sacrifice solemnly to the Gods, celebrate with him in a great company the nuptial Feast, and in the presence of all exchange kisses and embraces, and pass the night in the consummation of conjugal joys. Yet I frame no fiction to excite wonder, but only relate what from the living or written testimony of our fathers I have learned.

Horror seized the Prince's family, especially those who had the chief sway, who dreaded a Revolution, and, uttering no longer their indignation in secret, they stormed aloud, " That while the Emperor's
" bedchamber was polluted by a player, high re-
" proach was in truth incurred, but dissolution no
" wife, threatened the State. At present a young
" man of the prime Nobility, in the beauty of his
" person surpassing all men, of a spirit vigorous and
" capable, and just entering upon the Consulship,
" was pursuing views much higher; nor was it any
" riddle, what such a marriage tended to produce."
It is true, when they recollected the stupidity of Claudius, his blind attachment to his wife, and the many lives sacrificed to her fury, their own apprehensions dismayed them. But again, even the passive spirit of the Emperor revived their confidence, that, if they could first possess him with the horrid blackness of her crimes, she might be dispatched, without trial; or, if she obtained to be heard, and even confessed her guilt, they might yet stop his ears, and frustrate her defence.

But first it was in agitation, whether still to dissemble her past enormities, and by secret menaces deter her from her league with Silius. This was a project proposed by the particular freedmen, by Callistus, whom in relating the affaffination of Caligula, I have already mentioned, by Narciffus, who plotted the facrifice of Appius, and by Pallas, then the reigning favourite; but a project afterwards dropped, as from alarming Meffalina they apprehended their own doom. Pallas was faint-hearted, and Calliftus, a courtier in the laft reign alfo, had experienced, that power was fupported more fecurely by wary meafures, than by daring counfels. Narciffus perfifted in his purpofe, with this difference only, that fhe fhould be by no words of his pre-acquainted with the accufation or the accufer. Thus, watching all occafions, while the Emperor lingered at Oftia, he prevailed, by gifts and promifes, with two courtezans to undertake the accufation; fince, as they were the chief miftreffes of Claudius, the freedman urged to them, " That by the fall of his wife, their " own authority would become predominant."

Calpurnia therefore (for that was her name) upon the firft offer of privacy, falling at the Emperor's feet, cried out, " That Meffalina had married " Silius," and at the fame time afked Cleopatra, who purpofely attended to atteft it, " Whether " fhe had not found it to be true?" Claudius, upon a confirmation from Cleopatra, ordered Narciffus to be called. He, when he came, begged pardon, that he had concealed her adulteries with Vectius, and thofe with Plautius; " nor meant he now, he faid,
" to urge againft her any of her adulteries, nor even
" that the Emperor fhould reclaim his palace, his
" flaves, and the other decorations of his Imperial
" fortune. Let her adulterer ftill enjoy even thefe;
" let him only break the nuptial tables, and reftore
" the Emperor his wife. Knoweft thou, Cæfar,
" that thou art in a ftate of divorce? it is what all
" men know, the people, and Senate, and foldiery,
" and, if thou makeft not difpatch, her new huf-
" band is Sovereign of Rome.

He then sent for his most trusty friends, particularly for Turranius, Superintendant of the stores, next for Lusins Geta, Captain of the Pretorian Guards, and proposed the question to them. As they vouched it to be true, all the rest contended in clamour and importunity, that he should forthwith proceed to the Camp, secure the Prætorian Cohorts, and consult his preservation before his revenge. It is certain, that Claudius was confounded with such a degree of dread, that he incessantly asked, " Whether he were yet Emperor? Whether Silius " was still a private man?" As to Messalina, she never wallowed in greater voluptuousness; as it was then the middle of Autumn, in her house she exhibited a representation of the vintage. The wine-presses were plied, the wine-vats flowed, and round them danced women begirt with skins, practising the frantic agitations of the drunken sacrificers to Bacchus. She herself, with her hair loose and flowing, held a Thyrsus and waved it, accompanied by Silius, who was crowned with ivy, his legs in buskins, and brandishing his head; and about him revelled, in wanton postures, the chanting choir of mock Priests. It is reported, that Vectius Valens, having in a frolic vaulted to the top of an exceeding high tree, was asked, what he beheld, and answered, " a storm from Ostia." Whether he in truth saw a troubled sky, or spoke at random, it proved in effect a true presage.

For it was no longer a rumour only, but messengers were hourly arriving with tidings, " That " Claudius was apprized of all, and approached, " bent upon vengeance." Messalina therefore betook herself to the Gardens of Lucullus; and Silius, to dissemble his fear, resumed the offices of the Forum. As all the rest fled different ways, the Centurions caught and bound them, some abroad, some in private places, as fast as they could discover them.

Meſſalina, however, bereft of reſources under ſuch weighty calamity, yet formed no daſtardly purpoſe, even that of meeting her huſband, and moving him by her preſence, an expedient which had often proved her protection; ſhe likewiſe ordered that Britannicus and Octavia ſhould go forth and embrace their father; and beſought Vibidia, the oldeſt Veſtal, to intercede with the chief Pontiff, and implore his mercy. She herſelf the while wandered on foot all along the City, attended only by three perſons (ſo ſuddenly had her whole train forſaken her in diſgrace) and then, in a cart employed to carry dirt from the Gardens, took the road to Oſtia, but found no ſoul to pity her, as the deformity of her abominations had prevailed over all commiſeration.

The Emperor was, notwithſtanding, poſſeſſed with no leſs affright; for he could not intirely rely on the faith of Geta, Captain of his guards; a man equally fickle to embark in deſigns honourable or baſe. Narciſſus therefore, in concert with thoſe who entertained the ſame fears and miſtruſt, aſſured the Emperor, " That there was no other expedient to " preſerve him, than the transferring the command " of his guards upon one of his freedmen, for that " day only," and offered himſelf to undertake it. And that Lucius Vitellius, and Publius Largus Cæcina, might not, upon the road to Rome, prevail with Claudius to relent, he deſired leave to ſit in the ſame coach, and took it.

There was afterwards a prevailing report, that though the Emperor was agitated different ways, and wavered in his talk, now taxing the abominations of his wife, then recalling the endearments of their marriage, and the tender age of their children, Vitellius uttered nothing but, " Oh heinous! oh " the iniquity !" Narciſſus, in truth, laboured to drive him from his equivoques, and bring him to ſome expreſs declaration, but with all his labour

gained

gained nothing: Vitellius still answered indirectly, in terms that would admit of any construction, and his example was followed by Largus Cæcina. Besides, Messalina was already in sight, and importunately cried, "that he would hear the mother of " Octavia and Britannicus!" To drown her cries, the accuser stormed aloud against Silius, and her late marriage, and delivered at the same time to Claudius a memorial, reciting all her whoredoms, thence to divert him from beholding her. Soon after, as the Emperor was entering Rome, it was attempted to present him his children by her; but Narcissus ordered them to be taken thence; he could not, however, force away Vibidia, who insisted, with much earnestness, "That Cæsar would not surrender his wife to destruction without admitting " her defence." So that Narcissus was obliged to assure her, that the Prince would hear Messalina; who should have full opportunity of clearing herself; and advised the Vestal to retire, and attend the solemnities of her Goddess.

Wonderful, during all this, was the silence of Claudius. Vitellius affected astonishment, and the freedman controuled all things. By his command, the house of the adulterer was opened, and the Emperor carried thither, where first he shewed him, in the porch, the Statue of Silius the father, though the same had been decreed to be demolished by the Senate; and, within, all the sumptuous furniture belonging to the Neros and Drusi, now the price and monuments of his wife's prostitution, and of his own disgrace. Having thus inflamed him, and worked him up to threats and fury, he led him straight to the camp, where the soldiers being already assembled, Claudius, prompted by Narcissus, made him a short speech; for the eruptions of his displeasure, however just, were restrained by shame. Hence instantly began a general and importunate

clamour

clamour for the names and doom of the criminals, and Silius was presented before the Imperial Tribunal, where, neither offering any present defence, nor endeavouring to procrastinate, he only besought a dispatch of his doom. The like passion for sudden execution also stimulated several illustrious Roman Knights. He therefore commanded Titius Proculus, given by Silius as a guard to Messalina, Vectius Valens, who confessed his guilt, and offered to discover others, Pompeius Urbicus and Saufellus Trogus, as accomplices, to be all dragged to execution. On Decius Calpurnianus too, Præfect of the watch, Sulpicius Rufus, Comptroller of the Sports, and Juncus Virgilianus, the Senator, the same pains were inflicted.

Muester only created some hesitation; he tore off his garments and cried, " That the Emperor
' might behold upon his body the impressions of
' the lash; might remember his own commands,
' obliging him to gratify Messalina without reserve.
' Others have been tempted to the iniquity by great
' presents or mighty hopes; but his offence was
' only owing to compulsion, nor would any man
' have sooner perished had Silius gained the Sove-
' reignty." These considerations affected Claudius, and greatly biassed him to mercy; but his freedmen over-ruled him; " for that after so many illustrious
' sacrifices, he would by no means think of saving
' a Player, whose crime was of that enormity, that
' it availed not whether through choice or force he
' had committed it." As small effect had the defence of Traulus Montanus; this was a youth of signal modesty and loveliness, called by the express order of Messalina to her bed, and, after one night, cast off; with such equal wantonness was her passion surfeited and inflamed! To Suilius Cesoninus, and Plautius Lateranus, their lives were granted, to the last on account of the noble exploits of his uncle;

uncle; the other was protected by his vileness, as one who, in the late abominable revel, had prostituted himself like a woman.

Messalina was the while in the Gardens of Lucullus, still striving to prolong life, and therefore composing supplications to the Prince in a strain of some hopes, and even with sallies of resentment and wrath: such were the swellings of her pride, though encompassed with the horrors of her approaching fate. In truth, had not Narcissus hastened her assassination, the doom which he had prepared for her, would have rebounded upon his own head. For Claudius, upon his return home, having well feasted upon the rarities of the season, and becoming jovial, as soon as he became warm with wine, ordered them ' to go and acquaint the miser- ' able woman,' (for this was the appellation which he is said to have used) ' that to-morrow she should " attend and plead her cause." When these words were reported, as his resentment also visibly abated, and his wonted affections were returning; besides, since the impressions of the following night, and of the conjugal chamber, were apprehended as the certain effects of delay, Narcissus ran hastily forth, and directed the Tribune and Centurions then attending upon duty, ' to dispatch the execution, for ' such was the Emperor's command." With them he sent Evodus of the freedmen, as a watch upon them to see his orders strictly fulfilled: Evodus flew in a moment to the Gardens, and found her lying along upon the earth; by her sat her mother Lepida, who, during her prosperity, had lived in no degree of unanimity with her, but, in this her deadly distress, was overcome by compassion for her, and now persuaded her; " to anticipate the execu- ' tioner; the course of her life was now finally run, ' and she was now confined to one only pursuit, of ' dying with renown." But her soul, utterly corrupted

rupted by debauchery, retained no relish of glory. She continued bewailing herself with tears and vain complaints till the soldiers forced the doors. The Tribune stood before her without opening his mouth, but the freedmen abused her unmeasurably, with all the brutal invectives of a slave.

She was then first convinced of the fate that hung over her, and, laying hold on the steel, aimed first at her throat, then at her breast, but while an irresolute spirit and a quaking hand frustrated her aim, the Tribune ran her through. Her corps was granted to her mother. Claudius was yet pursuing his good cheer, when tidings were carried to him, " That Messalina had suffered her destiny," but without the addition of particulars, whether by her own, or another hand; neither did he enquire; he even called for a bowl of wine, and proceeded in the usual gaieties of banquetting; nor did he, in truth, during the following days, manifest any symptom of detestation or joy, of resentment or sadness, nor, in short, of any human affection; unmoved by beholding the accusers of his wife exulting over her death, untouched by the sight of his children bewailing the doom of their mother. The Senate helped him to forget her, by decreeing, ' That from ' all public and private places her name should be ' razed, and her Pictures and Statues removed." To Narcissus were decreed the decorations of the Quæstorship. This, however, was but a small monument of his grandeur, seeing he had now exerted an instance of power superior to that of Pallas and Callistus, an instance just in effect, but from whence, in time, arose most pernicious consequences, as the deserved punishment of Messalina proved the source of flagrant iniquities which escaped unpunished.

C 4. THE

THE ANNALS OF TACITUS.

BOOK XII.

The SUMMARY.

Contests amongst the Freedmen about the choice of a wife for the Emperor. Agrippina, his own niece, is preferred, and the marriage decreed lawful by the Senate. L. Silanus kills himself, and why. Seneca recalled from banishment. Octavia, the daughter of Claudius, betrothed to Nero, his wife's son. Deputies from Parthia apply to Rome for Meherdates to be their King. He is vanquished in battle by Gotarzes. Mithridates tries to gain the Kingdom of Pontus, without success. He is carried in chains to Rome. Lollia, a Lady of prime quality, condemned by the artifices of Agrippina. Claudius enlarges the circuit of Rome: Who they were that did so before him. Nero is adopted by Claudius for his Son. A colony settled amongst the Ubians. The Cattians commit great ravages and depredations, but are routed. Vannius

Vannius *King of the Suevians driven from his Kingdom.* Pub. Oſtorius *his exploits in Britain: A victory gained over King* Caractacus *there.* Britannicus *the Emperor's Son, by the arts of* Agrippina, *ſlighted and poſtponed to* Nero. *All his moſt faithful domeſtics removed from him. Prodigies. Dearth of grain at Rome. War between the Armenians and Iberians: The Romans and Parthians take different parts in it.* Furius Scribonianus *doomed to exile. Puniſhment decreed againſt Ladies marrying their ſlaves. Commotions in* Judæa. Claudius *cauſes a naval battle to be repreſented upon the lake Fucinus. With what power unlimited he inveſted his Comptrollers in the provinces. An utter exemption from taxes granted to the Iſle of Coos; alſo to the City of Byzantium, a remiſſion of tribute for five years.* Lepida, *a lady of high rank, doomed to die.* Claudius *poiſoned by procurement of his wife* Agrippina. Nero *her Son aſſumes the ſovereignty.*

UPON the execution of Meſſalina diſtractions ſhook the Prince's family, as amongſt the freedmen a ſtrife aroſe, which of them ſhould chuſe a wife for Claudius, one impatient of a ſingle life, and always abandoned to the dominion of his wives. Nor were the Ladies animated by leſs emulation, whilſt they endeavoured preferably to recommend their own quality, wealth, and beauty, and each boaſted her juſt claim to imperial wedlock. The chief competition, however, lay between Lolha Paullina, daughter to Marcus Lollius a Conſular, and Julia Agrippina the daughter of Germanicus, the latter ſupported by the intereſt of Pallas, the other by that of Calliſtus. But Ælia Petina, of the Tuberonian family, had the countenance of Narciſſus. For Claudius, as he was now bent upon one, then upon another, and always led by his laſt adviſer, he called together theſe his jarring counſel-

lors,

lors, and ordered them to produce their several proposals, and defend them.

Narcissus alledged " his former marriage with " Petina, and their common daughter" (for by her he had Antonia) " that such a wife would never ex" ercise the envious spirit of a step-mother towards " Britannicus and Octavia, in blood so nearly allied " to her own children." Callistus argued, " that, " to recall her, after so long a dislike and divorce, " would be the very means to heighten her indig" nation and pride. Lollia would be a much more " eligible match, who having no issue of her own, " was void of every motive of emulation to his, " but would use these her step-children with the " tenderness of a real mother." Pallas chiefly recommended Agrippina from these considerations, That, " with her she would bring the grandson of Germa" nicus, and was herself worthy of imperial for" tune, noble in her descent, and a proper band " to unite together to posterity the Claudian family; " that she was of tried fruitfulness, and in the " prime of her age; so that by this match would " be prevented her carrying into another house the " blood and splendor of the Cæsars."

The reasonings of Pallas prevailed, enforced, as they were, by the allurements and caresses of Agrippina; who under shew of consanguinity was assiduous in her visits to her uncle, and, though hitherto as she was only preferred to others, and not yet his wife, she already exercised the power of one. For as soon as she had secured her own marriage, she was framing higher purposes, and concerting a match between Domitius, her son by Cneius Ænobarbus, and Octavia, the Emperor's daughter, a design which without iniquity could not be accomplished, because the Emperor had betrothed Octavia to Lucius Silanus; a youth of signal quality, whom Claudius had distinguished with the triumphal ornaments, and, by the popular magnificence of an entertainment of gladiators in his name, recommended to the notice and favour of the people. But nothing appeared infurmountable to the undifcerning fpirit of a Prince, who had no judgment, nor choice, nor averfion, but fuch as were infufed and managed by others.

Vitellius therefore, who forefaw into whofe hands the fovereignty was haftening, to purchafe the favour of Agrippina, became engaged in her counfels, and, under the plaufible name of Cenfor covering his own fervile falfities, began to devife crimes againft Silanus, whofe fifter Junia Silana, a young lady gay and beautiful, and not long before been the daughter-in law of Vitellius. Hence he took the fource of the accufation and wrefted to a charge of inceft the mutual affection of brother and fifter, an affection no ways inceftuous, however too free and unguarded. The Emperor liftened to the charge, as his fondnefs for bis daughter rendered him the more prone to entertain fufpicions againft his fon-in-law. Silanus, unapprized of any machinations againft him, and happening to be Prætor that year, was all on a fudden, by an edict of Vitellius, degraded from the rank of a Senator, notwithftanding that the Senate was reviewed, and the number fixed a good while before. Claudius at the fame time withdrew his alliance, and Silanus was even compelled to renounce his magiftracy; infomuch that his Prætorfhip, which of courfe expired next day, was for that day conferred upon Eprius Marcellus.

i During the confulfhip of Caius Pompeius and Quintus Veranius, the contract of marriage between Claudius and Agrippina was already afcertained by the public voice, and indeed by their own criminal commerce. They durft not, however celebrate the nuptials, as there was no inftance of an uncle's taking to wife his brother's daughter. Befides, it was evidently inceſtuous, and if that conſideration were deſpiſed, it was apprehended that ſome avenging calamity might fall upon the ſtate. Theſe fears and delays continued, till Vitellius undertook to accompliſh it by his own dexterity. He aſked the Emperor, "whether he would ſubmit to the "expreſs pleaſure of the people, and to the autho- "rity of the Senate;" Claudius anſwered, "that he "himſelf was one of the people, and could not "withſtand the voice and conſent of them all." Vitellius then deſired him to continue within the palace, and went himſelf to the Senate, where, after a ſolemn declaration, that he had ſomewhat to communicate of the higheſt importance to the commonwealth, he demanded leave to be heard before any other; then alledged, "that "the exquiſite and inceſſant labours of the Prince, "even thoſe of governing the world, called for al- "leviation and ſupport, ſuch as, relieving him from "domeſtic cares, might leave him at full leiſure "to attend the intereſt of the whole. What, in "truth, was a more worthy conſolation to the "ſpirit of a Cenſor than that of a wife, a ſharer "in his croſſes and proſperity, one in whom he "could repoſe his moſt ſecret thoughts, and the care "of his tender infants? For as to the ways of "ſenſuality and voluptuous pleaſures, he had never "followed them, but from his early youth prac- "tiſed ſtrict obedience to the laws."

After this plauſible introduction, which he found received by the Senate with mighty ſycophancy and applauſe, he again proceeded; "that ſeeing they all "with one mouth perſuaded the Prince to marry, "a Lady muſt be choſen ſignal in her deſcent, of "diſtinguiſhed fruitfulneſs, and religiouſly virtuous; "nor for theſe qualifications needed there be long "ſearch, ſince Agrippina, in the illuſtriouſneſs "of her race excelled all others, had given proofs
"of

"of her fruitfulness, and was endowed with suitable purity of manners. It was indeed a happy circumstance, that through the providence of the Gods she proved then a widow, that the Prince might take her to his bed without violating that of another, he who had ever confined himself to his own wives. They had heard from their fathers, nay, themselves had seen, that Ladies were ravished from their husbands, at the lust and command of the Cæsars; a proceeding far from the moderate spirit of the present government, when the Emperor even established a precedent by what authority Princes ought hereafter to marry: But, amongst us, it seemed an innovation to marry our brother's daughters, which yet is a usage frequent in other nations, nor by any law forbidden to ours: The intermarriage of Cousin-germans was a practice long unknown, yet in time waxed frequent. Customs were to be suited to exigencies, and this very novelty was one of those things which would soon be followed and practised."

There were several Senators who declared with contending zeal, "that if the Emperor lingered longer, they would compel him," and rushed warmly out of the Senate. The mixed multitude were likewise assembled, and proclaimed with shouts, "that the same was the voice and demand of the Roman people." Nor did Claudius delay any further, but proceeded to the Forum, there to receive in person their acclamations, and thence entering the Senate, required "a decree to legitimate for ever the marriages between uncles and their brothers daughters." But notwithstanding the law, no man was found addicted to this kind of alliance, except Titus Alledius Severus, a Roman Knight, and he only, as many believed, in court to Agrippina. From this moment, the

the city assumed a different face, and all men tamely obeying a woman, one who did not, like Messalina, render the Roman State subservient only to her wantonness and amours, but over it established a complete and masculine bondage. Her carriage in public was severe, often haughty; at home she indulged no impurity, unless where the same served the purposes of her sway; and for a guise to her insatiate passion for money, she pretended the support of the sovereignty.

On the day of the nuptials Silanus slew himself; whether he had thus long entertained hopes of life, or invidiously chose that day to accumulate public hate upon his persecutors. His sister Calvina was banished Italy, and to her sentence Claudius added an injunction to the Pontiffs, ' that, accor-
' ding to the institution of King Tullus, they should
' offer expiatory sacrifices at the grove of Diana;" a source of mockery to all men, that penalties and lustrations for incest should be devised at such a conjuncture, when incest was established by law. For Agrippina, that she might not be distinguished and notorious only for the blackness of her deed, she obtained for Annæus Seneca a revocation from exile, and with it the Prætorship; favours which she supposed would prove well pleasing to the public, on account of his signal eloquence and accomplishments; besides her views to the education of her son Domitius under such a master, and to the use of his counsels for acquiring him the Empire. For Seneca, she believed, would continue faithfully attached to her from ties of gratitude, and in secret enmity to Claudius, through resentments of his sufferings.

It was now thought expedient to proceed without further delay, and Memmius Pollio, Consul elect, was gained, by vast promises, to move the Senate, that Claudius might be besought " to
" betroth

" betroth Octavia to Domitius," a match not unsuitable, indeed, to the equality of their ages, but introductory to the highest views. Pollio moved it much in the same words with those lately used by Vitellius; Octavia was betrothed, and Domitius, besides his former consanguinity with the Emperor, becoming also his son-in-law, was raised to a parity with Britannicus, an elevation derived from the efforts of his mother, and from the devices of those who having been the accusers of Messalina, dreaded the vengeance of her son.

I have before related that Embassadors from the Parthians were sent to Rome, to demand Meherdates for their King: they were at this time introduced into the Senate, where they opened their embassy to this effect; ' That they came not to seek
' the violation of treaties, which they were aware
' subsisted between us and them; nor as revolters
' from the family of the Arsacides, but to call home
' the son of Vonones, the grandson of Phrahates,
' as their deliverer from the tyranny of Gotarzes,
' equally insupportable to the nobility and people.
' Already he had utterly butchered his own brothers
' and his relations, and already extended the same
' cruelty to distant nobles and places; to their
' slaughter he was daily adding that of their wives
' and tender children, some of them yet unborn.
' He was a sluggard in peace, and of wretched for-
' tune in war, but would with acts of cruelty dis-
' guise his dastardly spirit. With us the Parthians
' had an ancient friendship, founded upon public
' leagues; and it behoved us to succour these our
' allies, in strength great as ourselves, and only in
' reverence yielding to us. It was true, the sons of
' their Kings were given as pledges to the Romans;
' but therefore only given, that when the govern-
' ment of Parthia became grievous, they might
' have recourse to the Emperor and Senate for a
' King

'King improved by the Roman manners, and thence
'worthier of the throne.'

When they had alledged thefe and the like arguments, Claudius made a fpeech concerning the grandeur of the Romans, and the deferences ever paid to the fame by the Parthians; and equalling himfelf with the deified Auguftus, reprefented that from him alfo they had fought a King. He omitted to mention Tiberius, though he too had fent them Kings. Upon Meherdates (who was prefent) he beftowed proper admonitions, ' not to confider his
' government as a lawlefs domination, nor his peo-
' ple as flaves, but to remember himfelf and them
' in the tender relation of magiftrate and fellow-
' citizens; to cultivate juftice and clemency, bleff-
' ings unknown to Barbarians, and thence the more
' likely to pleafe them." Then turning to the embaffadors, he enlarged upon the praifes of the young Prince, ' as one educated in the Roman difcipline,
' himfelf of diftinguifhed modefty,' yet advifed them;
' to bear with the humours of their Kings, for in
' frequent changes, they could never find their in-
' tereft. For the Roman State, it was arrived to a
' fatiety of glory, infomuch that fhe ftudied the
' repofe likewife of foreign Nations.' It was therefore given in commiffion to Caius Caffins, governor of Syria, to conduct the young King to the banks of the Euphrates.

This Caffius furpaffed all thofe of that time in the knowledge of the laws; for in a long and general recefs from war, the military arts were forgot, and, during a fettled peace, no difference appears between the daftardly and the brave. Yet he fedulouſly exercifed the legions, carefully revived the ancient difcipline, as far as without war the fame could be revived, and acted with the fame care and circumfpection, as if a formidable enemy had been at hand. Such conduct, he thought, became the

renown

renown of his anceſtors, and the Caſſian family, a family celebrated even amongſt thoſe nations. He now encamped at Zeugma, a place where the river is moſt paſſable, and having called together thoſe by whoſe advice a King was ſought, from Rome, as ſoon as the Parthian cheifs, and with them Agbarus King of the Arabs, were arrived, he repreſented to Meherdates, " that the Barbarians, in the firſt ſallies " of their ſpirit, were always violent, but cooled " by delays, or warped into treachery; ſo that it " behoved him to accelerate the execution of his " enterpriſe." This good counſel was fruſtrated by the fraud of Agbarus, who detained the young King many days at the city of Edeſſa, yet unexperienced, and believing that the eſſence of Royal fortune was placed in luxury and riot. So that, though Carrhenes preſſed them by meſſengers, and aſſured them, that ſucceſs was certain, if they advanced with ſpeed, yet they neglected entering directly into Meſopotamia, though they were juſt upon its borders, but choſe, by a long circuit, to march to Armenia, an unſeaſonable march, for winter was already begun.

As they deſcended into the plains, wearied with the deep ſnow and ſteep mountains, Carrhenes joined them with his forces; thence they paſſed the Tigris, and croſſed the country of the Adiabenians, Izates their King having publicly eſpouſed the intereſt of Meherdates, though ſecretly his inclinations were more ſincerely attached to Gotarzes. In paſſing the river, they took the city Ninos, the ancient ſeat of the Aſſyrian Empire, as alſo the caſtle of Arbela, ſo renowned in ſtory, for that the laſt battle between Darius and Alexander was there fought, and by it the Monarchy of Perſia diſſolved. Gotarzes the while was ſacrificing upon mount Sambulos to the Gods of the place: amongſt theſe Hercules is principally adored, who, at ſtated times, is wont to warn the prieſts in a dream, " to pre-
" pare

" pare him horses equipped for hunting, and place
" them by the temple;" and these horses, as soon
as they have fixed upon them certain quivers stuffed
with arrows, gallop off and scour the forests, nor
return till night; their arrows all spent, and themselves exhausted and blowing. Again, the God, in
another vision of the night, describes to the priests
the several tracts of the woods where he had ranged,
and in them are found scattered up and down the
beasts by him hunted down and slain.

As the forces of Gotarzes were not yet sufficiently
strengthened, he used the river Corma for a rampart,
and though daily by insults and heralds challenged
to battle, he still procrastinated, shifted stations, and
employed emissaries the while to bribe the enemy,
and wean them from their plighted faith; insomuch,
that first Izates, leader of the Adiabenians, presently after Agbarus, King of the Arabs, went off
with both their armies; a desertion agreeable to the
native fickleness of those barbarous people, and even
to their usual policy. We have learned too by several trials, that they would rather ask a King from
Rome, than be governed by him. Meherdates, thus
bereft of these powerful allies, and apprehending
treasonable purposes in those who continued, determined, as his only remaining resource, to commit
the issue to chance, and risque a battle; nor did
Gotarzes refuse it, who was grown resolute as his
enemy was become weak. The conflict was great
and bloody, and the event long in suspense, till
Carrhenes, having overthrown all that opposed him,
pursuing his victory too far, was surrounded in the
rear by a body of reserve. This Blow utterly blasted
all the hopes of Meherdates, who therefore trusting
to the faith and promises of Parrhaces, a dependent
of his father's, was by the traitor delivered in bonds
to the conqueror. Gotarzes disowning him " for
" a kinsman, or one of the family of the Arsacides,"
but

but reviling him, as "a foreigner and a Roman," ordered him to live with his ears cut off, as a vain instance of his own clemency, and towards us a monument of scorn. A disease soon after carried off Gotarzes; and Vonones, then governor of Media, was called to the throne, a Prince distinguished by nothing memorable, fortunate, or disastrous; his reign was short and inconsiderable, and the state of Parthia devolved upon his son Vologeses.

During this, Mithridates of Bosphorus, since the loss of his territories, wandered from place to place; but, having learnt that Didius the Roman commander was thence withdrawn with the strength of his army, and that Cotys, a young Prince void of experience, was left in his new kingdom with only a few cohorts under Julius Aquila, a Roman Knight, he slighted both, animated the neighbouring people to arms, drew over deserters, and having thus assembled an army, exterminated the King of the Dandarides, and seized his dominions. Upon these tidings, and an apprehension that he would instantly invade Bosphorus, Aquila and Cotys distrusting the power of their own forces, and being diverted too by Zorsines King of the Shacians, who had again taken up hostile arms, had recourse themselves to foreign aid, and dispatched embassadors to Eunones Prince of the Adorsians. Nor was it hard to accomplish this alliance, when they who sought it represented the imperial power of the Romans, in competition with Mithridates a vagabond and revolter. It was therefore accorded, "that Eunones " should make head with the cavalry, and the Ro- " mans besiege the towns."

The army was then formed, and marched in this order; the Adorsians composed the front and rear, the cohorts occupied the center, with those of Bosphorus, armed like Romans. Thus they discomfited the enemy, and arrived at Soza, a city of the
Dan-

Dandarides, now deserted by Mithridates, but in it a garrison was judged proper to be placed, as a bridle upon the doubtful affections of the people. Thence they proceeded against the Siracians, and crossing the river Panda begirt the city of Uspes, situated upon a hill and well fortified with walls and moats, only as the walls were not built with stone, but raised of rows of hurdles with earth between, they were unable to bear an assault; moreover, against them towers were raised high enough to overlook them, and from thence the besieged were infested with flights of darts and flaming torches, and, had not night parted the combat, the city had been attempted and stormed within the limits of a day.

Next day the besieged sent deputies to solicit, that to the free inhabitants their lives might be spared, and offering, as an atonement, ten thousand slaves: conditions rejected by the conquerors, since the massacring of such as were surrendered to mercy would have been inhuman; and to secure such an host of prisoners, extremely difficult. It was therefore deemed the sounder counsel to exercise the right of war, and put all promiscuously to the sword; hence to the soldiers, who already mounted the walls, the signal of slaughter was given. The overthrow of Uspes, and the doom of its inhabitants, terrified their neighbours, who now believed that nothing could be secure or impregnable against the Romans, since arms and bulwarks, heights and fastnesses, deep rivers and fortified towns, were with equal bravery vanquished by them. Hence Zorsines, after long deliberation, whether still to adhere to the desperate fortune of Mithridates, or consult the security of his own paternal crown, at last preferred the interest of his state, and having delivered hostages, came and prostrated himself before the image of Claudius, to the signal glory of the Roman army, who had advanced, in a course of victory without blood,

blood, within three days journey of the river Tanais. In their return, the same fortune did not attend them; for certain vessels, as they sailed back, were cast by a storm upon the coasts of the Taurians, and by these Barbarians surprized, who flew the leader of a cohort and most of the centurions.

Mithridates the while, now destitute of all resource from arms, was devising to what quarter he should have recourse for mercy. His brother Cotys he dreaded, as one who had formerly betrayed him, and became afterwards his open enemy. Amongst the Romans in those parts there was none whose authority and engagements could much avail him. To Eunones therefore he determined to apply, as one who bore him no personal hatred, and, by virtue of his late alliance with us, a Prince of prevailing credit. Thus, in a countenance and equipage suitable to his present desolate plight, he entered the palace, and throwing himself at the feet of Eunones, ' I am Mithridates, says he, the same who
' have been chased and persecuted by the Romans
' for so many years through sea and land; behold
' me before you, of my own choice. Use according to your pleasure a descendant of the great
' Achæmenes; it is the only advantage of which my
' enemies have not bereaved me."

Eunones was affected with the illustrious quality of the man, with the sad recollection of his fortune, and his magnanimous manner of supplication. He raised him up, and praising him for having thrown himself upon the friendship of the Adorsians, and chosen him as a mediator for pardon, dispatched embassadors to Claudius with letters to this purpose. ' The alliances of the Roman Emperors
' with the Kings of other mighty nations, were
' first founded upon a similitude of their fortunes;
' his own with Claudius was also confirmed by a
' joint victory. But all wars were then concluded
' with

' with most glory, when they ended in par-
' doning the vanquished. In this manner was
' Zorsines lately treated, beaten, but deprived of
' nothing. Mithridates, it was true, had offended
' more grievously: Hence for Mithridates he nei-
' ther besought new power or his former kingdom,
' but only an exemption from capital punishment,
' and from the ignominy of being led in triumph."

Claudius, though always benevolent to illustrious foreigners, was yet at a loss whether it were more adviseable to receive the captive on terms of mercy, or to have him by force of arms. For this last there pleaded the sense of injuries, and the gratification of revenge; but against it was alledged, ' That the war was to be undertaken in countries
' wild and trackless, upon a sea boisterous and
' destitute of havens, against fierce and warlike
' Kings, against rambling and vagabond nations;
' where the soil was indigent and barren, where
' hasty measures would be dangerous, procrasti-
' nation vexatious and wearisom; small would be
' the glory in victory, much infamy in a defeat.
' The Emperor ought therefore readily to embrace
' the overture, and agree to spare his life; he was
' indigent, and an exile, and the longer he enjoyed
' his desolate life, so much the severer would be
' his sufferings." These considerations convinced Claudius, and he writ to Eunones, ' That, in
' truth, Mithridates had merited the punishment
' of death, nor wanted he power to inflict it; but
' he chose to follow the rule of our ancestors, who,
' as they pursued obstinate enemies with unrelenting
' rigour, treated the supplicant with equal bene-
' volence. As to triumphs, they were only to be
' acquired by the conquest of entire kingdoms and
' nations."

Mithridates was thence delivered to Junius Cilo, the Imperial Procurator in Pontus, and by
him

him carried to Rome, where, in the presence of the Emperor, he is said to have spoke with more haughtiness than suited with the abjectness of his fortune; for, as the same was reported abroad, he thus expressed himself; " I am not brought " back to thee, Cæsar, but of my own choice have ' returned; or, if thou dost not believe me, dismiss ' me again, then try to recover me." Moreover, when he was exposed at the Rostrum to the view of the people, and encompassed with guards, his countenance continued perfectly undaunted. To Cilo were decreed the Consular ornaments, and to Aquila those of the Prætorship.

During the same Consuls, Agrippina, ever implacable in her hate, and enraged at Lollia for having disputed with her a right to the Emperor's bed, framed crimes against her, and suborned an accuser, who charged her; ' with dealings with ' the Magicians and Chaldæans, and even consult- ' ing the Oracle of the Clarian Apollo concerning that match." Claudius, without hearing her in her own defence, after a long preface to the Senate concerning the signal splendor of her birth, '· that ' by her mother she was niece to Lucius Volusius, ' Cotta Messalinus her great uncle, herself formerly ' married to Memmius Regulus," (for of her marriage with Caligula he purposely said nothing) added, ' that she pursued pernicious devices against ' the commonwealth, and must be divested of ' the means and opportunities of iniquity and trea- ' son, her estate be confiscated, and herself banished ' Italy." Thus, of all her immense wealth, only thirty thousand pounds were allotted her. Calpurnia too, another illustrious Lady, was doomed to ruin, because the Prince had praised her beauty, though from no passion for her person, but only in occasional discourse; a consideration, which so much abated the fury of Agrippina, that her punishment was on this fide death. To Lollia, a Tribune was difpatched, with orders to compel her to die. Cadins Rufus was likewife condemned for extortion, at the fuit of the Bithynians.

To the province of Narbon Gaul, it was now granted, in regard of the diftinguifhed reverence ever by them paid to the Senate, that to Senators of that province fhould be allowed the fame privilege with thofe of Sicily, of vifiting their eftates there without leave afked of the Prince; and the countries of Ituria and Judæa were, upon the death of their Kings Sohemus and Agrippa, annexed to the government of Syria. The augury too of divine protection, which for five-and-twenty years had been difufed, was judged fit to be revived, and thereafter regularly obferved; and the Emperor widened the circumference of Rome by virtue of an ancient inftitution, which impowered fuch as had extended the limits of the empire, to enlarge alfo the bounds of the city; a right which yet was never affumed by any of the Roman captains, though they had fubdued mighty nations, before Sylla the Dictator, and the deified Auguftus.

What was the ambition and practice of our Kings in this matter, or from what inftances of renown, the diverfity of tradition has rendered utterly uncertain. But I cannot think it impertinent to fhew where the firft foundations began, and what was the circuit fixt by Romulus. Now, from the Ox-market, where ftill is feen the brazen ftatue of a bull, becaufe by that animal the plough is drawn, a furrow was cut to defcribe the boundaries of the town, and extended fo as to include the great Altar of Hercules; from thence certain fpaces were left marked at proper diftances with ftones, and the line continued along the foot of Mount Palatine to the Altar of Confus, next to the *Curiæ veteres*, thence to the fmall Temple of the Lares, and laftly to the

great

great Roman Forum, which, as well as the Capitol, it is believed, was added to the city, not by Romulus, but by Tatius. With the increase of her empire the City afterwards continued to increase; and what were the boundaries now established by Claudius, is easily learnt, as they are inserted in the public records.

In the Consulship of Caius Antistius and Marcus Suilius, the adoption of Domitius was dispatched by the prevalent counsel of Pallas, who, as he had procured the match for Agrippina, and afterwards became engaged to her in a league of adultery, and thence wholly addicted to her interest, continually follicited Claudius " to provide for the exigency " of the Commonwealth, and support the infancy " of Britannicus with a collateral stay. Such had " been the policy of the deified Augustus, who, " though, for the support of his house, he had grand- " children of his own, yet he had distinguished with " power the sons of his wife. Thus too Tiberius, " notwithstanding he had issue of his own, adopted " Germanicus; and thus he also should fortify him- " self with the aid of a young Prince, fit to bear " in time a part of his public cares." To these considerations Claudius yielded, and adopted Domitius for his eldest son, though only three years older than his son, declaring the adoption to the Senate in a speech of the very same strain with that of his freedman to him. It was noted by men of observation, that never was any adoption made before this into the Patrician family of the Claudii, which, from Attus Clausus their first ancestor, had ever subsisted upon its own successive stock.

The thanks of the Senate were presented to the Prince, but conceived in strains of flattery still more exquisite towards Domitius; and a law passed decreeing his assumption into the Claudian family, and to him the name of Nero. Agrippina was also dignified with the title of Augusta. When these measures were thus accomplished, no mortal was found so void of compassion, as not to be affected with the sorrowful lot of Britannicus. By little and little he was even bereft of the attendance of his slaves, through the hollow officiousness of his step-mother, who would keep him unseasonably in a nursery; a treatment of great derision, which himself perceived, as he was capable of discerning deceit. For he is said to have wanted no quickness of understanding: whether the same was his real character, or whether his sad fortune was the only source of his praise, without living to give further proof, he still retained it.

Now Agrippina, that she might even to distant nations, our allies, signalize her power at Rome, procured a Colony of Veterans to be sent to the capital of the Ubians; a town in which she was born, and which she called by her own name. It had also been the lot of her grandfather Agrippa, when that people came over the Rhine, to receive them under the protection of the Romans. At that same time terror filled the Higher Germany, from the approach of the Cattians, exercising as they went rapine and depredations. Hence Lucius Pomponius, the Roman General, ordered the auxiliary Vangiones and Nemetæans, strengthened with some wings of horse, " to advance against those bands " of robbers, or, if they found them straggling, to " pour in upon them and beset them by surprize." The vigour of the soldiers was answerable to the scheme of the commander; separating themselves into two bands, that which marched to the left enclosed them just returned from the spoil, under the effects of a debauch, and sunk in sleep. To complete their joy, they now released from bondage some who had continued in it ever since the massacre of Varus and the Legions, forty years before.

The

The body that turned to the right, had made a shorter march, and, as the enemy ventured to fight, a greater slaughter. So that, laden with booty, and covered with glory, they returned to mount Taunus, where Pomponius waited with his Legions, prepared for battle, if the Cattians, from a passion for revenge, had ministered occasion. But as they dreaded being assaulted on every side, here, by the Romans, there, by the Cheruscans, with whom they have incessant enmity, they dispatched deputies and hostages to Rome. To Pomponius was decreed the honour of triumph, from which, however, he derives but a slender share of his surviving fame, since to posterity he is peculiarly known in the surpassing excellence of his Poems.

It was at this time too that Vannius, formerly created King of the Suevians by Drusus Cæsar, was driven from his kingdom. In the beginning of his reign, he lived in signal reputation, and in popularity with his people, but, intoxicated with long possession of power, grew afterwards imperious; so that he became at once exposed to the hate and hostility of his neighbours, and to a combination of his own subjects. It was conducted by his own sister's sons, Vangio and Sido, and by Vibillius their confederate, King of the Hermundurians. Nor would Claudius, though often entreated, engage in the quarrel of the Barbarians; he only answered the suit of Vannius, by a promise of a safe-refuge, in case of expulsion, and writ to Publius Palpelius Hister, governor of Pannonia, " to cover the banks of " the Danube with the Legion, and with a body of " auxiliaries raised in the same province, in order " to shelter the vanquished, and to awe the con- " querors; lest, elated by success, they might ven- " ture also to disturb the quiet of the Empire." For the Ligians and other nations were daily arriving in swarms, allured by the fame of the wealth of that kingdom, which for thirty years Vannius had been enriching by conftant depredations and exactions. His own army of natives were foot, and his horfe, the Jazigians of Sarmatia, a force unequal to the great hoft of his enemies. Hence he determined to confine himfelf to his ftrong holds, and protract the war. But the Jazigians, who could not reconcile themfelves to the reftraints of a fiege, roamed round the adjacent country, and being powerfully affailed by the Ligians and Hermundurians, brought him under a neceffity of fighting. So that, iffuing from his fortreffes to relieve them, he was overthrown in battle, but with this praife, notwithftanding his defeat, that with his own hand he had bravely fought, and was honourably wounded with his face to the foe. He then fled to his fleet, which ftaid for him in the Danube, and was foon followed by his adherents, who were fettled in Pannonia, and portions of land affigned them. Vanglo and Sido parted his kingdom between them, and towards us continued in fignal fidelity, paffionately beloved too by their fubjects, while they were yet acquiring royalty, and, after it was acquired, more vehemently hated, perhaps from the fickle temper of the people, perhaps from the genius of fervitude.

Now Publius Oftorius, Propraetor of Britain, found great uproar and combuftion there; for the enemy had in predatory bands broke into the territories of our allies, with the more violence, as they fuppofed that a new General would not, with an army which he had never proved, and in the depth of winter, dare to make head againft them. But as he was convinced that by the firft events of war, confidence or confternation was raifed in an enemy, he led forth his troops againft them with great fuddennefs, put to the fword all who refifted, and clofely purfued fuch as were broken, fo as to prevent their rejoining. And, fince a peace made by con-

ftraint,

ſtraint, and thence never ſincere, could enſure no repoſe to the General nor his troops; he determined to deprive of their arms all ſuch as he ſuſpected, and, by the means of forts, to confine them between the rivers Nen and Severn; a determination thwarted firſt by the Icenians, a powerful people, who having of their own accord become our confederates, were weakened by no invaſion nor aſſaults of war; they were now joined by the bordering nations, an army was formed, and the place of battle choſen, a place defended by a ditch, and the approach to it ſo narrow as not to be paſſable by the horſe. The Roman General, though, without the ſupport of the Legions, he only led ſome ſocial troops, yet drew up to ſtorm theſe ruſtic fortifications, and ranging his Cohorts in order, diſmounted the horſe and aſſigned them the duty of foot. Upon the ſignal given, they forced the ditch and broke the enemy, who were alſo hampered and entangled with their own incloſures. But they who, from the guilt of rebellion, were animated with deſpair, cooped in on all ſides, and no way left for eſcape, performed many and memorable feats of bravery. In this battle Marcus Oſtorius, the ſon of the General, having ſaved the life of a Roman citizen, acquired the Civic Crown.

For the reſt, the overthrow of the Icenians calmed all thoſe unſettled ſpirits, who before were wavering in their purpoſes between peace and war; and the army was led againſt the Cangians, waſted their territories, and committed general ſpoil. Nor durſt the foe encounter them openly, and were always beaten in their ſecret aſſaults. We had now approached near the ſea which waſhes the coaſt of Ireland, when commotions, begun amongſt the Brigantes, obliged the General to return thither; as he had determined to proſecute no new enterprize till his former were completed and ſecure. The Brigantes, in truth, became ſoon compoſed, by exe-

cuting.

cuting a few who raifed the revolt, and pardoning all the reft; but, no rigour nor mercy could reclaim the Silures, who were bent upon war, and only to be reduced by the force of the Legions. To facilitate this defign, a Colony, powerful in the number of Veterans, was conveyed to Camaloduńum, fituate in the conquered lands, as a bulwark againſt the rebels, and for inuring our allies to the laws and jurifdiction of the Romans.

Thence we marched againſt the Silures, a people refolute and fierce by nature, and moreover confiding in the affiftance and valour of Caractacus, one renowned for many difafters, fo that in credit he furpaffed all the other Britiſh commanders. In the advantage and fituation of the country he was more fubtle and expert than the Romans, but weaker in men, and therefore tranflated the feat of the war into the territory of the Ordovicans; and being joined by all fuch as feared an unequal peace with the Romans, ventured to try the decifion of the fword. In order to it, he chofe a place againſt which it was difficult to advance, and from which it was as difficult to retreat, every way incommodious to our army, every way favourable to his own. It was upon the ridges of mountains exceeding ſteep, and, where their fides were inclining and approachable, he reared walls of ſtone for a rampart. At the foot of the mountains flowed a river, dangerous to be forded, and a hoſt of men guarded his entrenchments.

Add to this, that the leaders of the feveral confederate nations were bufy from quarter to quarter, exhorting and animating their followers, with reprefentations proper to diffipate fear, to kindle their hopes, and to roufe in them all the fierceft incitements to war. Caractacus, particularly, flew through the whole army, and proclaimed, ' That ' from this day and this battle they muſt date their
' liberty

'liberty completely refcued, or their fervitude eternally eftablifhed. He called upon thofe of their anceftors who had exterminated Cæfar the Dictator, men by whofe valour they yet lived free from tribute and Roman axes, yet preferved free from proftitution the perfons of their children and wives.' As he thus harangued, he was anfwered by the acclamations of the multitude; and every particular bound himfelf by the oath moft facred to each different nation, ' Never to yield to arms, nor wounds, nor aught fave death.'

This loud alacrity of theirs amazed the Roman General. Befides, the river to be paffed, the rampart to be forced, the declivities of the high mountains to be climbed, and all defended by hofts of men, were terrible difficulties. But the foldiers urged for the attack: All things, they cried, were conquerable by courage, and the Tribunes and other officers expreffing the fame fpirit, heightened the ardour of the army. Oftorius, therefore, having carefully furveyed the fituation, where inacceffible, and where to be paffed, led them on thus animated; and, without much difficulty, gained the oppofite banks. In approaching the bulwark, while the encounter was yet managed by flights of darts, there were more of our men wounded, and many began to fall; but after they had formed themfelves into the military fhell, demolifhed the huge and fhapelefs ftructure of ftones, and encountered hand to hand upon ground equal to both, the Barbarians betook themfelves to the ridges of the mountains, and thither alfo mounted our foldiers after them, both the light and heavy armed. Here alfo was begun an unequal fight, by ours in clofe order againft the Britons, who only fought by difcharges of arrows, and, as they cover themfelves with no armour, were thence ftrait broken in their ranks; where they refifted the

the auxiliaries, they were flaughtered by the fwords and javelins of the foldiers of the Legions, and by the great fabres and pikes of the auxiliaries, where they faced thofe of the Legions. Signal was this victory; the wife and daughter of Caractacus were taken prifoners, and his brothers furrendered to mercy.

He himfelf had recourfe to the faith and protection of Cartifmandua, Queen of the Brigantes; but, as almoft all things confpire againft the unfortunate, was by her delivered in bonds to the conquerors, now in the ninth year after the commencement of the war in Great-Britain. So long had he fuftained it; hence his renown had reached all the ifles, fpread over the neighbouring provinces, and became celebrated even in Italy, where all longed to behold the man, who, for fo many years, had defied the Roman arms Nor, in truth, at Rome was the name of Caractacus without luftre and applaufe; and the Emperor, by exalting his own glory upon the conqueft, accumulated frefh glory in the conquered. For the people were affembled to fee him as a rare and important fpectacle; and the Prætorian bands ftood under arms in the field before their camp. There proceeded firft the fervants and followers of the Britifh King, with the military harnefs, golden chains, and the fpoils by him taken in the wars with his neighbours; next his brothers, his wife and daughter, and laftly himfelf expofed to view. All but he were dejected, and defcended, through fear, to fupplications unworthy of their quality. Caractacus, without either betraying a fupplicant look, or uttering a word that imploied mercy, as foon as he was placed before the imperial tribunal fpoke thus:

‘ If, to the height of my quality and fortune,
‘ I had joined an equal height of moderation in
‘ my

'my prosperity and success, I should have arrived
'in this city under another character, that of a
'friend, and not of a captive, nor would you then
'have disdained to have received a Prince born of
'illustrious ancestors, and governing so many na-
'tions, into terms of alliance. But different is
'my present lot, which derives upon you as emi-
'nent renown, as upon me disgrace and abasement.
'I was lately master of men and arms, horses and
'opulence. Where is the wonder, if against my
'inclination I was bereft of them? If you Romans
'aim at extending your dominion over all man-
'kind; it does not thence follow that all men will
'embrace voluntary servitude from Rome. Had
'I forthwith submitted to captivity, neither had
'my fall nor your glory been thus signal; and even
'now, if I am to suffer death, the fame of my story
'and of your conquest will die with my punishment;
'but if you preserve my life, I shall be a deathless
'example of your clemency.' Claudius upon this
pardoned him, his wife, and his brothers. Being
discharged of their chains; and having paid their
duty and acknowledgment to the Prince, they also
accosted Agrippina, exalted upon another tribunal
hard by, in the same strain of gratitude and veneration: A sight remarkably new, to our ancestors
utterly unknown, for a woman to preside amongst
the Roman Ensigns! she, in truth, assumed to call
herself a partner in the Empire which her ancestors
had acquired.

The Senate was thereafter assembled, where
many and pompous encomiums were pronounced
upon the taking of Caractacus, as an event 'no less
'illustrious than those of old, when Siphax was by
'Publius Scipio, Perses by Lucius Paulus, or any
'other conquered Kings were by any of our great
'Captains, presented in chains to the Roman
'people.' To Ostorius the triumphal ornaments

were decreed; and thus far his adminiſtration had been succcſsful, but was afterwards chequered with misfortunes. Whether it was, that upon the captivity of Caractacus the war was thought concluded, and thence our vigilance and diſcipline abated; or that the enemy, in compaſſion for ſo great a King, burned more vehemently for revenge. They aſſailed by ſurprize the camp-marſhal and legionary cohorts, left to rear forts amongſt the Silures, and, but for ſudden ſuccours from the circumjacent garriſons, our troops had been cut in pieces; as it was, the Marſhal himſelf and eight Centurions were there ſlain, with the moſt reſolute ſoldiers. Soon after they entirely routed our foragers, and even the troops ſent to guard them.

Oſtorius, it is true, diſpatched to their relief ſome cohorts lightly armed, who yet were not able to ſtay the flight, ſo that the Legions were drawn out to reſtore the battle, which by their ſtrength inſtantly became equal, and then favourable to us. The enemy fled, but, as night approached, with ſlight loſs. There continued thenceforward frequent encounters, many of them reſembling the parties and ſurprizes of robbers, ſometimes in the woods, ſometimes in moraſſes, conducted by chance or boldneſs, and with anſwerable ſucceſs, here at a venture, there in concert, now from reſentment, anon for booty, at times by command of their officers, and often without their knowledge. Of all others the Silures were the moſt implacable; they were incenſed by a ſaying of the Roman General current amongſt them, ' that their name muſt be ' utterly extinguiſhed, as was that of the Sugam-' brians, who had been partly cut off, and the ' reſt tranſplanted into Gaul.' Thus animated, they ſurprized and carried off two auxiliary cohorts, who were, without due circumſpection, plundering the country to ſatiate the avarice of their officers;
and

and by distributing the spoil and captives amongst the neighbouring nations, they were drawing them also into the revolt, when Ostorius, sinking under the weight of his anxieties, expired, to the great joy of the enemy, that a captain so considerable, though he had not fallen in battle, had yet perished in the war.

The Emperor, apprized of the death of his Lieutenant, that the province might not be without a governor, substituted in his room Aulus Didius; but he, notwithstanding his expeditious arrival, found not things in their entire state; for, the Legion commanded by Manlius Valens, had the while been engaged, and suffered a defeat, a disaster magnified by the enemy to terrify the new general, and even aggravated by him, thence to gain the greater glory, if he quelled the rebellion, or the juster excuse if it lasted. The late loss too we suffered from the Silures, who were daily making large incursions on all hands, till Didius now set upon them and repulsed them. Their ablest man of war, since the taking of Caractacus, was Venusius, of the city of the Jugantes, as I have above remembered, one long faithful to the Romans, and protected by their arms, during his marriage with the Queen Cartismandua; but being afterwards divorced from her, and thence instantly at war with her, he likewise began hostilities against us. Their arms at first were only employed against each other; but the Queen having by subtile stratagems possessed herself of the brother and other kindred of Venusius, the enemy became exasperated, and scorning the infamy of falling under the dominion of a woman, assembled all their ablest and most warlike youth, and invaded her territories; an event foreseen by us; so that we had sent some cohorts to her aid, and a fierce battle ensued, where the first onset was doubtful, but the end successful. With the like issue fought the Legion commanded

D 6   by

by Cesius Nasica. For Didius himself, unwieldy through age, and already satiated with a long train of honours, thought it sufficient to act by his Lieutenants, and only restrain the foe. All these transactions, though the work of several years, under two Proprætors Ostorius and Didius, I have thus connected, left the detail, if interrupted, might not have been so easily recovered. I now return to the order of time.

During the fifth Consulship of Claudius and that of Servius Cornelius Orfitus, to qualify Nero for entering into the administration of the state, the manly robe was presented him, while yet under age, and the Emperor concurred chearfully with the flattering decrees of the Senate, " that in his twen-
" tieth year, he should exercise the Consulship;
" that the while, as Consul designed, he should be
" invested with proconsular authority out of Rome,
" and be stiled Prince of the Roman Youth." Claudius moreover, in Nero's name, bestowed a largess upon the soldiers, and another upon the people: and, at the Circensian games, which were then solemnized, to draw upon him the eyes and affections of the populace, whilst Britannicus was carried along in the prætexta (the usual habit of boys) Nero appeared in the triumphal robe, the mark and ornament of imperial state. So that the people, beholding them thus differently attired, could thence conclude the difference of their future fortunes. At the same time, such of the Centurions and Tribunes as manifested any compassion for the partial lot of Britannicus were, some under colour of more honourable functions, all upon framed pretences, removed from the palace; even amongst the freedmen, those whose faith and constancy were found incorruptible, were discarded on the following occasion. The two young princes happening to meet, Nero saluted Britannicus by that name, and Britannicus

nicus him by his old name of Domitius.' This was by Agrippina represented to Claudius with grievous expostulations, as the first step to dissension, since by it ' the adoption of Nero was set at nought and ' condemned, the sanctions of the senate, with the ' authority of the people, were abolished within the ' walls of his own palace; and if the pravity of those ' who inspired into Britannicus such pernicious sen- ' timents were not repressed, it would break out ' into war and public ruin.' Claudius, alarmed and exasperated by these suggestions of his wife, as if the same had been crimes really committed by the tutors of his son, punished all the rest of them with exile or death, and entrusted him to the government of others chosen by his step-mother.

Agrippina however durst not yet proceed to the accomplishment of her great design, till from the command of the Prætorian cohorts were removed Lusius Geta and Rufius Crispinus, as men whom she believed grateful to the memory of Messalina, and zealously devoted to her children. When she had therefore alledged to the Emperor, ' that by the ' competition and cabals of two commanders, the ' guards were rent into factions, whereas, were ' they under the authority of one, they would be ' more easily subjected to the laws of discipline and ' obedience;' Claudius submitted to the reasoning of his wife, and the charge of these bands was transferred to Burrhus Afranius, an officer, in truth, of signal renown, but one however well apprized to whose credit he owed his advancement. Agrippina likewise began to signalize her grandeur still more, and even to enter the Capitol in a chariot, a distinction which of old was allowed to none but the priests and things sacred, and, being now assumed by her, heightened the reverence of the people towards a lady who was the daughter of a Cæsar, and the mother of one, sister to the last Emperor, and
wife

wife of the present; an instance of imperial fortune and nobility till then unparallelled. But in the mean time her chief champion Vitellius, in the height of favour, and extremity of age (upon such treacherous foundations great men stand!) was involved in an accusation, and, by Junius Lupus the Senator, charged with treason, and even with aspiring to the Empire. Claudius too would have listened to the charge, had not Agrippina prevailed by menaces rather than prayers, and turned his resentment upon the accuser, who was thence interdicted from fire and water. Further punishment than this Vitellius desired not.

Many were the prodigies that happened this year: upon the Capitol were seen birds of evil omen, frequent concussions of the earth were felt, and by them many houses overthrown. But as the dread was still more extensive than the calamity, in the throng of the flying multitude all the weak and decripit were trodden to death. For a prodigy also was reckoned the barrenness of the season, and the effect of it, famine. Nor were the complaints of the populace confined to houses and corners; they even gathered in tumultuous crowds round the Prince, then engaged in the public administration of justice, and with turbulent clamours drove him to the extremity of the forum; so that, to escape their violence, he was forced with his guards to break through the incensed multitude. It is certain, there was then in Rome but just provision for fifteen days, and by the signal bounty of the Gods and the mildness of the winter, it was that the public was relieved in that its urgent distress. It was, in truth, otherwise with Italy in former days, when from her fruitful fields foreign provinces too were furnished with supplies; nor, at this time, is the sterility of soil any part of our misfortune; but we now rather chuse to cultivate Africa and Egypt, and the

the lives of the Roman people are entrusted to ships and the casualties of the year.

The same year, the war which arose between the Armenians and Hiberians, begot also mighty broils between the Parthians and Romans. Over the Parthians reigned Vologeses, who, though the son of a Greek concubine, had, by the concession of his brothers, obtained the diadem. The kingdom of Hiberia had been long held by Pharasmanes, and his brother Mithridates was, by our aid and procurement, possessed of Armenia. Pharasmanes had a son graceful and tall, of signal strength of body, trained up in all the politics of his father, and in high renown with the bordering nations. His name was Rhadamistus, a young prince who, impatient that the small kingdom of Hiberia should be so long detained from him by the great age of his father, declared this his discontent with so much frequency and passion, that his ambition could not be concealed. Pharasmanes therefore, in regard of his own declining age, and fearing the spirit of his son; eager of himself to reign, and supported besides with the affections of his subjects, chose to divert his thoughts upon another pursuit, and tempted him with the prospect of Armenia; ' a kingdom which, ' having expulsed the Parthians, he said, he had ' given to Mithridates; but, in gaining it now, all ' methods of violence were to be postponed; and ' those of guile first to be tried, in order to oppress ' him unawares.' Thus Rhadamistus, feigning to quarrel with his father, and to fly the persecutions of his step-mother, withdrew to his uncle, and, while he was by him cherished like a child, with transcendent complacency drew the nobility of Armenia into the conspiracy; Mithridates being so ignorant of his conduct, that upon him he was still multiplying honours.

Then,

Then, under shew of being reconciled to his father, he returned, and informed him, ' that what ' fraud could effect, was accomplished, the rest arms ' must execute.' Hence Pharasmanes set himself to devise colours for the war, and declared, ' that ' whilst he was at war with the king of the Albani- ' ans, he had applied to the Romans for aid, but his ' brother opposed its coming; and this injury he ' was now about to revenge with his utter destruc- ' tion.' At the same time, he committed a numerous army to the conduct of his son, who, by a sudden invasion, utterly dismayed Mithridates, and forced him out of the field into the fortress of Gorneas, a place strong in the situation, and defended by a garrison of our soldiers, under the command of Cælius Pollio Governor, and Casperius a Centurion. The Barbarians are strangers to nothing more than the use of machines, and the dexterity of assaulting places, a part of military skill which to us is throughly familiar. Rhadamistus therefore, having without effect, or with loss to himself, attempted the fortifications, changed his efforts into a siege, and when all his attacks were despised, purchased with a price the avaritious Governor, notwithstanding the adjurations of Casperius, ' that he would not sell a ' confederate King, not sell Armenia, the gift of ' the Roman people, and convert his own trust ' into perfidiousness and money.' But at last, since Pollio persisted to plead the multitude of the enemy, and Rhadamistus the orders of his father; the Centurion procuring a truce departed, in order either to deter Pharasmanes from pursuing the war, or otherwise to proceed to Numidius Quadratus, Governor of Syria, and lay before him the condition of Armenia.

By the departure of the Centurion, Pollio being, as it were, discharged from the restraint of a keeper,

ex-

exhorted Mithridates to an accommodation. He alledged, ' the natural ties between brothers, the ' seniority of Pharasmanes, and their other mutual ' bonds of affinity; that he was himself espoused to ' his brother's daughter, and to Rhadamistus had ' espoused his own; that the Hiberians, however ' then superior in forces, refused not peace; and ' the perfidiousness of the Armenians was sufficiently ' known; neither had he any other sanctuary but ' that castle, destitute of stores. He therefore ' ought not to scruple to prefer terms gained with- ' out blood to the casualties and violence of war.' But, as Mithridates still procrastinated, suspecting the counsels of the Governor, as one who had debauched a concubine of his, and was reckoned of a vile spirit, purchaseable by money into every baseness, Casperius the while reached Pharasmanes, and urged him ' to recall his Hiberians from the ' siege.' That Prince returned him openly equivocal answers, sometimes such as were more gentle and plausible, and, during these amusements, warned Rhadamistus by secret messengers, ' to dispatch by ' whatever means the taking of the place.' Hence the price of the treason was augmented to Pollio, who also privately corrupted the soldiers, and prompted them to demand peace, or otherwise to threaten that they would relinquish the garrison. Mithridates, pressed by this extremity, agreed to the time and place of capitulation, and went forth from the castle to meet Rhadamistus, who instantly flew to embrace him, feigned all the marks of duty and obedience, and called him his father: he even swore that he intended him no violence either by poison or the sword, and drew him at the same time into a neighbouring grove, where a sacrifice, he said, was by his orders prepared, that by the solemn presence of the Gods their league of peace might be confirmed.

It

It is a custom amongst the Kings of those countries, whenever they strike alliances, to tie together with a hard bandage the thumbs of their right hands, till the blood, starting to the extremities, is by a slight cut discharged. This they mutually suck, and a league thus executed is esteemed most awful, as mysteriously solemnized with the blood of the parties. But upon this occasion, he who was applying the bandage pretending to fall, seized Mithridates by the legs, and overthrew him, and instantly he was oppressed by many, then bound, and haled away, dragging his chain, a circumstance of consummate contumely amongst the Barbarians! The people too, over whom he had exercised rigorous tyranny, assaulted him with bitter reproaches, and even threatened him with blows. Yet there were some of a different temper, who uttered their commiseration for such a mighty change of his fortune; besides, his wife following him with her little infants, was by her doleful lamentations every where heard. They were thrust apart into covered carriages, till the commands of Pharasmanes were known. With him the passion for a kingdom was more prevalent than his regard for a brother or daughter, and he possessed naturally a spirit prone to every cruelty. He however considered the indecency of the spectacle, and ordered them to be put to death, but not in his sight. Rhadamistus too, as if from an exact observance of his oath, employed neither sword nor poison against his sister and uncle, but caused them to be thrown upon the ground, and stifled with a vast weight of coverings. The children also of Mithridates, for bewailing the murder of their parents, were butchered themselves.

Quadratus, as soon as he knew the treason, with the doom suffered by Mithridates, and that they who took his life held his kingdom, assembled his council, and representing these events, sought their advice

advice whether vengeance ought to be purſued. Few had at heart the public honour, and moſt of them reaſoned from conſiderations of ſecurity, ' that all ' the injuries and cruelties committed by foreign na- ' tions upon each other, ought to the Romans to be ' matter of joy; nay, the ſeeds of diſſenſion were ' induſtriouſly to be ſown amongſt them; a policy ' frequently practiſed by the Roman Emperors, who ' under colour of beſtowing from time to time that ' ſame kingdom of Armenia upon Princes Barba- ' rians, deſigned thence to furniſh them with matter ' of reciprocal feuds and hoſtilities. Rhadamiſtus ' might therefore enjoy a crown wickedly acquired, ' ſince with it he enjoyed public deteſtation and ' infamy, circumſtances which better ſerved the ' purpoſes of Rome, than if by methods of glory he ' had obtained it.' With this advice they all con- curred; but that they might not ſeem to have aſ- ſented to a wickedneſs ſo flagrant, and left contrary orders ſhould arrive from the Emperor, they diſ- patched a meſſage to Pharaſmanes, ' to retire from ' the frontiers of Armenia, and recall his ſon.'

Over Cappadocia then ruled Julius Pelignus, with the title of Procurator, one equally deſpicable for his daſtardly ſpirit and the deformity of his perſon, but in great intimacy with Claudius, who, while yet a private man, was wont to ſpend his idle life in liſtening to the drollery of ſuch buffoons. This Pelignus drew together a body of auxiliary forces from the adjacent provinces, and declared he would reconquer Armenia; but as he committed greater ſpoil upon our allies than upon the enemy, he was by his own men abandoned, har- raſſed by the inceſſant incurſions of the Barba- rians, and, thus bereft of all defence, betook him- ſelf to Rhadamiſtus, by whoſe liberalities he was ſo intirely ſubdued, that of his own accord he exhorted him to aſſume the royal diadem, and even aſſiſted in perſon that ſolemnity, as the author of the advice,

and

and his vassal at arms. When this vile transaction came to be divulged, that the character of the other Roman Commanders might not be judged by that of Pelignus, Helvidius Priscus was dispatched at the head of a legion, with general orders to apply such remedies to the present combustions, as their circumstances would bear. He therefore, having with much celerity crossed mount Taurus, had already made many pacifications, rather by mildness than force, when an order overtook him, ' for his ' return into Syria, by it to avoid ministering to the ' Parthians any ground of war.'

For, Vologeses believing that an occasion now offered for invading Armenia, a kingdom inherited by his ancestors, but now treasonably occupied by a foreign usurper, drew together an army, and prepared to instate his brother Tiridates in the throne; that none of his house might be destitute of dominion. The march of the Parthians terrified the Hiberians; they were expelled without fighting a battle, and the Armenian cities of Artaxata and Tigranocerta, without a struggle, received the invaders. But a tempestuous winter, or want of provisions, and the pestilence arising from both, constrained Vologeses to relinquish his conquests. So that the throne of Armenia being once more vacant, was again invaded by Rhadamistus, now more outrageous and bloody than ever, as incensed against a people that had already abandoned him, and were still ready, on the first occasion, to revolt. They too, though inured to servitude, lost all patience, betook themselves to arms, and begirt the palace; nor had Rhadamistus any resource save in the fleetness of his horses, and by them he escaped with his wife.

She was great with child, yet, from dread of the foe, and tenderness to her husband, bore at first, as well as she could, the fatigue of the flight; but when, by continued hurrying, her heavy womb was

sorely

sorely agitated, and all her bowels bruised, she besought him ' to save her by an honest death from the ' reproach and misery of captivity.' At first, he embraced her, comforted and encouraged her, now admiring her heroic spirit, then struck with fear, left, if. be left her, some other might possess her; at last, in the rage of love, and well trained in acts of blood, he drew his scymetar, and wounding her deeply, haled her to the banks of the Araxes, committing her body to the flood, that even of her corps none might ever be master. He himself pursued his flight full speed, till he reached Hiberia, the kingdom of his father. Zenobia the while (for that was her name) was descried by the shepherds, floating gently on the surface with manifest appearances of life; and as they gathered from the beautiful dignity of her aspect that she was of no mean rank, they bound up her wound, and to it administered their rustic medicines. Having then learnt her name and disaster, they carried her to Artaxata, from whence, at the charge and care of the city, she was conducted to Tiridates, by him courteously received, and entertained with all the marks of Royalty.

In the Consulship of Paustus Sylla and Salvius Otho, Furius Scribonianus suffered exile, upon a charge of having ' consulted the Chaldæans about ' the term of the Prince's life.' In his crime was involved his mother Junia, ' as, having borne with ' impatience her own lot;' for she too had been banished. Camillus, the father of Scribonianus, had levied war in Dalmatia; hence Claudius vaunted his own clemency, that to a hostile race he persisted to grant their lives. That, however, of the present exile, remained not long; whether he died naturally or by poison, was differently reported as each differently believed. For expelling the Astrologers from Italy, a decree of Senate was made full of rigour, but never executed. The Emperor thereafter

after uttered a discourse in praise of those Senators, who, from the narrowness of their fortunes, of their own accord renounced their dignity; and such as, by adhering to their order, added confidence to their poverty, were degraded.

During these transactions, in the Senate was proposed a penalty to be inflicted upon Ladies who married slaves, and ordained, ' That she who thus ' debased herself, unknown to the master of the slave, ' should be adjudged herself in a state of slavery; ' but, where he consented, she should be held for ' a slave manumitted.' To Pallas, who was by Claudius declared to be the deviser of this scheme, the ornaments of the Prætorship, and three hundred seventy five thousand crowns, were adjudged by Bareas Sornus, Consul designed. Cornelius Scipio added, ' that the public thanks ought likewise to be paid him; for that, being descended ' from the old Kings of Arcadia, he postponed the ' regard of his most ancient nobility to the service ' of the state, and deigned to be numbered amongst ' the ministers of the Prince.' Claudius avowed, ' that Pallas was content with the honour only, and ' resolved to live still in his former poverty.' Thus a decree of Senate was published engraven in brass, in which a franchized slave, possessing an estate of more than seven millions, was extolled for observing the parsimony of the ancients.

His brother sirnamed Felix, he who for some time had governed Judæa, acted not with the same restraint, but as one who, relying upon such potent protection, supposed he might perpetrate with impunity every kind of villainy. The Jews, in truth, by their sedition, in the time of Caligula, had ministered some appearances of an insurrection; and, after they were apprized of his assassination, scarce returned to obedience. Their dread remained, lest some of the succeeding Emperors might subject
them

them to the like odious injunctions. Felix too, the while, by applying unseasonable remedies, inflamed their offence and disaffection; a conduct imitated by Ventidius Cumanus, who held under his jurisdiction part of the province, and emulated Felix in all his worst courses; for such was the division, that Galilæa was subject to Cumanus, and Samaria to Felix, two nations long at variance, and now, from contempt of their rulers, less than ever restraining their mutual hate. Hence depredations on both sides were committed, bands of robbers employed, ambushes formed, and sometimes battles fought, and all the spoil and booty presented to these their Governors, who, at first, rejoiced over it; but when, after the mischief grew outrageous, they interposed their armed troops, their men were slain, and, but for the aid of Quadratus, ruler of Syria, the whole province had been in a blaze of war. Nor, as to the Jews, who had carried their violence so far as to kill our soldiers, did any obstacle arise against punishing them with death. The affair of Cumanus and Felix created some delay; for Claudius, upon a hearing of the causes of the revolt, had also granted a power to try and sentence the Governors; but Quadratus taking Felix up to the Tribunal, and shewing him amongst the Judges, awed the accusers, and stopped one part of the prosecution: So that, for the guilt and evil-doings common to both, Cumanus alone was doomed to punishment. Thus the repose of the province was restored.

Shortly after this, the boors of Cilicia, they who are sirnamed Clitæans, and had before raised many insurrections, betook themselves now, under the leading of Throsobor, to their steep and inaccessible mountains, and there encamped. From thence in prædatory bands they made excursions as far as the shore, and round the adjoining cities, boldly committing ravages upon the villagers and husband-

men,

men, and daily spoiling the merchants and seamen. They even besieged the city of Anemurium, and repulsed a body of horse sent from Syria to its relief, under the command of Curtius Severus; for the rocky situation of the place proved a defence to an army of foot, and scarcely admitted the attacks of the horse. But afterwards Antiochus, King of that territory, having by many courtesies gained the multitude, and by stratagem secured their leader, effectually disjoined the forces of the Barbarians; and putting to death Throsobor, and a few more of the chiefs, pacified the rest by methods of clemency.

About the same time, a naval fight was prepared upon the lake Fucinus, and to accommodate the greater numbers with the advantage of beholding the mighty magnificence of the work, a mountain between the lake and the river Liris was levelled: in imitation of Augustus, who once exhibited the like spectacle upon an artificial pool on this side the Tiber, but with light ships, and fewer men. Claudius armed light gallies, some of three, some of four banks of oars, and manned them with nineteen hundred combatants. The circle assigned for the combat was surrounded with an inclosure of great rafts of wood, to obstruct all means of flight or escape: space sufficient was however allowed for the velocity of rowing, for the stratagems of the pilots, the mutual encounters of the ships, and for all the usual feats in naval battles. Upon the rafts stood the Emperors guards, foot and horse, with platforms before them, for wielding and discharging the engines of battery: all the rest of the lake was possessed by the combatants upon covered vessels. The shore, the adjacent hills, and the tops of the mountains, were crowded with a mighty multitude, many from the neighbouring towns, others from Rome itself; some from a passion to behold the spectacle,

tacle, some in compliment to the Prince; and the whole represented a vast theatre. The Emperor presided in a splendid coat of mail, and with him Agrippina in a mantle woven of pure gold. The battle, though between malefactors, was fought with a spirit becoming brave soldiers; so that, after many wounds and much blood, they were redeemed from utter slaughter.

When the spectacle was concluded, and the water discharged, the negligence of the workmen became manifest, and the insufficiency of the work, which was not sunk sufficiently low about the center of the lake. Its bed therefore some time after was hollowed deeper; and, to draw the multitude once more together, a shew of Gladiators was exhibited upon bridges laid over it, in order to display a foot fight. But as a banquet was prepared just at the fall from the lake, the same proved the occasion of great affright; for the weight of the water breaking out with violence bore down with it whatever was near it, shook what was more distant, and by its impetuosity and roaring dismayed all that were present. Agrippina laying instant hold of the Emperor's fright, charged Narcissus, the director of the work, with avarice and rapaciousness; nor did Narcissus spare Agrippina, but attacked and upbraided " the domineering spirit of the woman with her " aspiring and boundless views."

During the Consulship of Decimus Junius and Quintus Haterius, Nero, now in the sixteenth year of his age, espoused Octavia the daughter of Claudius, and, to signalize his accomplishments in polite learning, and acquire the glory of eloquence, undertook the cause of the Ilians, and having floridly represented the Romans as descendants from Troy, and Æneas as the founder of the Julian race, with other old traditions little remote from fables, he obtained for the Ilians entire immunity from all public charges. By the rhetoric of the same advocate, the Colony of Bologne, which had been utterly consumed by fire, were relieved by a bounty of two hundred and fifty thousand crowns. To the Rhodians too their liberty was restored, which had been often withdrawn, and often re-established, as a punishment or reward for their different behaviour, when they obliged us by their assistance in our foreign wars, or provoked us by their seditions at home. And to the city of Apamea, overturned by an earthquake, a remission of tribute was granted for five years.

The policy all this of Agrippina, who pushed Claudius on the contrary upon all the most detested measures of cruelty. As she panted inordinately after the gardens of Statilius Taurus, a nobleman of illustrious fortune, who had been Proconsul of Africa, she procured his bane by the ministry of Tarquitius Priscus, who was his Lieutenant there. After their return, he charged him with some few crimes of extortion, but the sum of the accusation were the practices of Magic. Neither did Taurus deign longer to bear the unworthy lot of prosecution from that traiterons accuser, but, without waiting for the decision of the Senate, laid violent hands upon himself. Tarquitius was, however, expelled the Senate: such was the detestation of the fathers towards the accuser, that they carried his condemnation against the intrigues of Agrippina.

This year, what the Prince had frequently declared, " That to the decisions of his Imperial Pro-
" curators the same force should be allowed as to
' his own," was moreover confirmed and established by a decree of Senate (as a proof that the same was no declaration at random) nay, with more fulness than heretofore and greater enlargements. For the deified Augustus had ordained too, that the Knights who ruled Ægypt, should act judicially, and that the sentences by them pronounced should
be

be equally valid with those of the Roman Magistrates. Soon after this jurisdiction of the Knights was extended to other Provinces, and even in Rome itself to their Tribunal were referred may things formerly determined by the Prætors. Claudius now conferred upon them universal jurisdiction, that jurisdiction for which so many seditions had been raised and so much blood shed, when, by the popular ordinances of the Tribune Sempronius, the Equestrian Order was invested with the power of judicature, and when Servillus the Consul, by a contrary establishment, restored to the Senate the judicial authority. This too chiefly was the end and incitement of the bloody wars betweem Marius and Sylla. But in those days, the several Orders of the State were engaged in different and interfering pursuits, and the party that prevailed made public regulations at their pleasure. Caius Oppius and Cornelius Balbus were the first particulars, who (enabled by the power of Cæsar the Dictator) arbitrated matters of peace and war. It would little avail to recount after this the names of Matius and Vedius, and other Roman Knights, who once bore sway; when to his franchized slaves, such as were entrusted with his domestic concerns, Claudius thus asserted a power equal to his own and to that of the laws.

Thereafter, he proposed for the inhabitants of Coos, a general immunity from impositions, and recounted their antiquity in a long detail; "how
" the Argives, or at least Ceus the father of La-
" tona, first cultivated that island; and thither soon
" after arrived Æsculapius, and with him the art
" of medicine and healing, an art which had great
" applause amongst his descendants," whose names he rehearsed, and marked the several ages in which they flourished. He even said, that " Xenophon
" his own physician, was a branch of the same

" a ily,

"family, and to his fupplications it ought to be
" granted, that his countrymen the people of Coos
" fhould be for ever difcharged from all tribute,
" and only attend the cultivation of an Ifland folely
" devoted to the miniftry of that Deity." It is
without queftion, that many good offices of theirs
towards the Roman people might have been alledged, and even victories gained by their aid; but
Claudius, led by his wonted weaknefs, coloured
under no public confiderations what he had thus
perfonally granted to his phyfician.

The deputies from Byzantium being heard, befought of the Senate to be eafed of their heavy im-
pofitions; and recapitulating things from the firft,
began with the confederacy which they had ftruck
with us fo long ago as the war which we maintained againft that King of Macedon, who from the
degeneracy of his fpirit was diftinguifhed by the
name of Pfeudophilippus; next they recounted the
forces by them fent againft King Antiochus, Perfes,
and Ariftonicus; as alfo how they had fupported
Antonius in the war to fupprefs the Pyrates, with
the feveral aids which they had beftowed upon Sylla, Lucullus, and Pompey. They added the fer-
vices which more lately they had rendered to the
Cæfars, during their encampments and abode in
thefe their territories, where our armies and their
leaders, in all their progreffes by land and water,
were well accommodated, and all their ftores carried after them.

For Byzantium was founded by the Greeks, in
the extremity of Europe, upon a ftreight which dif-
joins Europe from Afia. Thither the founders were
directed by an Oracle of the Pythian Apollo, who,
when confulted by them where to build a city,
replied, " That they fhould feek a fituation oppo-
" fite to the habitations of the blind-men." By this
riddle the Chalcedonians were reprefented; for they,

who

who were the first comers into those parts, and had viewed the advantages of this shore, had yet chosen the opposite and the worst. Byzantium, in truth, stands upon a fertile soil and a plentiful sea; since, into her port are borne all those infinite shoals of fish, which breaking out of the Euxine, shun the other coast, as they are feared by the rocks which, under the waters, shoot from it. Hence, at first the gain and wealth of the Byzantines, but afterwards pressed by the excess of their impositions, they now besought that the same might be abolished or abated. The Emperor too was their advocate, who represented them as late sufferers in the war of Thrace, and in that of Bosphorus, and worthy to be relieved. They were therefore acquitted from tribute for five years.

In the Consulship of Marcus Asinius and Marcus Acilius, a change of affairs for the worse was portended, as was gathered from the frequency of Prodigies. The Ensigns of the soldiers and their tents were scorched with fire from heaven; a swarm of Bees pitched upon the summit of the Capitol; children were born of compounded forms, and a Pig was farrowed with the talons of a hawk. Amongst the prodigies it also was reckoned, that the number of every order of Magistrates was then curtailed, one of the Quæstors, one of the Ædiles, a Tribune, a Prætor, and a Consul, being all deceased within a few months. But more particular was the fear of Agrippina. She was alarmed by a saying of Claudius, uttered heedlessly in his wine, "That it was a fate upon him, to bear the iniqui-" ties of his wives, but at last to punish them." Hence she determined to be quick and prevent him, but first to destroy Domitia Lepida, upon motives derived from the pride and resentments of women. For Lepida, who was the daughter of the younger Antonia, the great niece of Augustus, cousin german

man to Agrippina the elder, and sister to Cnæius Domitius (once husband to the present Agrippina) accounted herself of equal nobility with the other; neither were they much differing in beauty, age, or wealth, both prostitutes in their persons, infamous in their manners, and violent in their tempers, nor less rivals in vices than in the lustre and advantages of their fortune. Hence, however, arose the most vehement struggle, whether the aunt or mother should acquire the ascendant over the spirit of Nero. Lepida laboured to engage and govern his youthful mind by caresses and liberalities: Agrippina, on the contrary, treated him with sternness and threats, like one who would, in truth, confer the sovereignty upon her son, but not bear him for her sovereign.

The crimes therefore charged upon Lepida were, " That by charms and imprecations she had sought " to destroy the Emperor's Consort, and that by " neglecting to restrain the tumultuous behaviour " of her numerous slaves in Calabria, she disturb- " ed the public peace of Italy." For these imputations she was doomed to die, notwithstanding the laboured opposition of Narcissus, who was now become more and more distrustful of Agrippina, insomuch that he is said to have lamented amongst his intimates, " That to himself nothing but cer- " tain destruction remained, whether Britannicus " or Nero succeeded to the Empire; but such to- " wards him had been the favour of the Emperor, " that for the service of his master he would lay down " his life. Under Claudius he had procured the con- " viction and doom of Messalina and of Silius; and " under Nero (if Nero came to reign) there would " be the like causes for the like accusation. If Bri- ", tannicus was to succeed, neither from that Prince " had he any claim to favour, since he had, by " the death of his mother, made room for a step-
mother,

" mother, who by infidious plots was ruining all
" his houfe with fuch notable wickednefs, that bet-
" ter it were he had never divulged to the Empe-
" ror the proftitutions of his former wife, though
" neither, in truth, was the prefent free from prof-
" titution, as Pallas was notorioufly her adulterer;
" infomuch that with no mortal could any doubt
" remain, but to the luft of rule fhe poftponed her
" fame, her modefty, her perfon, and all things."
Repeating thefe and the like fpeeches, he tenderly embraced Britannicus, and fupplicated for him full and fudden ripenefs of age; now to the Gods, then to the young Prince, he lifted up his hands and poured out prayers, " That he might attain
" vigour of years; that he might exterminate the
" enemies of his father, and even be revenged on
" thofe who flew his mother."

Amidft all thefe mighty agitations and anxieties, Claudius was taken ill, and for the recovery of his health had recourfe to the foft air and falubrious waters of Sinueffa. It was then that Agrippina, long fince bent upon the parricide, greedy of the prefent occafion, and well furnifhed with wicked agents, confulted concerning the quality of the poifon: " If it were fudden and rapid in its operation,
" the dark deed might thence be betrayed; if one
" flow and confuming were adminiftered, there
" was danger that Claudius, when his end approach-
" ed, and perhaps having the while difcovered
" the deadly fraud, would recall the tendernefs and
" partiality of a father for his fon." A fubtle poifon was therefore judged beft, " fuch as would
" diforder his brain, and not prefently kill." An experienced artift in fuch preparations was chofen, her name Locufta, lately condemned for poifoning, and one long entertained amongft the other machines of the Monarchy: by this woman's fkill the poifon was prepared; to adminifter the fame

was the part of Halotus, one of the Eunuchs, steward of the Emperor's table and his taster. Indeed, all the particulars of this deed were soon afterwards so thoroughly known, that the writers of those times are able to recount, " how the poison was " seethed in a delicious mess of mushrooms, but, " whether from the natural stupidity of Claudius, " or that he was drunk, he felt not instantly the " virulence of the dose;" a looseness too at the same time seemed to relieve him, and to defeat the operation. Agrippina became terribly dismayed; but, as her own life lay at stake, she despised the stain and odium which must accompany her present proceedings, and called in the aid of Xenophon the physician, whom she had already engaged in her guilty purposes. It is thought that he, as if he had meant to assist Claudius in his efforts to vomit, thrust down his throat a feather dipt in outrageous poison, as one who well knew, that the most daring iniquities are attempted with hazard, but accomplished with rewards.

The Senate was in the mean time assembled, and the Consuls and Pontiffs were offering vows for the recovery of the Emperor, when he was already dead; though coverings and restoratives were still applied, till matters were disposed for securing the Empire to Nero. And first, Agrippina, personating unconquerable sorrow, and one who sought on all hands for consolation, clasped Britannicus in her arms, stiled him ' the genuine image of his father," and, by various and feigned devices, with-held him from leaving the chamber. There she likewise detained Antonia and Octavia, his sisters, and, by posting guards, shut up all the passages From time to time too she declared that the Prince was upon recovery, thence to encourage the hopes of the soldiery till the fortunate moment, according to the calculations of the Astrologers, were at hand.

At

At laſt, on the thirteenth of October, at noon, the gates of the palace were ſuddenly thrown open, and Nero, accompanied by Burrhus, walked forth to the cohort, which, according to the cuſtom of the army, was then upon guard: there, upon ſignification made by the Præfect, he was received with ſhouts of joy, and inſtantly put into a litter. It is reported, that there were ſome who heſitated, diligently looking and frequently aſking, where was Britannicus? but that as no one appeared to propoſe him, they preſently embraced the choice which was offered them. Thus Nero was borne to the camp, where, a'ter a ſpeech ſuitable to the exigency, and the promiſe of a largeſs equal to that of the late Emperor his father, he was ſaluted Emperor. The declaration of the ſoldiers was followed and confirmed by the decrees of the Senate; nor was there any reluctancy in the ſeveral provinces. To Claudius were decreed cœleſtial honours, and the ſolemnity of his funeral the ſame as that of the deified Auguſtus, ſince in it Agrippina would needs emulate the magnificence of her great grandmother Livia. His teſtament, however, was not rehearſed in public, leſt the preference there given from his own ſon to the ſon of his wife, might grate and provoke the ſpirit of the populace.

THE ANNALS OF TACITUS.

BOOK XIII.

The SUMMARY.

Silanus, *Proconsul of Asia, poisoned at the instigation of* Agrippina. Narcissus, *freedman to the late Emperor, doomed to die. The funeral of* Claudius. Nero's *Panegyric upon him.* Nero's *reign begins well. The Senate left to act independently. The Parthians aim at the possession of Armenia.* Corbulo *employed against them.* Nero *his passion for* Acte. Agrippina *provoked by it, and thence loses credit with her son.* Pallas *removed from the administration.* Britannicus *poisoned.* Agrippina *grows obnoxious to* Nero; *is accused before him, and acquitted.* Nero's *wild revellings during the night. Debate about recalling insolent freedmen to their former bondage. Some eminent men condemned. Natural deaths. New broils with the Parthians about Armenia.* Corbulo *inures his men to severe and primitive discipline; invades Armenia, storms several strong-holds, takes the city of Artaxata, and burns*

' *burnt it.* Tiridates *flies before him.* P. Suilius *condemned.* Octavius Sagitta, *in the rage of love, stabs* Pontia, *his former mistress, upon her refusing to marry him. His freedman takes the fact upon himself.* Nero *conceives a passion for* Poppæa Sabina *Her history, character, and arts.* Cornelius, *through the Emperor's jealousy, banished to Marseilles. The exorbitance of the publicans restrained. The Frisians endeavour to settle near the Rhine, but are driven thence by the Roman horse and routed. The Ansibarians make the same attempt, with the same ill fortune. Fierce war between the Hermondurians and Cattians; the latter almost utterly cut off in a great battle. Strange eruption of fire in the territory of the Jubones.*

THE first victim under the new Prince was Junius Silanus, proconsul of Asia, dispatched unknown to Nero, by the fraud of Agrippina: not that he had provoked his fate by any turbulence of spirit, having lived in such sloth and even such scorn, during the late reigns, that Caligula was wont to call him the golden sheep. But Agrippina feared that he might prove the avenger of the murder of his brother Lucius Silanus, by her formerly procured. For it was now the current rumour amongst the populace, that, " as Nero was " scarce past his childhood, and by iniquity had ac- " quired the Empire, such a man was to be pre- " ferred to him, one of composed age, spotless in- " tegrity, noble, and (which was then highly pri- " zed) descended from the Cæsars:" for he too was the great grandson of Augustus. Such was the cause of his doom; the instruments were Publius Celar a Roman knight, and Helius the freedman, both employed to manage the Emperor's domestic revenue in Asia; by them the proconsul had poison given him at a banquet, so openly, as if they meant not to disavow it. Nor was less haste used to dispatch Narcissus, the late Emperor's freedman, whose bold invectives against Agrippina I have mentioned. In a rigorous prison, and through the miserable extremity of want, he was constrained to die, sore against the mind of Nero, who, however he hitherto smothered his vices, bore a wonderful conformity to the temper to Narcissus, profuse and rapacious like his own.

A torrent of slaughters was about to have followed had not Afranius Burrhus and Annæus Seneca prevented it: these were the governors of the Emperor's youth, and though engaged in partnership of power, yet, by a rare example, well united, men different in their accomplishments, but of equal weight and authority. Burrhus his instructor in lessons of arms and the gravity of manners, Seneca in the precepts of eloquence and polite address. In this office they helped and supported each other, the easier to manage between them the dangerous age of the Prince; or if he rejected the pursuits of virtue, to restrain him at least within the bounds of guiltless pleasures. One constant struggle they both had against the tempestuous spirit of Agrippina, who was transported with every lust of lawless dominion, and in her designs upheld by Pallas, the same who had led Claudius into that incestuous match, then into the fatal adoption, and by both, into his own destruction. But Nero's temper was not such as to be controuled by slaves; and Pallas too having exceeded the liberties of a slave manumised, and by his horrid arrogance provoked Nero's disgust. Upon Agrippina however, in public, he accumulated all kinds of honours, nay to a Tribune once, who, according to the discipline of the soldiery, desired the word, gave that of *excellent mother*; by the Senate too were decreed her two Lictors, with the character of Priestess to Claudius. To him at the same time was ordained a cenforial funeral, and afterwards deification.

The day of burial, his funeral praifes were pronounced by Nero, who, whilft he carefully recounted the antiquity of this lineage, the many Conful-fhips, the many triumphs of his anceftors, others as carefully liftened. The difplay too of his acquirements in Letters was heard with attention and pleafure, as alfo the obfervation, that during his reign no calamity from foreigners had befallen the ftate: but when he fell into a commemoration of the wifdom and providence of Claudius, not a foul could refrain from laughter, though the fpeech was of Seneca's compofing, and difcovered much accuracy and finenefs, as he had, in truth, a beautiful genius, and ftile well fuited to the tafte of that time. Old men, who make it their recreation to draw parallels between things prefent and paft, took notice, that Nero was the firft Roman Emperor who needed the aid of another man's eloquence. For Cæfar the Dictator was ranked with the moft diftinguifhed Orators. Auguftus too had an eafy and flowing elocution, fuch as became a Prince. Tiberius alfo poffeffed the art of marfhalling words; his fentiments were likewife ftrong, and it was from policy that fometimes his expreffions were obfcure. Even the difordered fpirit of Caligula impaired not his addrefs and energy in fpeaking. Nor was Claudins wanting in elegance of difcourfe, when his difcourfe was the effect of ftudy. Nero, even from his childhood, had abandoned his lively imagination to other occupations and diverfions, to graving, painting, finging, and managing the horfe, at times too in compofing poems, whence fome grounds of fcience appeared to have been in him.

Having finifhed this mimickry of mourning, he repaired to the Senate, where, after an introduction concerning his eftablifhment in the Empire by the authority

authority of the fathers, and the common concurrence of the soldiery, he declared with what worthy purposes, and upon what good examples he assumed the Sovereignty; that his youth being never ruffled nor engaged in any of the animosities of civil wars, or any domestic dissensions, he brought with him no spirit of hatred, no sense of injuries, nor appetite of revenge. He then proposed the scheme of his future rule, and in it avoided carefully all those late measures of reigning, which were still fresh and odious; 'for that he claimed not the judgment and
' decision of affairs, nor would allow the shutting
' up those who were accused in the same house with
' their accusers, and by it sustained the impotent
' tyranny of a few. Nothing should be saleable
' within his walls, nor any access there to intrigues
' of ambition. Between his family and the republic
' a just distinction should be maintained; the Senate
' should uphold her ancient jurisdiction; Italy, and
' all those provinces which depended upon the
' People and Senate, should apply only to the tri-
' bunal of the Consuls, and by them proenie ac-
' cess to the Fathers. To himself he reserved what
' was especially committed to his trust, the direc-
' tion of the armies'

This declaration wanted no sincerity, and by the Senate many regulations were made, agreeable to their own good liking, particularly, that no advocate should defend a cause for gift or payment, and that those who were designed Quæstors, should be no longer obliged to exhibit public shews of Gladiators. All this was opposed by Agrippina, as what rescinded the acts of Claudius; but the Fathers prevailed, though by her contrivance they were purposely assembled in the palace, that there posted by a door, behind a curtain, secure from sight, she might yet easily overhear. Nay, at a time when the Embassadors from Armenia were pleading before Nero a cause of their nation, she was advancing to ascend the Imperial Tribunal, and to sit in joint judgment with the Emperor, if Seneca, seeing all the rest mute through fear, had not remembered him 'to descend and meet his mother.' Thus, under the guise of filial reverence, that public disgrace was prevented.

At the end of the Year, tidings were brought by the flying alarms of rumour, 'that the Parthi-
' ans having broke out into fresh hostilities, had seiz-
' ed Armenia, and exterminated 'Rhadamistus,' who, often Sovereign of that Kingdom, and as often a fugitive, had now too abandoned the war. At Rome therefore, a city fond of descanting upon the public, they began to inquire, ' how a Prince, scarce
' passed his seventeenth year, could undertake so
' mighty a charge, how repulse such a potent foe?
' what protection to the State from a youth govern-
' ed by a woman? would he, upon this occasion also,
' act by the ministry of his tutors? would his tutors
' fight battles, storm towns, and execute the other
' functions of war?' Others, on the contrary, alledged, ' that it had thus better happened, than if the
' weight and care of that war had fallen upon Clau-
' dius, under all the defects of old age and stupidity,
' one who would have blindly obeyed the dictates of
' his slaves. Burrhus and Seneca were known for men
' of long and various experience in affairs, and to
' the emperor himself how little was wanting of
' mature age? when Pompey in his eighteenth
' year, Octavius Cæsar in his nineteenth, each sus-
' tained the weight of a civil war? Under public
' rulers, more was accomplished by counsels and
' influence, than by arms and force. Nero besides
' would soon exhibit a manifest proof, whether he
' employed worthy or unworthy Counsellors, if his
' choice of a General fell, without pique or parti-
' ality, upon a man of signal reputation, rather than
' upon

"upon one that was only wealthy, and trusted to favour and intrigues."

Whilst these and the like discourses employed the public, Nero, to supply the Legions in the East, ordered recruits to be raised through the neighbouring provinces, and the Legions themselves to be posted near to Armenia; as also that the ancient Kings, Agrippa and Antiochus, should make ready their forces, such as might enable them to invade the territories of the Parthians; and that bridges should be forthwith made upon the Euphrates. To Aristobulus he moreover committed the Lesser Armenia, and the region of Sophenes to Sohemus, with the ensigns of Royalty and title of Kings. There arose likewise to Vologeses a competitor for his Crown, even for his own son Vardanes. Hence the Parthians withdrew from Armenia, so as if they meant to return, and only postponed the war.

But, in the Senate, all this was extolled above measure, by such as voted, "that days of public supplications should be decreed to the Gods, that on those public days the Prince should wear the triumphal robe, that he should enter the city in the pomp of *Ovation*, that to him a statue should be erected of the same bulk with that of Mars the Avenger, and in the same temple." Besides their habitual proneness to flattery, they sincerely rejoiced that, for the reconquest of Armenia, he had preferred Domitius Corbulo, whence a door seemed to be opened for the reward of virtue and merit. The forces in the East were so divided, that part of the auxiliaries, with two Legions, were to remain in Syria under the command of Numidius Quadratus governor of the province; an equal number of Romans and allies were assigned to Corbulo, with an addition of the cohorts and other troops, which wintered in Cappadocia. The Confederate Kings were ordered to obey either, according to the
exigencies

exigencies of the war; but their affections were much more devoted to Corbulo, who, in order to take advantage of fame, which in all new enterprizes has ever most powerful influence, marched with expedition, and at Ægeas, a city of Cilicia, was met by Quadratus, who advanced purposely thus far, lest Corbulo, if he had entered Syria to receive his forces there, should draw upon himself the eyes of all men, large as he was in his person, a magnificent speaker, and, besides the esteem of his wisdom and great experience, even things empty in themselves, his air and fashion, served powerfully to recommend him.

' Both, however, warned Vologeses by messages,
' to prefer peace to war, and by delivering hos-
' tages to preserve towards the Roman people
' that reverence which was wont to be paid by
' his ancestors.' Vologeses too, in order to make the more effectual preparations for war, or perhaps to remove under the name of hostages, such as he suspected of aiming at the Diadem, yielded the most illustrious of the family of Arsacides. They were received by Histeius the Centurion, who had been for this very end dispatched to the King by Numidius. When this became known to Corbulo, he ordered Arrius Varus, Prefect of a Cohort, to go and take them; hence a quarrel arose between the Centurion and the Prefect, but, to prevent the same from becoming the sport of foreign nations, to the hostages themselves and deputies who conducted them, the decision of the difference was committed, and they preferred the pretensions of Corbulo, in regard of his late exaltation, and even from a certain bias towards him in the hearts of our enemies. Hence a source of discord between the Generals. Numidius complained that he was bereft of what he had by his own counsels atchieved; Corbulo, on the contrary, maintained that the King

had

had not inclined to yield hostages, till he himself being appointed to conduct the war, had changed his hopes into fear. Nero, to compose their jarrings, ordered public declarations to be made, " that for the successful conduct of Quadratus and " Corbulo, the laurel should be annexed to their " fasces." These transactions, though they reached into the year of the succeeding Consuls, I have thus laid together.

The same year, Nero applied to the Senate for a statue to his father Domitius, and for the Consular ornaments to Asconius Labeo, who had been his Tutor. Statues to himself of solid silver and gold he refused, and opposed such who proposed them; and, notwithstanding an ordinance of Senate, that the year for the future should begin on December, the month in which Nero was born, he preserved the ancient solemnity of beginning the year with the first of January; neither would he admit a criminal prosecution against Carinas Celer the Senator, upon the accusation of a slave; nor against Julius Densus of the Equestrian Order, charged as a delinquent for his devotion to Britannicus.

In the Consulship of Nero and Lucius Antistius, as the Magistrates were swearing upon the acts of the Emperors, he with-held Antistius his colleague from swearing upon his; an action copiously extolled by the Fathers with design that his youthful spirit, first animated by the glory resulting from light things, might proceed to court the same in things which were greater. There followed an instance of his Mercy towards Plautius Lateranus; formerly degraded from the order of Senator, for adultery with Messalina, but now by Nero restored. He chose to make many professions of clemency in the frequent speeches with Seneca, either to manifest what worthy counsels he gave, or in ostentation

of

of his own wit, uttered in public by the mouth of the Emperor.

In the mean while, the authority of his mother became by little and little flight and impaired; for Nero having fallen into a paſſion for a franchiſed damſel, her name Acte, at the ſame time aſſumed as confidents in his amour Otho and Claudius Senecio, the firſt of a Conſular family, the other a ſon of one of the Emperor's freedmen, both youths of graceful perſons, who firſt unknown to his mother, then in ſpight of her, had by fellowſhip in luxury and ſecret pleaſures crept into an unbounded intimacy with him. Nor did even his ſevereſt miniſters thwart this intrigue, when with a woman of low condition, to the injury of no man, the Prince ſatisfied his youthful inclinations and pleaſures. For Octavia his wife, however illuſtrious in her birth, however celebrated for her virtue, he intirely nauſeated, whether from blind fatality, or that forbidden purſuits are more prevalent and attractive. Beſides it was dreaded, that had he been with-held from that gallantry, he would have daringly polluted Ladies of high quality.

Now Agrippina ſtormed, ' that a manumiſed ' ſlave was become her competitreſs, a handmaid ' her daughter-in law,' with other the like angry invectives of an incenſed woman. Nor would ſhe practiſe the leaſt patience, till her ſon were reclaimed by being aſhamed or ſurfeited; though the fouler her reproaches were, the more vehemently ſhe fired his paſſion; ſo that, overcome at laſt by its ſuperior force, he ſhook off all reverence for his mother, and ſurrendered himſelf intirely to Seneca, who had a friend named Annæus Serenns, that had hitherto cloaked the Prince's paſſion for Acte, by feigning one of his own, and furniſhed his name, that in it he might openly preſent to her whatever Nero in ſecret beſtowed upon her. And now Agrippina,

grippina, changing her arts and address, assailed his youthful spirit with softness and blandishments, she offered him ' her own chamber, that there, and ' even within her own arms, he might more co- ' vertly accomplish whatever the warmth of his ' youth and sovereign fortune prompted him to.' She even acknowledged her unseasonable rigour, and tendered him the disposal of all her wealth, not far short of the imperial treasures. For as she had lately been over strict in checking her son, so now she was become beyond measure submissive and condescending. This sudden change deceived not Nero; and his closest friends dreading it, besought him, " to beware of snares from a woman always " implacable, and then both implacable and dis- " sembling." It happened about that time, that as Nero was surveying the precious ornaments in which the wives and mothers of the Emperors were wont to shine, he chose out certain rich rai- ment with many jewels, and sent them as presents to his mother; nor were the same any wife stinted, since the choicest things, and such as others pas- sionately covet, were by him, unasked, presented to her. But Agrippina waxed violent, and said, ' that by these gifts, the adorning of her person ' was not intended, but rather her exclusion from ' all besides: and her son would thus divide with ' her what he had wholly received from her.' Nor were there wanting those who related these her words with aggravations.

Nero therefore, provoked with those who mana- ged and upheld the imperious spirit of Agrippina, dismissed Pallas from the employment which he had received from Claudius, and in it had acted like the sovereign director of the Empire. It is reported that, as he departed the palace, attended by a mighty throng of followers, Nero said, not unpleasantly, " Pallas is going to abdicate his soveregnity."

Pallas

Pallas had, in truth, stipulated, 'That he should be questioned for no part of his past behaviour; and, for his accounts, the public should have no more demands upon him, than he upon the public.' After this Agrippina quite abandoned herself to a stile of threats and terrors, nor spared she to utter them in the Emperor's hearing, but declared, 'that Britannicus was now grown up, the natural descendant from Claudius, and worthy to assume the Empire of his father; an Empire which one, who was a son only by adoption and ingraftment, swayed by trampling upon his own mother. She freely consented that all the crying calamities brought upon that unhappy house, should be laid open to the world, and first in the list her own incestuous marriage with her uncle, then her own guilt in poisoning her husband. One only consolation, by the providence of the Gods and her own, remained to her, that her step-son was still left alive; with him she would repair to the camp, where, on one side, would be heard the daughter of Germanicus, on the other Burrhus and Seneca, the first with his maimed hand, the second with the stile of a pedagogue, both engaged in a contest with her about the sovereign rule of human kind.' At the same time she tossed her menacing hands, accumulated reproaches, invoked the deified Claudius, with the manes of the Silani, and of so many others whose murders she had in vain perpetrated!

All this alarmed Nero, and as the following day was that of the nativity of Britannicus, who on it accomplished his fourteenth year, he revolved, within himself, now upon the violent spirit of his mother, then upon the promising genius of that youth, of which, during the late Festival of the Saturnalia, he had given a remarkable specimen, and by it acquired universal esteem. Besides other sports, on

that

that occasion, amongst them and others of the like age and condition, as they drew lots who should be King of the play, the lot fell upon Nero: he therefore, in that quality, gave to all the rest distinct commands, yet such as exposed them to no ridicule; but that to Britannicus was, to stand forth in the center of the company, and there begin some song. From attempting this task he hoped the boy would become an object of laughter, untrained as he was even in the parts of sober conversation, much more in the rants of drunkards. Britannicus, however, with an address steady and undisturbed, raised his voice to some verses which imported, how he ' was bereft of his natural inheritance and the Im- ' perial power.' Hence he drew compassion from those who heard him, which was the more unrestrained, for that their gaiety and the night had banished hypocrisy. Nero was struck with the invidious application, and grew into still more mortal hate; but, however urged to dispatch by the menaces of Agrippina, yet as his brother was without crime, and openly he dared not command his execution, he set about a secret machination. He ordered poison to be prepared, and as his agent in it employed Julius Pollio, Tribune of a Prætorian Cohort, in whose custody was kept a woman under condemnation for poisoning, Locusta, 'famous for many black iniquities in that art. For, as to any obstacle from those who were nearest about the person of Britannicus, care had been long since taken that they should be such as were to have no sense of common honesty, or conscience of their faith and duty. The first poison he took was even administered by the hands of his governors, but without effect, being voided in a looseness; whether in itself it wanted energy, or, to prevent a discovery by its sudden rage, had been qualified. Nero, who was impatient of slow progress in his cruelty, threatened

ened terribly the Tribune, and was dooming the Sorceress to execution, 'for that, whilst they only 'apprehended the out-cries of the people, and 'were meditating ways to acquit themselves, they 'postponed the security of the Prince.' Hence they undertook to prepare a dose which, sudden as a dagger, should dispatch him, and in a chamber next to the Emperor's the deadly potion was seethed, compounded of several poisons, all of experienced rapidity.

At meals, it was the manner of the children of Princes, accompanied with other young nobles, to be served in a sitting posture, in the sight of their nearest kindred, at a separate table, and more sparingly covered. While Britannicus was thus at meat, the opportunity was taken; but forasmuch as whatever he eat or drank was first tried by a special officer of his, a taster, to the end therefore that neither this usage might be omitted, nor by the death of both the iniquity be detected, the guile was thus concerted. To Britannicus drink was presented, such as was yet free from all infection, and tried by the taster, but scalding hot, and for that reason returned by Britannicus; hence it was qualified with cold water, in which the poison was poured, which seized all his organs with such sudden efficacy, that he was at once bereft of speech and life: fear and trembling possessed his companions; such too as comprehended not the mystery, instantly retired, but those of deeper discernment remained, with their eyes fixed stedfastly upon Nero, who, as he lay in a reclining posture, declared, with the air of one utterly ignorant, "That it was a usual 'fit of the falling-sickness, with which Britannicus 'from his early childhood had been afflicted, and 'by degrees his sight and understanding would re-'turn.' But in Agrippina such tokens of dread and consternation of spirit broke out, though by disguised

looks

looks she laboured to smother the same; that it was manifest she was as much a stranger to the doom of Britannicus as was his own sister Octavia; for by his death she was sensible, that her last refuge was snatched from her, and saw an awakening example of parricide before her. Even Octavia, however raw in years, had learnt to hide under dissimulation her grief and tenderness, and every other affection of her soul. So, after a short silence, the pleasantry of the entertainment was resumed.

Upon one and the same night were seen the untimely fate of Britannicus and his funeral pile; for beforehand had been prepared all the appointments for his burial, which itself proved but moderate and stinted. In the Field of Mars, however, his remains were reposited, during such tempestuous rains as the populace believed to be denunciations of the wrath of the Deities against the crying deed; a deed which yet was in the judgment of many men entitled to pardon, whilst they considered the wonted dissensions eternally happening between rival brothers, and the incommunicable genius of sovereignty. It is related by most of the writers of those times, that, for some time before the murder, Nero had defiled the youth by frequent constupration; so that this his death, however suddenly procured during the inviolable hospitality of the table, and so precipitately that to his sister not a moment was allowed for a last embrace, and under the eye of his capital enemy, yet could not appear too early incurred, nor even cruelly inflicted, though by it the last branch of the Claudian race was extirpated, since it was a branch vitiated by unnatural pollution before it perished by poison. Nero, by an edict, justified the hasty dispatch of the obsequies; the same, he said, was the institution of our ancestors, ‘ presently to withdraw from the eyes of the pub‘ lic the corses of such as fell before their prime,

nor

' nor to stay to lengthen the solemnity by pomp and
' funeral orations. He too in Britannicus had lost
' the support of a brother; hence all his surviving
' hopes rested solely in the Commonwealth, and
' hence with the greater tenderness ought the Se-
' nate and people to cherish a Prince, who alone
' survived of a family born to sustain sovereignty.'

He then distinguished his most noted friends with great donations; nor were there wanting such as severely censured some, who, notwithstanding their avowed gravity, were yet parting amongst themselves, like spoils taken in war, the possessions of Britannicus, his palaces in Rome, and his manors and villas throughout Italy. Others believed, that they were constrained to accept them by the authority of the Emperor, who, stung with the guilt of his own conscience, hoped that his crimes would be overlooked, if by largesses he could engage in his interest the most powerful men in the state. But his mother's wrath, no liberalities could assuage; she was still caressing Octavia, still holding secret cabals with her confidents; and, besides the usual cravings of her inherent avarice, she was on all hands exacting and amassing treasure, as if by it she had some great design to support. The Tribunes and Centurions she received with great court and affability, and to the quality and merit of such of the virtuous nobility as even then remained, she paid distinguished honour, as if she were thus studying to create a party and find a leader. These her measures were known to Nero; and therefore the guards which attended at her gate (a pre-eminence which she held as consort to the late Emperor, and had continued to her as mother to this) were by his order withdrawn, together with the band of Germans which, as an additional honour, had been joined to the former. Moreover, to prevent her being followed by such a throng of courtiers, he

Vol. II. F sepa-

separated her habitation from his, and conveyed her into the house which had belonged to Antonia. There, as often as he visited her, he went always surrounded with a crowd of officers, and after the short ceremony of returning her salute, immediately departed.

Of all mortal things there is nought so unstable and transitory as the name of power, which stauds not upon its own native vigour and basis. Instantly the house of Agrippina was deserted; none appeared to give her consolation, none to visit her, except some few Ladies, and whether from affection or hate they did it, is uncertain. Amongst these was Junia Silana, she who was by Messalina divorced from Caius Silius, as above I have recounted, a Lady signal in her quality, beauty, and lewdness, and one, for a long while, very dear to Agrippina; but between them afterwards secret heart-burnings and resentments arose, for that Sextius Africanus, a noble youth, purposing to espouse Silana, was diverted by Agrippina, who urged, ‘that she was ‘ lewd, and past her prime:’ not that she meant to reserve Africanus for herself, but left by marrying Silana. he should, as she had no children, with her possess all her wealth. Silana, who thought she saw a prospect of vengeance, instructed two of her own creatures, Iturius and Calvistus, to accuse her; neither did she attack her with stale charges often before alledged, such ‘ as her bewailing the
‘ fate of Britannicus, and publishing the wrongs
‘ done to Octavia, but with designs to stir up Rube-
‘ lius Plautus to make a revolution in the state, a
‘ nobleman who, by his mother, was in blood as
‘ nigh as Nero to the deified Augustus; that by
‘ espousing him and investing him with Empire,
‘ she meant once more to seize the Common-
‘ wealth.’ All this was by Iturius and Calvisius imparted to Atimetus, freedman to Domitia, Nero's aunt:

aunt: Atimetus, overjoyed at the discovery, (for between Agrippina and Domitia a passionate competition was maintained) instigated Paris the player, who was also Domitia's freedman, to proceed with all haste to the Emperor, ' and there in tragical ' colours to announce the crime.'

It was far in night, and Nero was wasting the remainder in carousing, when Paris entered, who else was wont at such seasons to heighten the voluptuous gaieties of the Prince; but now, with a face carefully framed into sadness, he laid before Nero a minute and orderly detail of the conspiracy, and by it so thoroughly affrighted him, that he not only determined the death of his mother and of Plautus, but also to remove Burrhus the captain of his guards, as one who owed his promotion to the favour of Agrippina, and would be ready to return her the like good office. We have it upon the authority of Fabius Rusticus, ' That to Cæcina Tuscus a codi-
' cil was already dispatched, intrusting him with
' the command of the Prætorian bands, but that,
' through the credit and mediation of Seneca, Bur-
' rhus retained his dignity.' According to the account of Cluvius and Pliny, no jealousy was entertained concerning the fidelity of the Præfect. But it must be owned, that Fabius manifests a constant zeal to extol Seneca, by whose friendship his own fortune flourished. As my own purpose is to follow the general consent of authors, so I shall insert under the name of each whatever they diversly publish. Nero, possessed with dread, and with a blind passion to slay his mother, could not be brought to defer his cruel purposes, till Burrhus undertook for her execution, in case she were convicted of the imputed crimes; ' but to every one, whoever it were, a
' liberty of defence, he said, must be granted, how
' much more to a mother? Nor, in truth, against
' her did any accusers appear, but only the hearsay
' of

' of one man, and by him brought from the house
' of her enemy, a hearsay too which the circum-
' stances and unseasonable hour contributed to re-
' fute; it was during the dead darkness and solitude
' of the night, and during a night spent in the festi-
' vity of banquetting, when all things conspired to
' produce only rash judgment and uncertainty.'

The Emperor's fears being thus in some measure assuaged and day returned, recourse was had to Agrippina herself, that, having notified to her the several charges against her, she might invalidate the same, or bear the punishment. These orders were performed by Burrhus in the presence of Seneca; there attended likewise some of the Emperor's freedmen to watch his discourse. Burrhus, after he had to her explained her crimes, and given her the names of those who alledged them, proceeded to high words and menaces. Agrippina retained still the wonted fierceness of her spirit; ' I wonder not, said she,
' that to Silana, who never bore a child, the tender
' affections of a mother are thus unknown; for
' children are not so easily changed by their parents,
' as by a harlot are her adulterers; nor, because
' Iturius and Calvisius, after having riotously de-
' voured their whole fortunes, prostitute themselves,
' for their last resource, to gratify the vengeance
' of an old woman, by turning my accusers, does
' it therefore follow that I am to undergo the foul
' infamy of parricide, or that any apprehensions
' should thence alarm the mind of Cæsar. As to
' Domitia, I would thank her even for all the ef-
' forts of her enmity to me, if in instances of tender-
' ness towards my child Nero she would strive to
' exceed me. At present, by the ministration of
' Atimetus her minion, and of Paris the player, she
' is framing a plot, like one for the stage; but she
' was occupied in trimming the canals of her villa
' at

' at Baiæ, at a time when by my councils and ma-
' nagement he was adopted into the Claudian name,
' invested with the Proconsular authority, designed
' to the Consulship, and all other measures taken
' proper for acquiring him the Empire. In short,
' produce the person, who can charge me, either
' with attempting the faith of the guards at Rome,
' or with shaking the allegiance of the provinces,
' or with suborning the Prince's slaves and freedmen
' to treason against his person. Under the reign of Bri-
' tannicus, indeed, had he possessed the sovereignty,
' I could have preserved my life; but, were Plautus
' or any other to gain the supreme rule, and thence
' a power of pronouncing judgment upon any
' process against me, is it likely that I should want
' accusers, when, even under Nero, there are those
' who stand up to accuse me, not of words, some-
' times by me incautiously uttered in the heat of
' affection and pity, but of treason so flagrant, that
' only through the bowels of a son for his mother
' can I be acquitted by mine?' Compunction seized
all who attended her; they voluntarily strove to
allay the swellings of her heart, and she demanded
an interview with her son. During it, she alledged not a syllable in behalf of her innocence,
like one who mistrusted herself, nor of his engagements to gratitude, like one who could reproach
him for want of it, but insisted that vengeance
should be done upon her accusers, recompences be
conferred on her friends, and obtained both. To
Fenius Rufus was granted the superintendance of
provisions, to Arruntius Stella the direction of the
public shews which the Emperor was preparing to
exhibit, and to Caius Balbillus the government of
Ægypt; that of Syria was assigned to Publius Anteius, but by various feints and stratagems he was,
from time to time, eluded of the possession, and at

last detained for good and all at Rome. Silana was sent into exile: Calvisius too and Iturius were banished. Upon Atimetus capital pains were inflicted; but Paris was of too prevailing consequence to the Emperor in his debauches, to be subjected to punishment. Plautus was for the present passed over in silence.

A charge was thereafter brought against Pallas and Burrhus, 'for having engaged in a design of 'advancing to the Empire Cornelius Sylla, in re- 'gard of his splendid descent and alliance with Clau- 'dius,' whose son-in-law he was, having espoused his daughter Antonia. This accusation was supported by one Pætus, a fellow infamous for busily promoting confiscations in the exchequer, and purchasing the effects of such as were condemned. Equally notorious too, upon this occasion, was the vanity and falshood of his allegations; yet the apparent innocence of Pallas proved not so well pleasing, as his arrogance proved shocking; for upon naming to him those of his freedmen who were said to have been his accomplices, he answered, 'That 'at home he never used any other way of signifying 'his pleasure than sometimes by a nod, sometimes 'by a motion of his hand; or, if his commands 'consisted of many particulars, he then committed 'the same to writing; so that, at all adventures, 'he ever avoided to mix in discourse with his dome- 'stics.' Burrhus, notwithstanding he was arraigned, sate and voted with the other judges, and upon the accuser the doom of banishment was inflicted. His duplicates too were burnt, the instruments by which he was wont to exact fresh payment to the cancelled claims of the exchequer.

Towards the close of the year was removed the band of men which, as a guard, was wont to attend at the celebration of the public plays, thence to exhibit

hibit a more plaufible appearance of popular liberty; as alfo to preferve the foldiery from tainting their difcipline by the diffolute licentioufnefs of the theatre, and moreover ' to prove, whether the populace ' would still retain the fame modefty of behaviour ' now the guards were removed.' At the admonitions of the foothfayers, the Emperor purified the city by luftration, for that the temples of Jupiter and Minerva had been ftruck with lightning.

In the Confulfhip of Quintus Volufius and Publius Scipio, while profound quiet reigned all over the Empire abroad, abominable revellings prevailed at Rome, under the leading of Nero, who, difguifed into the habit of a flave, went roaming about the ftreets, and fcoured the public inns and ftews, followed by a fet of companions, who feized as prey whatever ftood expofed to fale, and affaulted whomfoever they met; and all thefe violences were committed upon people fo unapprized of the author, that he himfelf was once wounded, and bore the fear in his face. When afterwards it came to be divulged, that it was the Emperor who rioted thus, and as frefh outrages were daily done to men and ladies of illuftrious quality, the name of Nero being once ufed to warrant licentioufnefs, was faifly affumed as a cloak by others, and many with their own feparate gangs boldly practifed the fame exceffes: fo that fuch were the nightly combuftions at Rome, as if the city had been ftormed and the inhabitants taken captive. Julius Montanus, one in the rank of Senators, but hitherto invefted with no Magiftracy, having cafually encountered the Prince in the dark, refolutely repulfed his affaults, and afterwards difcovering him, implored his forgivenefs; but, as if he had reproached the Emperor, by owning that he knew him, he was compelled to die. Thenceforward, however, Nero became more fearful,

ful, and in thefe his rambles fortified himfelf with a party of foldiers and a great train of Gladiators; thefe interpofed not in the beginning of a fray, nor while the fame continued but moderately high, as if it were only a quarrel between particulars, and they were unconcerned; but if fuch as were infulted refifted with vigour, inftantly the men of arms fell on. Nay, at the diverfions of the theatre, the feveral parties that favoured particular players, were by him turned into hoftile factions, encountering as it were in battle, animated, indeed, by the influence of impunity and rewards. Befides, he greedily attended thofe broils, fometimes concealed, and often as an avowed fpectator. Thefe tumults went on, till the people being heated and rent into diffenfions, and commotions ftill more terrible apprehended, no other remedy was found but that of driving the players out of Italy, and of recalling the foldiers to guard the theatre.

About the fame time the Senate had under confideration the infolence and bafe dealings of the Freedmen towards their Lords; and it was demanded with great eagernefs, 'That to patrons a pri'vilege fhould be granted of revoking the liberty 'of fuch as ungratefully ufed it.' For this many were ready to vote; but the Confuls were afraid to propofe the queftion, without apprizing the Prince: they, however, acquainted him by writing with the concurrence and biafs of the Senate, and confulted him whether he would be declared the author of this decree, which was oppofed by fo few. They laid before him the reafonings on both fides, as fome urged with great vehemence and refentment, 'That fince their inveftiture with liberty to fuch 'an excefs of infolence they had foared, that they 'fcarce allowed their patrons the common treat'ment of equals, but affailed them with infults 'and violence, fpurned at their motions in the Se'nate,

'nate, lifted up their hands againſt them, threat-
' ened them with blows; and with outrageous im-
' pudence warned their patrons from proſecuting
' the delinquencies of theſe their former ſlaves.
' And, in truth, what higher ſatisfaction or amends
' was permitted to the abuſed patron, than to baniſh
' his criminal freedmen an hundred miles off, into
' the pleaſant confines of Campania? in every other
' circumſtance the privileges of the freedman were
' the ſame with thoſe of his patron. It was there-
' fore expedient to arm the patron with ſome prero-
' gative not to be deſpiſed; nor could it be deemed
' any grievance upon ſlaves manumiſed, to pre-
' ſerve their liberty by the ſame dutiful obſervances
' by which they attained it. And for thoſe al-
' ready notoriouſly guilty, it was but juſt to remand
' them to the yoke of ſervitude, that through their
' example fear might curb ſuch as benefits could
' not amend.'

On the other ſide it was argued, "That the
' tranſgreſſion of a few ought to prove pernicious
' only to themſelves, and nothing be derogated
' from the eſtabliſhed rights of all; they were a
' body widely diffuſed; from thence in a good mea-
' ſure the tribes were ſupplied, and the colleges of
' ſcribes often filled. From the ſame ſource aroſe
' the ſeveral officers attending the Magiſtrates and
' Pontiffs; from thence too the city cohorts were
' enrolled, nor from any other original did a multi-
' tude of Knights and many Senators derive their
' pedigree. Now if from the ſeveral ranks the de-
' ſcendents of freedmen were ſeparated, there would
' quickly be diſcovered a manifeſt ſcarcity of ſuch
' as were originally free. Not without good ground
' had our anceſtors, when they aſcertained the diſ-
' tinction and privileges of the three orders, award-
' ed undiſtinguiſhed liberty to all men. Beſides,
' there were two kinds of manumiſſion appointed,

' on

'on purpose to reserve a latitude for revoking liber-
'ty, where the grant was repented, or for the ex-
'ercise of fresh generosity, by rendering the favour
'irrevocable. Those who had not been by their
'patron regularly freed before the Prætor, remained
'still bound to him by a certain tye of servitude.
'.Every patron must examine carefully the merit of
'such as he meant to discharge, and grant with de-
'liberation an immunity, which once granted he
'could never annul.' This opinion prevailed; and Nero wrote to the Senate, that they should try the offences of freedmen singly, whenever they were prosecuted by their patrons, but in nothing retrench from the rights of the body. Not long after Nero bereft Domitia, his aunt, of Paris her freedman, an act done by pretended law, to the great infamy of the Prince, since by his special authority was obtained the judgment which asserted him free born.

There, however, subsisted still some resemblance of the ancient Republic: for in the contest which arose between Vibullius the Prætor and Antistius Tribune of the people, about some turbulent partizans of the players, by the Prætor cast into irons, and by order of the Tribune released; the Senate affirmed the judgment of Vibullius, and reprimanded the arbitrary conduct of Antistius. The Tribunes were moreover, prohibited from entrenching upon the jurisdiction of the Prætors and Consuls, as also from summoning before them out of any quarters of Italy such as might be tried at tribunals of their own. It was added by Lucius Piso, Consul elect, ' That
' in their own houses they should not be allowed to
' exert any act of power, nor that under four months
' the Quæstors of the Exchequer should register the
' mulcts by them laid; that in the interval there
' should be privilege to controvert their sentence,
' and that by one of the Consuls the contest should
' be determined.' The jurisdiction too of the
Ædiles

Ædiles was further ſtraightened, and it was ſettled how high the Patrician Ædiles, how high the Plebeian, might exact ſureties, and to what value impoſe penalties. Theſe proceedings encouraged Helvidius Priſcus to gratify his own perſonal pique againſt Obultronius Sabinius, Quæſtor of the Exchequer, by charging him, ' that by his prerogative of ' confiſcating-goods for taxes, he unmercifully ex- ' torted upon the poor and inſolvent.' After this, the management of the Exchequer was by the Prince removed from the Quæſtors, and committed to the Præfects.

Various had been the regulations of this office, and its form often altered; for Auguſtus had left to the Senate the power of chooſing the Præfects. Thereafter, as the ſuffrages were ſuſpected to have been gained by caballing, out of the liſt of Prætors were drawn by lot ſuch as were to preſide there. Neither held this expedient long; for that the blind lot often ſtrayed, and fell upon thoſe who were little qualified. Claudius therefore once more reſtored the Quæſtors; and that the fear of raiſing enemies might not ſlacken their activity and inſpection, he promiſed them, by ſpecial diſpenſation, an immediate deſignation to the greater Magiſtracies; but as this was the firſt which they ſuſtained, ripeneſs of age was found wanting in them ; hence Nero choſe into their places ſuch as had exerciſed the Prætorſhip, and were of tried abilities.

Under the ſame Conſuls was condemned Vipſanius Lenas, for his rapacious adminiſtration in Sardinia. Ceſtius Proculus, charged with extortion (his accuſers acquieſcing) was acquitted. Clodius Quirinalis, Admiral of the galleys which rode at Ravenna, as he ſtood convicted, ' for having by his pro- ' fligate manners and acts of cruelty infeſted Italy, ' and treated it as the moſt abject of all nations,' prevented by poiſon his impending condemnation.

Canninius Rebilus, one of the firſt rank in Rome for his abilities in the law, and his abundant treaſures, choſe a quick releaſe from the torments of an old age broken with infirmities, by opening his veins, a man never before eſteemed of magnanimity ſufficient to encounter a voluntary death, infamous as he was for a life of laſciviouſneſs and effeminacy. But illuſtrious and amiable in fame departed Lucius Voluſius, after a long life of ninety-three years, and the upright acquiſition of ſignal opulence, with the ſingular felicity of having never rouſed the cruel ſpirit of ſo many Emperors.

During the ſecond Conſulſhip of Nero, and that of Lucius Piſo his colleague, few events occurred worthy commemoration, unleſs any writer liked to fill pages in magnifying the vaſt foundations and wooden ſtructure of the new Amphitheatre, an immenſe pile then erected by the Emperor in the Field of Mars. But to the dignity of the Roman people it belongs, that in their Hiſtory ſhould be inſerted illuſtrious events only, and in the City-Journals ſuch deſcriptions as thoſe. The Colonies however of Capua and Nuceria were ſtrengthened by a ſupply of Veterans; to the populace was diſtributed a largeſs of four hundred ſmall ſeſterces * a man; and into the Exchequer was conveyed the ſum of four hundred thouſand great ſeſterces †, as a fund to ſupport the credit of the Roman people. Moreover, the duty of four in the hundred upon the ſale of ſlaves was remitted, an act rather ſpecious in appearance than of any efficacy; for as the ſeller was obliged to pay it, he thence raiſed the price upon the buyer. The Emperor too iſſued an edict, ‘ that no Procurator, or any other Magiſtrate, who

---

* Betwixt twelve and thirteen Crowns.

† Three Millions one hundred and twenty-five thouſand pounds.

‘ had

'had obtained a charge in any province, should
'exhibit a spectacle of Gladiators or of wild beasts,
'nor any other popular entertainment whatsoever.'
For, before this, they had by such acts of munificence no less afflicted those under their jurisdiction, than by plundering them of their money, whilst, under the influence of such court to the multitude, they sheltered their arbitrary delinquencies and rapine.

A decree of Senate also passed, equally tending to the avenging of crimes, and providing for domestic security, ' that if any one was killed by his slaves,
' those too, whom by his last will he had made free,
' if they still continued under the same roof, should
' amongst his other slaves suffer execution.' Lucius Varius, one who had been Cousul, but for the crimes of rapine formerly branded with degradation, was now restored to his primitive dignity, and Pomponia Græcina, a Lady of signal quality, arraigned of having embraced an extraneous superstition, was preferred to the inquisition of her husband; for she was married to Plautius, the same who upon his return from Britain entered the city in the pomp of *Ovation*. Plautius assembled her kindred, and, in observance of primitive institution, having in their presence taken cognizance of the behaviour and reputation of his wife, adjudged her innocent. To a great age this Lady lived, and under incessant sorrow; for ever after the untimely fate of Julia (the daughter of Drusus) procured by the perfidious snares of Messalina, she wore, for the space of forty years, no habit but that of mourning, entertained no sentiments but those of grief, a temper which during the reign of Claudius escaped with impunity, and redounded thereafter to her glory.

The same year produced many arraignments, and amongst them one against Publius Celer, prosecuted by the province of Asia, with such incontestible evidence, that the Emperor, finding no pretence to discharge him, lengthened out the process till he died of old age. For Celer having, as is above remembered, dispatched by poison the Proconsul Silanus, skreened under that mighty iniquity all his other enormities. Coffutianus Capito was impleaded by the Cilicians, ' as a man utterly abominable and 'infamous, one who claimed authority to commit ' in his province the same bold exorbitancies which, ' in Rome he had committed.' And he found himself so sorely beset with the vigour of the accusation, that at last he wholly abandoned his defence, and was condemned by the law against extortion. But for Eprius Marcellus, who was charged by those of Lycia with the violation of that very law, a faction so powerful was formed, that some of his accusers were punished with exile, ' as if they had conspired ' the ruin of an innocent man.'

With Nero, now in his third Consulship, Valerius Messala commenced colleague, he whose great grandfather Corvinus the Orator, was by some old men (very few) remembered to have been colleague in the same Magistracy with the deified Augustus, who, by one degree more remote, was ancestor to Nero. But, as an additional honour to that illustrious family, a yearly pension was presented to Messala of about twelve thousand crowns, that by it he might relieve his honest poverty, and still support his integrity. To Aurelius Cotta also, and Haterius Antoninus, annual appointments were assigned by the Prince, though they had wasted in voluptuousness their paternal wealth. In the beginning of this year the war between the Parthians and Romans for the mastery of Armenia, though it had commenced with faint efforts, and hitherto lingered, was prosecuted with vigour; for Vologeses would neither suffer his brother Tiridates to be bereft of the monarchy by himself conferred upon him,

nor

nor to hold the same as a gift from any other power and Corbulo esteemed it becoming the grandeur of the Roman people to re-establish the conquest formerly made by Lucullus and Pompey. Moreover the Armenians, a people of double and faithless minds, invited the arms and protection of both, though, from the situation of their country and similitude of manners, they stood in nearer conformity to the Parthians, being besides commonly linked with them in conjugal alliances; and, being destitute of all experience or sense of liberty, they were thence rather addicted to Parthian slavery.

But to Corbulo it proved greater labour to struggle with the degenerate sloth of his soldiers, than against the perfidious dealings of his enemies. For the Legions brought out of Syria, and enervated by long peace, bore with much impatience the laborious occupations of war. It fully appeared that in that army there were those who had served to the age of Veterans, and yet had never kept guard, never stood sentry, men who beheld entrenchments and pallisades as sights new and wonderful, and who, in spruce apparel and pursuit of gain, without ever wearing helmet or body-armour, had amongst the delicacies of cities fulfilled the term of their service. Having therefore discharged such as were enfeebled by sickness or age, he sent to demand recruits. Hence levies were made through Cappadocia and Galatia, and to these was added a Legion from Germany, with some wings of horse and a detachment of infantry from the Cohorts. The whole army too was incamped; though such was the rigour of the winter, and so stubbornly had the frost bound the earth, that without digging they could not pierce it in order to pitch their tents: many had their limbs utterly scorched up by the raging cold, and some, as they stood sentry, were frozen to death. More remarkable still was the fate of one particular soldier,

soldier, whose hands, as he carried in them a bundle of wood, stiffened and mortified so suddenly, that still clasping their burden they dropped from his arms. The General himself, in a thin habit and his head bare, whether they marched or worked, was hourly amongst them, commending the magnanimous, heartening the weak, and exhibiting an example to all. Next, as many refused to bear the asperity of the weather and service, and began to depart, he had recourse to severity for a cure; for he proceeded not as in the other armies, where the first or second offence was forgiven, but whoever deserted his colours, was instantly put to death; a course which was by experience proved to be wholesome, and preferable to that of clemency, since from his camp there were fewer desertions than from those in which acts of mercy were wont to prevail.

Corbulo the while, holding his Legions encamped, waited the advancement of the spring, and, having quartered the auxiliary Cohorts in convenient places, expresly forewarned them that they should not venture to engage first in a battle. The superintendance of these garrisons he conferred upon Pactius Orphitus, one who had served as Lieutenant-Colonel of a Legion. This officer, although he acquainted the General by letter, that the Barbarians acted negligently, and thence an opportunity presented of assailing them with success, was ordered to abide within his entrenchments, and wait for greater forces; but he broke through his orders; for upon the arrival of some few troops of horse, who, assembling from the neighbouring castles, rashly demanded battle, he encountered the enemy, and was routed. Those too, who ought to have reinforced him, being themselves terrified with his disaster, betook themselves to a cowardly and tumultuons flight, and returned to the several fortifications; an event which grievously affected Corbulo.

Hence,

Hence, after he had bitterly reproached Paetius himself and the captains and common soldiers, he expelled them all from the camp, doomed them to lie on the other side its inclosure, without tents or defence; and under this contumelious punishment they were held, till at the universal supplications of the whole army they were released.

Now Tiridates, who over and above the forces which he drew from his own vassals, was supported by the might of his brother Vologeses, proceeded no longer against Armenia by disguised efforts, but attacked it with open war, and, upon all such as he suspected* of attachment to us, committed depredations, but, where troops were drawn out against him, eluded the encounter, scouring to and fro, and effecting greater matters by the fame and terror of his incursions, than by any exploits in fight. Corbulo therefore, having long laboured to come to an engagement, and being still frustrated, found himself obliged to follow the method of the enemy, and make a circulatory war. Hence he distributed his forces so that his several Lieutenants might at once attack diverse quarters; he at the same directed King Antiochus to fall into the Armenian districts which lay contiguous to his own. For as to Pharasmanes, King of Hiberia, having for the imputation of treason slain his son Rhadamistus, he was already, in order to display his fidelity towards us, renewed with the more acrimony against the Armenians the exercise of his inveterate hate. The Insechians too, a people since singularly attached to the Roman interest, were then first engaged in our alliance, and over-run the wilds of Armenia. Thus all the measures of Tiridates proved abortive and contradictory, so that he dispatched Embassadors to expostulate, in his own name and that of the Parthians, ' upon
' what score it was, that after he had so lately de-
' livered hostages to the Romans, and with them
' re-

'renewed his former amity, which might reason-
'ably have proved to him a source of new friend-
'ship, he must yet be chased out of Armenia, a
'Kingdom so long in the possession of his ancestors?
'Hence it was, that Vologeses had not hitherto
'taken arms in person, because they both desired
'to commit the justice of their cause to the way of
'accommodation rather than to that of violence.
'But if war were still to be obstinately pursued, the
'Arsacides would not find themselves forsaken of
'that victorious bravery so often tried by the Ro-
'mans, in many bloody overthrows.' Corbulo was
well informed, that what engaged Vologeses was
the revolt of Hyrcania: He therefore, in answer to
Tiridates, persuaded him to apply to the Emperor
with supplications; 'hence he might enjoy his
'Kingdom in security, and an establishment with-
'out the expence of blood, if rejecting his remote
'and tedious hopes, he would close with sounder
'measures already concerted.'

But as the business of peace was nothing advanced by an intercourse of messengers, it was at
last judged proper to ascertain a time and place for
an interview between the two chiefs. Tiridates declared, 'that he would come attended only by a
'guard of a thousand horse, but would not restrain
'Corbulo to any number of troops of any kind,
'provided they came without armour, as a proof
'of their disposition to peace.' This perfidious wile
of the Barbarian must have appeared manifest to
every man breathing, especially to an old and cau-
tious Captain, since, by limitting the number of men
on one side, and leaving liberty for a greater number on the other, nothing but a snare could be intended. For against a body of Parthian horsemen,
constantly trained in the use of the bow, any numbers whatsoever, when naked of armour, would avail
nothing. Corbulo, however, disguised all his apprehensions

Book XIII. OF TACITUS. 115

prehensions of guile, and returned answer, 'that
'matters which concerned the interest of both their
'states, would he more properly discussed in pre-
'sence of both armies.' Hence he chose a station
consisting partly of hills rising with a gentle slope,
fit for embattling his infantry, partly of a large plain,
affording scope for ranging the squadrons of horse.
On the day appointed, Corbulo advanced first, on
the wings he posted the social troops and the auxiliary forces sent by the confederate Kings, in the
center the sixth Legion, which he had strengthened
with three thousand men of the third, led by night
from another camp, all mixed together under one
Eagle, to preserve still the appearance of a single
Legion. Tiridates at last appeared, but late in the
day, and afar off, from hence he could be easier
seen than heard. So that the Roman General, having
obtained no conference, ordered his men to retire
to their several camps.

The King too retreated in haste, whether it were
that he apprehended a design to surprize him, for
that the Romans filed off in different routs, or, that
he meant to intercept their provisions which were
coming from Trebizonde and the Euxine sea. But
as the provisions passed over the mountains, which
were secured by several bands of our men, he found
no means to attack them; and Corbulo the while,
that the war might not thus linger without action,
and in order to force the Armenians to defend their
own dwellings, set himself to raze their strong holds.
The attack of the strongest of all those in that quarter, the fort named Volandum, he reserved to himself; and to Cornelius Flaccus his Lieutenant, and
Insteius Capito, Camp Marshal, committed those of
smaller note. Having therefore viewed the fortifications and prepared all things requisite for storming the place, he exhorted his men 'to extermi-
'nate that base and vagabond foe, never prepared
'for

' for war, yet never difpofed to peace, but ftill by
' flight confeffing faithleffnefs and cowardice; do
' this, faid he, and at once purfue a harveft of fpoil
' and glory.' He then diftributed his forces into four
divifions; one he formed clofe under their fhields
into the military fhell, in order to overthrow the
pallifade and undermine the rampart; others were
ordered by ladders to mount the walls, and a party
to manage the engines, and thence annoy the for-
trefs with fhowers of darts and artificial fire. To
the archers too and flingers a quarter was affigned
whence they might from afar difcharge volleys of
ftones and bullets. So that every part of the for-
trefs being affailed, and the confternation everywhere
equal, no one quarter of the befieged might be at
leifure to relieve another. All this was executed
by the befiegers with fuch fpirit and vigour, that in
a few hours the defendants were entirely driven from
the walls, the gates were forced, the bulwarks fcaled,
and all that were arrived to full age put to the
edge of the fword, without the lofs of one of our
men, and very few were wounded. The weak and
mixt multitude were fold by the public cryer, and
to the conquerors remained all the reft of the fpoil.
Equal fuccefs attended the Lieutenant General and
Camp Marfhal; in one day they took three caftles
by ftorm, infomuch that all the others, fome from
dread, others from the inclination of the inhabitants,
furrendered. Such a feries of good fortune infpired
a refolution to attempt the fiege of Artaxata, the
capital of Armenia. The Legions were not however conducted thither the fhorteft road; for that,
in paffing the bridge over the Araxes, which wafhes
the walls of the city, they would have been expofed
to be galled by the enemy; fetching therefore a
long circuit, they forded over upon the large fhal-
lows.

As

As to Tiridates, he struggled between shame and fear; if he gave way to the siege, it would appear that there was no reliance upon any relief or force from him; if he attempted to prevent it, he must be hemmed in with his cavalry in close and intricate places. At last, he determined to shew himself in order of battle, and at break of day begin the onset, or by a feigned flight try to draw the Romans into a snare; with great suddenness therefore he beset them, but without any surprize to our General, who had formed his army as well for a fight as a march. On the right marched the third Legion, on the left the sixth, and in the center a chosen detachment from the tenth: the baggage was secured between the ranks, and a thousand horse guarded the rear. These last were ordered ' to repulse the ' foe, if they made any close attack, but not to ' pursue them when they fled.' The foot archers and remainder of the horse were placed on the wings, but the left was the most extended, and reached to the roots of the hills, that if the enemy attempted an onset there, he might be encountered at once by our front and by the heart of the army. Tiridates on his side pickeered about, yet never approached within the throw of a dart, but now braving us with the countenance of an assailant, then assuming an air of dismay, provoked us to loosen our ranks, that he might fall upon us when we were disjoined. When he saw no unwary relaxation in our order, and that only one captain of horse, who had adventured too rashly, was by a volley of arrows slain, and by his fate had confirmed all the rest in submission to discipline, he marched off at the close of the evening.

Corbulo encamped upon the place, and, supposing that Tiridates had retired to Artaxata, was unresolved whether he should march thither the same night with his Legions unincumbered by baggage, and immediately invest it; but, upon tidings brought him

him by his spies that the King had undertaken a long rout, though it was uncertain whether towards the regions of Medea or Albania, he waited for the morning, and dispatched his troops lightly armed to beset the city, and begin the storm of the place by a distant attack. But the citizens voluntarily opening their gates, made an unreserved surrender to the Romans; by this their persons were secured. The city was fired, and laid level with the ground, for such was the wide circuit of its walls, that without a powerful garrison they could not be defended, nor were our forces sufficiently large to fill the garrison, and yet to prosecute the war; or, had it been left untouched and destitute of a guard, there had been no profit nor glory in having taken it. To this relation of the fall of the city is added a Phænomenon, which was deemed miraculous, as a signal sent immediately from heaven, for that, while all the region round the walls and close to them was gloriously irradiated by the sun, the whole space incompassed by them was so suddenly darkened by a thick cloud, spangled with lightening and roaring with thunder, that it was believed the angry Gods, to satiate their vengeance, had consigned that city to utter destruction.

For these prosperous exploits Nero was proclaimed *Imperator*, and, by decree of Senate, days of public devotion were appointed, with statues of victory to the Prince, triumphal arches, and perpetuity of the Consulship. It was moreover decreed, that the day when the city was won, the day when the news arrived at Rome, and the day that produced this decree, should all be inrolled amongst the annual festivals, with several other particulars of the same stamp, so much beyond all measure, that Caius Cassins, though he had agreed to the former, yet argued here, ' That were every instance of
' public prosperity to be attended with public thanks-
' giving, the whole year would not afford days
enough

'enough for days of devotion; a just distribution
'ought therefore to be made between days of de-
'votion and days of business, in such sort that the
'worship of the Gods might be solemnized with-
'out interfering with the secular business of men.'

Thereafter was impleaded a man, who had passed through various revolutions of life, and justly incurred much hatred, and many enmities; yet obnoxious as he was, his condemnation drew an imputation and blemish upon Seneca. It was Publius Suilius, he who, during the reign of Claudius, had borne such terrible sway, and exercised such a venal spirit, and though now by the change of times considerably sunk, yet not so low as his enemies wished. Besides, he was one who chose rather to bear the character of a criminal, than descend to that of a supplicant. Hence the decree of Senate made at this time for the revival of the Cincian law, which subjected to penalties all those who had pleaded for pay, was thought to have passed on purpose to ruin him. Nor did Suilius, on his part, spare to retort complaints and recriminations, but, vehement as he ever was in his temper, now too extremely old, and thence indulging avowed freedom, upbraided Seneca, ' as an inveterate foe to all the
'friends of Claudius, during whose reign he had
'been justly doomed to exile; as one who, being
'himself conversant in stupid and insignificant studies,
'and in teaching scholars, was actuated by envy
'towards all such, who in defending the rights
'of their fellow-citizens exercised vigorous elo-
'quence, free from pedantry and corruption. For
'himself; he had been Quæstor to Germanicus,
'but Seneca the adulterer of Germanicus's
'daughter. Now, was it to be judged a more
'heinous offence to pursue the advantages of a
'worthy vocation, by accepting a reward from a
'suitor, who freely gives it, than to contaminate
'the beds of Princesses? By what precepts of wis-
'dom,

' wifdom, by what principles of philofophy, had
' he, during four years of imperial favour, amaffed
' a treafure of more than feven millions? Through
' Rome he hunted after teftaments and inheritances,
' the rich and childifh were catched, as it were, in
' his net, and all Italy and the Provinces were
' by his mighty and exceffive ufury exhaufted. But
' fmail is my own wealth, and with induftry ac-
' quired; and upon the whole, I am determined
' rather to undergo the heavieft profecution, the
' fevereft fentence and doom, and every degree of
' hardfhip and fuffering, than debafe a diftinguifhed
' reputation, the acquifition of a long life, and bend
' to this fudden fon of felicity,'

There were fome too, who failed not to relate to Seneca all thefe reproaches in the fame angry ftrain, or in one ftill more embittered. Accufers, moreover, were found, who arraigned him, ' for
' his exceffes in Afia, when he ruled as Quæftor
' there, for plundering the inhabitants, and robbing
' from the public revenue.' But as a whole year was granted them for preparing their evidence, it was deemed a quicker expedient to proceed upon his enormities at Rome, of all which there were in ftore ready witneffes. By thefe it was urged, ' That
' by a virulent accufation he had driven Quintus
' Pomponius upon the neceffity of raifing a civil
' war; by him was procured the violent death of
' Poppæa Sabina, and of Julia the daughter of Dru-
' fus; of his framing was the doom of Valerius
' Afiaticus, of Lufius Saturninus, and of Cornelius
' Lupus. Add to thefe, whole bands of Roman
' Knights at his inftigation condemned; with all
' the long train of cruelties during the reign of
' Claudius.' For upon Suilius they charged the whole. In his defence he began to alledge, ' That
' of all thefe accumulated profecutions, he had of
' his own inclination engaged in none, but purely
' in

'in obedience to the Prince.' But Nero checked this plea, and testified that, from the memoirs of Claudius, he had found, that no accusation whatsoever had ever been undertaken by compulsion from him. The accused then pleaded the uncontroulable orders of Messalina; an impotent defence! 'for why had 'no other advocates but only Suilius been singled 'out to have lent their eloquence for accomplish- 'ing the purposes of that bloody prostitute? In ' truth, the ministers and promoters of such black ' deeds must be punished, they who, having re- 'ceived the wages of their iniquities, would upon 'others father the iniquities themselves.' A part of his estate was therefore confiscated; for to his son and grand-daughter the other part was granted, besides that from the sentence were also exempted the fortunes left them by the will of their mother, and that of their grand-father. He himself was banished to the isles Baleares; but neither during the heat and peril of the prosecution, nor after his condemnation, was his spirit in the least sunk or dismayed. He was even said to have passed his solitary exile in a life of voluptuousness and pleasure. In hatred to him, Nerulinus his son was also arraigned, upon the crimes of public rapine; but Nero interposed, and alledged, that by the doom of the father public vengeance was sufficiently satiated.

About the same time Octavius Sagitta, Tribune of the people, intoxicated with a passion for Pontia, a married woman, gained her by vast presents, first to consent to the adultery, afterwards to quit her husband, engaging himself and her in a promise of marriage after the divorce. But the woman, when she found herself single, framed delays from time to time, pleaded the opposition of her father, and then, having discovered some hopes of a wealthier husband, quite renounced her engagement. Octavius failed not to combat this resolution; one moment broke into complaints, the next into menaces; he adjured her by the reputation which for her he had shipwrecked, by the wealth which upon her he had totally confumed; lastly, he told her, that his life and person was the only fortune left him, and of that too the disposal lay wholly in her breast. At length, perceiving her deaf to all his reasonings, he requested the consolation of one parting night; for that thus calmed and gratified, he would thenceforth be able to govern his passion. The night was granted and named; and Pontia appointed a maid, her confidant, to secure the chamber. Sagitta brought with him one freedman, and a dagger concealed under his robe. The interview began, as usual, in combinations of love and anger, with a medley of chiding and beseeching, of reproaches and submissions; and part too of the night was devoted to joy and embraces: at last, he became enraged with expostulations and despair, and suddenly plunged his dagger into her heart (free as she was of all dread) beat down and wounded the maid, who was flying to her assistance, and burst out of the chamber. Next day the murder was divulged; and by what hand was apparent; for it was proved they had lodged together. But the freedman adopted the guilt; he averred, that the assassination was of his own committing, to procure just vengeance to an injured master; and, by the exemplary greatness of such behaviour, many were induced to believe him, till the maid, when she was healed of her wound, fully disclosed the author, and all the particulars; so that the Tribune was arraigned before the Consuls by the father of the deceased, and at the expiration of his office, condemned by the Senate to the penalties of the Cornelian Law.

An instance of lewdness no less notorious proved this year the source of heavy calamities to the Roman state. In the city lived a daughter of Titus Ollius,

Ollius, but as Poppæus Sabinus, her mother's father, had shone in the Commonwealth, and, from the Consular dignity and glory of a triumph, acquired an illustrious name, from his she took her own, that of Sabina Poppæa; for Ollius, ere yet he had overtaken any public dignity, was swallowed up by the fatal friendship of Sejanus. This Lady possessed every ornament but that of a virtuous soul; for from her mother, who in beauty had excelled all the women of her time, she derived her loveliness, as well as the glory of descent; the lustre of her birth was supported by proportionable wealth; her speech was soft and engaging, her wit pertinent, modesty the part she personated, lewdness that she practised. It was rare that she appeared abroad, then too part of her face hid under her veil, the more to stimulate the curious beholders, or, perhaps, because thus she was still more charming. By the awe of fame she was never controuled; between husband and adulterer, she made no distinction; by no man's passion was she ever biassed, nor even by her own; wherever her interest appeared, thither she transferred her lewd pleasures. Hence, though she was married to Rufius Crispinus, a Roman Knight, and by him had brought forth a son, she was carried away by the gay youth and profuseness of Otho, especially for that he was esteemed to reign, beyond all others, in the affection of Nero, nor was it long ere this commerce of adultery was followed by their intermarriage.

It became now the ordinary language of Otho to extol to the Prince the beauty and delicate charms of his wife, either as he was prompted by the indiscreet warmth of a lover, or designed to enflame Nero with the like passion, and from their common enjoyment of the same woman hoped to find an additional support to his present authority. It was usual to hear him boast, as he rose from the Em-

peror's table, 'That he now retired to the sum
'of all noblenefs and lovelinefs, her who was the
'centre of every joy and felicity, the defire of all
'men, but happily his own peculiar lot.' After
thefe and the like incitements, Nero deferred not
long his own gratification; an interview was appointed, where Poppæa, at firft, employed all her foft
arts and careffes, and by them intirely fubdued him;
fhe feigned herfelf fmitten with his fine perfon, and
wholly overcome by her paffion for him. But when
fhe had worked up the Prince's affection to a pitch
of impatience, fhe changed her former behaviour
into haughtinefs and defpite. If fhe were detained
above a night or two, 'fhe was a married woman,
'fhe cried, nor could fhe relinquifh her hufband,
'as to him fhe was engaged by a way of living,
'which no other man could equal. Otho was magnificent in his perfon, generous in his spirit; in
'him fhe beheld every thing worthy the moft exalted fortune. Nero was attached to Acte, thence
'inured to the embraces of a flave, and could from
'a fellowfhip fo wretched and fervile derive nothing
''but fordidnefs and fervility.' Upon this, Otho
became degraded from his ufual intimacy with the
Emperor, then debarred of all intercourfe, and even
accefs; and, at laft, to prevent all his rival practices in Rome, was preferred to the government of
Lufitania, a government which he adminiftered, till
the beginning of the civil wars, with eminent uprightnefs and honour, and wide of all the courfes
of his former diffolute life; a proof of his various
character, that of an unbridled voluptuary in a private ftation, in authority obferving gravity and juft
reftraints.

 Nero as yet endeavoured to find difguifes for his
vileneffes and crimes. He, whom of all others he
apprehended moft, was Cornelius Sylla, miftaking
the heavy fpirit of the man for deep artifice and dif-
'fimulation.

simulation. These apprehensions were inflamed by Graptus, a freedman of his, an ancient domestic of the court, ever since the reign of Tiberius, and being well practised in the dark devices of the Emperors, he, upon this occasion, framed the following forgery. The Milvian Bridge was then the famous scene of nocturnal revellings, and thither Nero frequently resorted, that there he might more licentiously riot without the city. Graptus therefore feigned, 'That a plot had been laid for him, as
' he should return from thence by the Flaminian
' Way, but, by the benignity of fate, he had es-
' caped it in coming home through the Gardens of
' Sallust, and of this treason Sylla was the author.'
The fact was, that as some of the Emperor's attendants were repairing back to the palace, certain young companions, indulging a sort of licentiousness then universally practised, had filled them with causeless fears. But amongst these companions not a slave of Sylla's was observed, nor one of his dependants; and for himself, his courage was so utterly despicable, and so unequal to any enterprize; that his very nature was repugnant to every attempt of treason; nevertheless, as if he had been a traitor fully convicted, he was banished his country, and confined within the walls of Marseilles.

During the same Consuls were heard the deputies from Puzzoli, some dispatched by their Senate, others by the populace; the former inveighing against the violence of the multitude, the latter against the oppression and avarice of the Magistrates and Nobles; and as the sedition was so violent, that the factious had already combated with stones, threatened the firing of houses, and were betaking themselves to arms and massacre, Caius Cassins was appointed to apply a remedy; but they could not bear the severity of his proceedings; so that, at his own request, that charge was transferred to the two brothers Scribonii, affisted by a Prætorian Cohort, by the terror of which and the execution of some few incendiaries, concord was restored amongst the inhabitants.

The decree of Senate now made, for permitting the Syracusians in their shews of Gladiators to exceed the number formerly limited, is a matter so common, that I should not insert it here, had not Pætus Thrasea opposed it, and thence administered to his revilers matter of invective. ' For, if he be-
' lieved that the condition of the Commonwealth
' called upon the Senators to exert liberty of speech,
' why were his censures and pursuits confined to
' things of such trivial moment? How came it,
' that he stood not forth to advise or controul mea-
' sures of war and peace, the administration of the
' revenue, that of the laws, and whatever else con-
' cerned the support and governance of the Roman
' state? To every Senator, as soon as invested with
' the privilege of voting, full freedom was allowed
' of propounding whatever he would, and of claim-
' ing that what he propounded might be put to the
' vote. Now, did nothing else in the state want
' check or amendment, but only that the specta-
' cles at Syracuse should be exhibited with no en-
' largements? Was, in truth, all the rest of the
' administration throughout the Empire so excel-
' lent, as if by Thrasea himself, and not by Nero,
' it were swayed? But if all these were passed over
' in profound dissimulation, how much more rea-
' sonably to be forborne were things utterly void
' of all use and significancy?' To his friends, who asked him the meaning of his conduct, Thrasea answered, ' That he had, from no ignorance in
' the situation of the public, interposed against a
' decree of that sort, but in it consulted the honour
' of the Senate, by making it appear, that an in-
' spection into the greatest affairs was not like to be
' disa-

'disavowed by those who thus applied their thoughts 'to the most insignificant.'

In the same year, so importunate were the cries of the people against the exactions of the Tax-gatherers, that Nero was deliberating about the intire suppression of all taxes and duties, as the most illustrions bounty he could bestow upon human kind. But the Senate, after many high praises upon his greatness of soul, restrained his rash resolution, by apprizing him, ' That the dissolution of the Empire ' must ensue a reduction of the revenues which sus- ' tained it; and were the public duties once an- ' nulled, it would be a precedent for labouring the ' discharge of all the public tributes. The compa- ' nies for administering the taxes were for the most ' part established by the Consuls and Tribunes, even ' then when popular liberty was in its prime at ' Rome, and the regulations which followed were ' so concerted, that the public impositions might ' just balance the public exigencies. But the ra- ' venous extortions of the publicans did, in truth, ' require to be stopped, that so the rates borne by ' the people for so many years without murmuring, ' might not be embittered by new grievances.'

The Emperor therefore by an edict ordained, ' That the laws of the revenue, which had till then ' been kept secret, should now be committed to ' the public tables; the publicans should exact no ' claims for above a year backward; in all suits a- ' gainst them, the Praetor at Rome and in the Pro- ' vinces, the Propraetor or Proconsul for the time ' being, should proceed to discretionary judgment; ' but to the soldiers should be reserved the usual ' exemption in all instances save those of traffic;' with other the like injunctions, which, being intirely equitable, were for some short time obeyed, but soon grew neglected and obsolete. The suppression, however, of the Quadragesima (fortieth penny) and of the Quinquagesima (fiftieth) continues still in force, as also that of other impositions with the like titles, invented by the publicans to cover their lawless exactions. Moreover, a regulation was made about the importation of grain from the provinces beyond sea, and it was ordained that the ships of traders should not be rated with the commodities which they carried, nor any duty be paid for the same.

Two men accused of male-administration in Africa, where they had both ruled as Proconsuls, were acquitted by the Emperor, Sulpicius Camernius and Pomponius Silvanus. Against the former there appeared only a few private prosecutors, who charged him rather with particular acts of rage than those of general rapine. But Silvanus was beset with a mighty train of impleaders, who required time to procure their witnesses, as did he to be instantly admitted to his defence; and, by being wealthy, ancient, and childless, prevailed, yet outlived and disappointed those who saved his life to merit his estate.

Till this time Germany had continued in a state of tranquillity, secured by the temper of our commanders there, who, at a time when the honours of the triumph were so miserably prostituted, judged that higher glory was to be reaped by preserving peace. These commanders were Paulinus Pompeius and Lucius Vetus. To keep, however, the soldiers employed, the former now perfected the dam which had been begun by Drusus threescore and three years before, to restrain the overflowing of the Rhine, while Vetus was digging a canal of communication between the Arar and Moselle, that the armies from Italy, having sailed by sea into the Rhone, and thence into the Arar, might fall through this canal into the Moselle, thence through the Rhine into the Ocean; so that, all impediments of the passage being thus removed, a naval intercourse
might

might be opened from West to North between the two seas. But this great work was marred through the envy of Ælius Gracilis, Lieutenant of Belgic Gaul, who warned Vetus against bringing his Legions into another man's province, and courting the affections of the Gauls, for that such conduct would alarm the Emperor; an apprehension which frequently serves to frustrate many worthy enterprizes.

But, from the continued inaction of both armies, a report spread, that their Generals were enjoined not to lead them against the enemy. In confidence of this the Frisians possessed the forests and morasses with their youth, and carrying over the lakes all such as were weak through sex or age, placed them along the banks of the Rhine, then proceeded to settle themselves upon those tracts of land which, being void of inhabitants, were appropriated to the uses of our soldiers. In this enterprize they were counselled and conducted by Verritus and Malorigis, who were sovereigns over this nation, as far as the Germans are wont to submit to sovereignty. They had already founded their dwellings, sown the fields, and were cultivating the lands, as if the same had been their native soil, when Dubius Avitus, who succeeded Paulinus in the province, threatened them with the vengeance of the Roman sword, unless they retired to their ancient territories, or obtained from the Emperor a new settlement. By these menaces he forced Verritus and Malorigis to the ways of supplication. On this negociation therefore they proceeded to Rome, where, while they waited for access to Nero, who was engaged in other affairs, amongst the sights which are usually shewn to Barbarians, they were conducted into Pompey's Theatre, that they might there survey the multitude of the Roman people. Here, gazing round them (no wise interrupted by the diversions of the stage, which they understood not) while they were intent upon the arrangement of the audience, and informing themselves about the distribution of ranks, 'which were the Roman Knights, and where sat 'the fathers of the Senate;' they spied certain persons in a foreign habit, sitting upon the benches of the Senators, and asked who were these? When they had learnt that this was a distinction conferred upon the Ambassadors of such nations as signalized themselves by their merit and friendship towards the Romans; 'There is not amongst men, they 'cried, that nation which, in good faith and feats 'of arms, surpasses the Germans;' and thus, leaving their seats, placed themselves among the Senators; a proceeding courteously taken by the spectators, as a flight of ancient liberty, and the effect of an honest emulation. Nero bestowed upon both the privileges of Roman citizens, but ordered that the Frisians should abandon their new possessions; and, as they refused to obey, they were forced by a sudden irruption of the auxiliary horse, who put in bonds, or to the sword, all who obstinately resisted.

The Ansibarians too took possession of the same lands, a more potent people, not in their own multitudes only, but also from the sympathy of the neighbouring nations; for that they had been exterminated by the Chaucians, were destitute of all settlement, and, like exiles, besought only a quiet shelter and retreat. They were likewise led by a man of signal renown amongst these nations, and even of approved fidelity towards the Romans, his name Boiocalus, who, in behalf of himself and his people, upon this occasion alledged, ' That ' upon the revolt of the Cheruscans he had been ' thrown into bonds by order of Arminius, afterwards carried arms under Tiberius, then under ' Germanicus, and to the merit of fifty years service
' and

'and adherence to the Romans, he was still ready
' to add that of submitting his people to their Em-
' pire. Was not the territory in dispute large and
' waste? or reserved for any other use than that of
' occasional pasture for the soldiers cattle, and
' how small a portion sufficed for this? yet the
' Romans might still, if they pleased, retain wide
' exclusive tracts only for their beasts to range in,
' although by feeding their beasts they even famish-
' ed men; provided they did not wilfully devote all
' the rest to desarts and solitude, rather than allow
' it for an habitation to a people disposed to their
' friendship and alliance. The possessing of this
' territory was no new thing; formerly it was held
' by the Chamavians, next by the Tubantes, after-
' wards by the Usipians. As the heavens were ap-
' propriated to the Gods, so was the earth to the
' children of men, and such portions of it as none
' possessed were free and common to all.' Here
he lifted up his eyes to the sun, and invoking, as if
they had been present, that and the other celestial
luminaries, he asked them, ' Could they bear to
' survey a desolate soil? or would they not more
' justly let loose the sea to swallow up usurpers, who
' thus engrossed the earth?'

This language warmed Avitus, who replied,
' that to the orders of the most powerful, submission
' must always be paid; even the Gods, to whom
' they now appealed, had so appointed, that to the
' Romans should appertain the sovereign judgment,
' what to bestow and what to take away, and other
' judges than themselves they would suffer none.'
This was his public answer to the Ansibarians;
but to Boiocalus he privately promised, that in
acknowledgment of his long attachment to the Romans he should have lands for himself assigned him,
an offer which he considered as a price proposed for
betraying his people, and, rejecting it with indigna-

G 6 tion,

tion, added, ' A place to live in we may want, but
' a place to die in we cannot.' Thus they parted
with animosity on both sides. The Ansibarians, to
prepare for the impending war, invited into a confederacy the Bructerians, Tencterians, and even other
nations more remote. Avitus too, after he had written to Curtilius Mancia, who commanded the upper army, to pass the Rhine, and to appear with
his forces upon their rear, marched himself with his
Legions into the territories of the Tencterians, and
threatened them with desolation and slaughter unless they departed from the league. Hence they
were forced to acquiesce; and, as the like terrors
awed the Bructerians, the rest too relinquished a hopeless cause, whence ruin to themselves was threatened from their attachment to others. So that the
forlorn Ansibarians retreated back to the Usipians
and Tubantes, but by them also were exterminated.
They then withdrew for reception first to the Cattians, afterwards to the Cheruscans, and in these
long and various wanderings from nation to nation,
thus vagabond, indigent, and treated as enemies
and intruders, all their youth fell by the sword, and
the promiscuous multitude were utterly dispersed
according to the various lot of captivity.

Between the Hermundurians and the Cattians,
during the same summer, a mighty battle was
fought about the propriety of a river which divided their territories, and which, yielding abundant
store of salt, each people was labouring by force to
appropriate to themselves. To this quarrel, besides
their passion for committing all disputes to the decision of the sword, they were further animated by
an inherent superstition, ' that these places were
' doubtless in the neighbourhood of heaven, and no
' where quicker than there did the supplications of
' men reach the ears of the Gods. Hence, through
' a special indulgence of the Deities, in this river
' and

' and in these groves salt was produced, not, as
with other nations, from the foam of the sea crust-
ed upon the shore, but by pouring the water of
' this river upon flaming piles of wood, and thus
' condensed by a combination of opposite elements.'
The issue of the war was prosperous to the Hermundurians, and to the Cattians the more bloody and
destructive, for that presuming upon victory they
had devoted the adverse host to Mars and Mercury,
a vow by which men and horses, with whatever
else appertains to the vanquished, are doomed to be
burnt or slain. Thus upon their own heads returned their cruel menaces against their foes.

The people Juhones, a state in alliance with us,
were at this time afflicted with a calamity altogether
sudden and alarming, by the eruption of a subterra-
neous fire, which caught and consumed on every
side their towns, farms, and particular dwellings,
and was advancing with fury to the late-built walls
of Cologn; neither could it be extinguished even by
the falling of rain, nor by the throwing of water, or
by any other usual expedient, till certain boors, de-
spairing of remedy, and enraged at the devouring
conflagration, vented their wrath in attacking it at
a distance with vollies of stones; as the flames came
thus to abate, they proceeded to a closer approach,
and by dint of clubs and blows, as in an encounter
with fierce beasts, quite repulsed it. At length, utterly to smother it, they stripped themselves of their
cloaths, which the more soiled and worn they were,
the more effectual they proved.

During the same year the tree Ruminalis, standing in the place assigned for the election of magistrates,
the same which after the birth of Romulus and Re-
mus had yielded shelter to these exposed babes,
eight hundred and forty years ago, began to decay
with withered branches and a deadened trunk; a
change which passed for an omen of evil portent, till
it revived again into fresh blossoms and verdure

THE

THE ANNALS OF TACITUS.

BOOK XIV.

The SUMMARY.

Nero *hates and dreads his mother, and causes her to be murdered. He gives a false account of that murder to the Senate. What strange applause he finds there, and his encouragement from thence to every excess and enormity. He drives chariots, nay mounts the stage. Quinquennial games instituted, with popular observations upon that institution. The brave conduct of* Corbulo *in Armenia; he takes* Tigranocerta, *and establishes* Tigranes *King there. A great massacre of the Romans in Britain during the absence of* Suetonius Paulinus, *then employed in subduing the Isle of Anglesey. Thence the province almost lost, but recovered again by the vigorous efforts of the Governor, and in one great combat. The Governor of Rome slain at home by one of his slaves; the rest punished. The law of Majesty revived. The death of* Burrhus. *Attempts to ruin* Seneca; *who is aware of them, and sues*

sues to be dismissed, but is refused. Tigellinus *his mischievous credit with the Emperor;* causes Plautus *and* Sylla *to be killed.* Nero *dismisses his wife* Octavia, *and marries* Poppæa. *Hence a popular tumult, which hastens the murder of* Octavia.

DURING the Consulship of Caius Vipstanus and Caius Fonteius, Nero determined to accomplish, without more delay, the parricide which he had been long devising, as from the permanence of his power he was become resolute and hardened, and his passion for Poppæa waxed daily more flaming. She too, who could never hope to see Octavia divorced, nor herself espoused during the life of Agrippina, teased him with incessant reproaches, nay, sometimes jeered him by the sarcastical name of ' pupil, one blindly
' subject to the controulment of another, so far from
' being suffered to sway the Empire, that he was
' not allowed even private liberty: for upon what
' other motives could he delay to marry her? Had
' he any objections to her person and beauty, or to
' her blood and ancestors, men of renown, distin-
' guished with triumphal honours? was he unsatis-
' fied about the fruitfulness of her body, or the sin-
' cere affections of her soul? No; the truth was,
' it was dreaded, that when she was become his
' wife she would be laying open the grievances
' of the Senate, the resentment of the people against
' the pride and rapaciousness of his mother. But
' after all, if Agrippina would bear for a daughter-
' in-law no other than one who would prove to
' her son a vexatious and malevolent wife, she de-
' sired to be restored again to the conjugal embra-
' ces of Otho; for she was ready and resolved to
' withdraw to any quarter of the earth, there rather
' to hear of the Emperor's abasement and reproach,
' than stay to behold it, and expose herself to a part-
' nership

'nership of the perils which surrounded him.' These and the like expostulations, enforced with sighs and tears, and all the soft artifices of the adulteress, pierced the soul of Nero; nor did any one check their operation, as all earnestly wished to see the authority of Agrippina crushed, and as no mortal believed that ever the son would wax so hardened in his hate as to spill the blood of his mother.

It is recorded by Cluvius, that such was the flaming passion of Agrippina for retaining her wonted dominion, to such extravagant lengths was she transported, that often in the face of the day, at a season when Nero was heated with wine and banqueting, she accosted him gaily attired, and, while he was thus drunk strove to prompt him to incest; that their obscene kisses, gestures, and other such signals and incitements to that abomination, being well observed by those who were present, Seneca, for an antidote against the inticements of one woman, had recourse to another; hence Acte was introduced, a franchised damsel, one who being equally anxious for her own danger and the infamy of Nero, warned him, that already the incest was every where published, and his mother gloried in the publication, and that the soldiery would never bear the rule of a Prince contaminated with such unnatural pollution. Fabius Rusticus ascribes this strange appetite not to Agrippina, but to Nero, and recounts, that by the cunning of the same Acte he was weaned and rescued. But the detail given by Cluvius is the same with that of the other writers, and on this side too is the testimony of popular fame; whether she really nourished in her heart an impurity so monstrous, or whether the concerting of this unheard-of prostitution appeared the more credible in her, who almost in her childhood had, from thirst of dominion, consented to be debauched by Lepidus, with the like spirit of power
aban-

abandoned herself to the lust of Pallas, and during her incestuous marriage with her uncle Claudius had been practised in a course of wickedness of every kind and degree.

Thenceforth Nero began to avoid all private encounters with his mother, and upon every occasion of her retiring to any of her gardens out of Rome, or to her seats at Tusculum or Autium, used to applaud her for thus employing her leisure: at length, considering her as his dread and torment wherever she resided, he assumed a resolution to kill her, and was only in suspense about the means, whether by poison or the sword, or any other effectual violence. That of poison was preferred at first, but to administer the same was difficult: if it were done at the Prince's table, its operation could never pass for accidental death, since in the like manner Britannicus had already perished: to apply to her own domestics appeared a great risque, as she was a woman who, from her own long intimacy with frauds and blood, was wary and vigilant against all snares and circumvention, and moreover always secured herself by counter-poisons against the efforts of poison. How to dispatch her with the sword, and yet cover the appearances of the execution, no one pretended to devise; it was feared too, that the orders would be rejected, to whomsoever they were given, for the perpetration of such hideous iniquity. Here Anicetus proffered his service and dexterity, a franchised slave, tutor to Nero in his infancy, but now Commander of the fleet which rode at Misenum, one virulently hated by Agrippina, and with equal virulence hating her; he therefore explained, ‘ how
‘ a vessel might be so contrived, that by the sud-
‘ den bursting of one particular quarter in the open
‘ sea,’ she might be overwhelmed without the least
‘ warning or apprehension. Nothing, he said, was
‘ so fertile of disasters as the sea, and if she were
‘ thus

' thus difpatched by fhipwreck, who could be fo in-
' jurious as to afcribe the malignity of wind and
' waves to the malice and contrivance of men?
' Moreover, the Prince would of courfe beftow on
' his deceafed mother a temple and altars, and all
' other honours proper to create an oftentation of
' filial grief and piety.'

Nero was pleafed with the device, which was alfo favoured by the juncture of time, the Feftival of Minerva, called *Quinquatrus*, which he was then celebrating at Baiæ: thither he inticed his mother; for he was frequently declaring, ' that the hafty
' humours of parents were to be borne withal, and
' towards her it behoved him to fupprefs every irri-
' tation of his own fpirit;' as by fuch declarations he meant to raife a general rumour of his own reconcilement to her, a rumour which he hoped would reach Agrippina and find credit with her, from the credulous genius of women, prone to believe whatever feeds their wifhes and promifes matter of joy. When fhe approached, he met her upon the fhore (for fhe came by fea from Antium) prefented her his hand, and embraced her, then conducted her to Bauli, fo the villa is called, which, lying between the Cape of Mifenum and the Gulf of Baiæ, is wafhed by the fea which winds round the point: here, amongft feveral other veffels, there lay one more gaudy and ornamental than the reft, as if, in this particular too, he meditated frefh honour to his mother; for fhe had been always wont to be carried in a galley with three banks of oars, rowed by mariners from the fleet. Moreover, the banquet to which fhe was invited was fo timed, that under the dark fhades of night the horrid execution might be covered: it was, however, apparent that fome body had betrayed the defign, and that Agrippina, upon hearing the perfidious machination, though fhe was doubtful whether fhe ought

to

to believe it, had yet chosen to be carried by land to Baiæ in a sedan; but upon her arrival there the plausible behaviour of Nero assuaged her fears; for besides placing her at table above him, treating her with all tenderness and caresses, he amused her with great variety of conversation, now breaking out into sallies of youthful frankness, then with an air composed and grave discoursing of weighty affairs, and having thus drawn out the banquet into a great length, he attended her to the shore, there more ardently than before he kissed her eyes, kissed her bosom, and left it uncertain whether by such passionate behaviour he only meant to complete this scene of dissimulation, or whether the last sight of a mother just going to perish really checked his spirit however savage.

The night proved clear, the stars shone in full lustre, the sea was smooth and calm, as if all this had been concerted by the providence of the Gods for the more incontestable detection of the murder. Agrippina, of all her numerous domestics, was when she embarked attended only by two, Crepercius Gallus, who stood by the steerage, and Acerronia, who, as her Lady reposed, lay at her feet, and was recounting to her with much joy the remorse of her son, and the favour which by it he had regained from his mother: nor had the vessel yet made much way, when suddenly, upon a signal given, the deck over that quarter was loosened, and being purposely loaded with a great quantity of lead sunk violently down, and instantly crushed Crepereius to death: Agrippina and Acerronia were defended by the posts of the bed, which happened to be too strong to yield to the descending weight; neither did the structure of the vessel burst, for the mariners were all embarrassed, and those of them who were not entrusted with the fraud obstructed the measures of such as were. The next expedient con-

concerted by the latter was to bear her down on one fide, and fo fink her; but neither amongft thefe accomplices was there an inftant concurrence in executing a project thus haftily propofed, and there were others at the fame time ftruggling contrariwife to preferve her: hence it proceeded that fhe was not fwallowed up at once in the deep, but defcended more leifurely. Now Acerronia, while fhe declared herfelf to be Agrippina, and called upon them paffionately to fuccour and fave the Prince's mother, was purfued with poles, and oars, and whatever other naval weapons came accidentally to hand, and fo flain. Agrippina kept filence, and being therefore the lefs known, efcaped with one wound however upon her fhoulder. What with fwimming, what with the affiftance of fome fifher-boats, which rowed out to fuccour her, fhe reached the lake Lucrinus, and was thence conducted to her own villa.

Here fhe revolved upon her danger, that for this very end fhe had been inveigled by the fraudulent letters of her fon, for this treated by him with fuch fignal marks of honour, that the veffel, even under the fhelter of the fhore, without the agitation of winds, without concuffion from rocks, had yielded in its upper part, and tumbled down like a frail ftructure of earth. She confidered the fate of Acerronia, miftaken for herfelf and defignedly flain, and fhe beheld her own wound. From the whole however fhe inferred that her only refource againft thefe black machinations was to act as if fhe faw them not. With this view fhe difpatched Agerinus, her freedman, to notify to her fon, ' that through the
' benevolence of the Gods, and the aufpicious in-
' fluence of his fortune, fhe had efcaped a grievous
' cafualty, but befought him that, however terri-
' fied with the danger which had threatened his
' mother, he fhould yet poftpone the trouble of
' vifiting

' visiting her, for what she only needed at present
' was rest.' In the mean while, counterfeiting perfect security and fearlessness, she had medicines applied to her wound, and her body chafed and anointed; she called too for the last will of Acerronia, and ordered all her effects to be registered and sealed up; in which proceeding only she acted without counterfeiting.

As to Nero, while he was hourly expecting expresses, that the parricide was executed, tidings arrived ' that she had escaped only with a slight hurt,
' having so far felt the danger as to remain in no
' uncertainty who it was that sought her life.' At this he became mortally struck with dismay, and swore in passionate terms, ' that without peradventure she would presently be at hand, bent
' upon taking hasty vengeance, whether by arming
' the slaves, or by stirring up against him the rage
' of the soldiery, or by flying to the Senate and
' people with a tragical representation of the vessel
' wrecked, herself wounded, her friends murdered,
' and her son the author of all: and against this
' menacing event what resource, what protection
' had he, unless some such could be proposed by
' Burrhus and Seneca?' For the instant he received the news of the disappointment, he had called for them both to consult them; neither is it certain whether before this they were unacquainted with the conspiracy. Upon this emergency they both kept long silence, as they apprehended that it was in vain to persuade him to drop the design, and perhaps believed it to be already pushed so far, that unless Agrippina soon perished, Nero certainly must: at length Seneca proved the more forward of the two; yet no further than to look at Burrhus, and ask, ' whether the orders for this execution were
' not to be trusted to the soldiery?' Burrhus answered, that ' the Prætorian guards were so zealously
' attached

' attached to the whole family of the Cæfars; fo fond
' in particular of the name and memory of Germa-
' nicus, that against any defcendent of his they
' could never be animated to aught that were cruel
' and bloody; it therefore behoved Anicetus to ac-
' quit himfelf of his engagement:' neither did Anicetus paufe one moment, but even demanded the office of completing the murder. Nero became revived with thefe words, and declaring himfelf to be that day prefented with the Empire, owned his franchifed flave for the author of the mighty prefent, and urged him to difpatch, leading with him for his affiftance fuch as were moft prompt to obey. The freedman however having heard that Argerinus was arrived from Agrippina, with the news of her difafter and efcape, contrived a plot to turn the treafon upon her; and therefore as the other was delivering his meffage dropped a dagger between his legs, then, as if he had caught him in the terrible fact, called for irons to be inftantly caft upon him. By this fable he purpofed to fupport another, by feigning that the deftruction of the Prince had been concerted by his mother, and that being ftruck with confufion upon the difcovery of her treafon fhe had defperately put an end to her own life.

During thefe tranfactions, while the danger which threatened Agrippina at fea flew abroad (for it was underftood as the effect of chance) the people flocked impatiently to the fhore, each as foon as he heard it. Some climbed up the mounds which fhoot out into the fea, fome crowded into barks and fkiffs, others entered the floods and waded as deep as their height would permit; nay, there were thofe who ftretched out their arms, as it were to catch and receive her; fo that with lamentations for her misfortune, with vows for her deliverance, and with the indiftinct clamour of a multitude, many afking different queftions, or returning uncertain anfwers, the whole coaft
re-

resounded: there ran, moreover, to the rest a great crowd with lights in their hands; and as soon as it was confirmed that Agrippina was out of danger, they were speeding with all zeal to offer her their congratulations, till by the sight and menaces of an armed band they were terrified and dispersed. Anicetus beset the villa with a guard, and, bursting open the gates, seized and secured all such of her slaves as appeared to stop him; he then advanced towards her chamber, where he found the door guarded by very few; all the rest were scared away by the terror and violence of his entrance. In her chamber was a small light, and only one of her damsels; Agrippina too herself was more and more tossed with anxious thoughts, that no soul had yet arrived from her son, nor had even Agerinus returned; she perceived from without strange vicissitudes and an unusual scene, the desertion of her own people, and the sudden violence and tumult of strangers, with all the warnings of her last fate; insomuch that seeing her maid too about to depart, she said, ' thou ' likewise art going to abandon me;' and that moment spied Anicetus, accompanied with Herculeus, Captain of a galley, and Oloaritus, a Centurion of the navy; she told him, ' If he came from the ' Emperor to be informed of her health, he should ' acquaint him she was well recovered; if upon ' any bloody design, she would no wise believe him ' commissioned by her son; her son could never give ' unnatural orders for parricide.' The assassins having placed themselves round her bed, the Captain was the first that wounded her, striking her upon the head with a club; for to the Centurion, as he was drawing his sword to dispatch her, she presented her belly, and with a loud voice, ' Strike ' thy sword into my womb,' she cried, and was instantly assassinated with a multitude of wounds.

In

In these particulars authors are unanimous; but that Nero afterwards surveyed the body of his murdered mother, and magnified its symmetry and loveliness, there are those who have related, and those who deny. That very night her corps was burned with sordid obsequies, upon no other bed than such as she used to recline upon at meals; neither during the reign of Nero were her relics reposited, or covered with common earth, till afterwards, from the benevolence of her domestics, she received a slight and vulgar grave upon the road to Cape Misenum, adjoining to a villa of Cæsar's the Dictator, which from its elevated situation overlooks the coast and bays below. Mnester, a freedman of hers, as soon as her funeral fire was lighted, run himself through with a sword, whether from affection for his lady or from dread of his own doom, is altogether uncertain. This violent end of Agrippina was foretold her many years before, and believed, and yet set at nought by her; for as the Chaldæans, whom she consulted concerning the fortune of Nero, answered, that ' he would certainly reign, and cer-
', tainly kill his mother;' ' Let him kill me, said
' she, so he do but reign.'

The scene of this horrible iniquity being over, the Emperor became terribly struck with its crying enormity, and for the rest of the night was now dumb, motionless, with his eyes fixed, then started up amazed and trembling, and thus waited in distractions of mind the approach of day, a day from which he expected some direful doom. What first raised his assurance was the flattery of the Tribunes and Centurions, who at the instigation of Burrhus grasped his hand, with congratulations, ' That he had thus escaped such unforeseen peril, ' and the mortal snares of his mother.' Next, his friends and intimates betook themselves with thanksgiving to the several Temples; and the example
being

being thus begun was followed by the adjacent towns and communities of Campania, who gave public testimonies of their joy, by sacrifices to the Gods, and embassies to the Prince. For himself, his dissimulation took a different turn from theirs: Sad and dejected was his mien, he seemed to hate a life thus saved, and bewailed with many tears, the death of his mother. However, as places cannot change their aspect, like the supple countenances of men, and as the tragical prospect of that deadly sea and coast was incessantly reproaching him (besides there were those who believed, that from the high cliffs round about they heard the shrill sound of trumpets, and shrieks and wailings from Agrippina's grave) he withdrew to Naples, and there sent letters to the Senate, of which these are the heads:

'That Agerinus, a freedman of Agrippina's, in intimate trust with her, had been seized, ready armed to assassinate him; whence she had undergone the pains of parricide, from the same guilty conscience that prompted her to contrive it.' To this he added a catalogue of her crimes, traced a long way backwards; how 'she had aimed at a co-ordinate power in the Empire, with an oath from the Prætorian bands, an oath of allegiance to a woman, nay, to the abasement of the Senate and people, had expected the like mark of subjection from them; and finding her ambition disappointed, she became enraged against the soldiery, against the fathers, and the populace, opposed a donative to the guards, and a largess to the people, and devised destruction against the illustrious chiefs of Rome. Nay, it was with great difficulty that he defeated her design of usurping a seat in the Senate, and of returning answers to the Ambassadors of foreign nations.' He even obliquely lashed the transactions under Claudius, and cast upon his mother all the acts of tyranny in that reign, ascribing her fall

VOL. II. H to

to the good fortune of the State; for he recounted the particulars of the shipwreck. But where lived there a soul so stupid to believe it to be the blind work of chance; or that a forlorn woman, just saved from a wreck, should employ a single assassin to break through an armed fleet and the imperial guards, and slay the Emperor? Hence it was not now upon Nero that the popular censure fell (for Nero's brutal barbarity surpassed all censure) but upon Seneca, for that, by such a representation to the Senate, he had in writing avowed the deed.

Wonderful, however, was the competition of the Grandees in decreeing the following solemnities; ' That at all the altars public devotions should be ' performed; the feast of Minerva, during which the ' conspiracy was detected, should be celebrated with ' anniversary plays for ever; in the Senate-house ' should be placed the statue of that Goddess in gold, ' and close by her, that of the Emperor; and in ' the list of unhallowed days, Agrippina's anniver-' sary should be inserted.' Thrasea Petus, who was wont either to pass over the like sallies of servility in utter silence or with a short word of assent, walked now out of the Senate, and thence awakened future vengeance against himself, and yet to the rest opened no source of liberty. There happened, moreover, at the same time frequent prodigies, from which arose many prognostics, but no consequences. One woman brought forth a serpent, another, in the embraces of her husband was struck dead with a thunder-bolt; the sun became suddenly darkened, and the fourteen quarters of the city felt the effects of lightning. All which events came to pass so apparently without any providential design in the Deities, that for many years after this, Nero continued safe in his sovereignty and enormities. Now, in order to heighten the popular hate towards his mother, and withal to magnify his own clemency, as if the

same

fame were enlarged now she was removed, he reſtored to their native country and inheritance, Junia and Calpurnia, Ladies of illuſtrious quality, with Valerius Capito and Lucinius Gabolus, men of Prætorian dignity, all formerly doomed to exile by Agrippina: He likewiſe permitted the remains of Lollia Paullina to be brought home, and a ſepulchre for them to be built; Iturius too and Calviſius, whom he had lately baniſhed, he now pardoned and releaſed; for Silana had already yielded to the lot of mortality at Tarentum, whither, from her remote baniſhment, ſhe had returned, either becauſe the authority of Agrippina, by whoſe enmity ſhe fell, was then declining, or her wrath by that time aſſuaged.

While Nero lingered in the towns of Campania, full of anxiety how to conduct himſelf upon his return to Rome, whether he ſhould find the Senate obſequious, or zeal in the people, his doubts were combated by all the profligates of the court (and no court upon earth abounded with more). They argued ' that the very name of Agrippina was deteſted,
' inſomuch that by her death the affections of the
' people were more powerfully kindled towards him:
' He ſhould therefore proceed confidently, and in
' perſon receive proofs of popular adoration.' As they demanded too, that, for trial, they might arrive ſomewhat before him, they found, in all reſpects, a more forward and officious zeal than they themſelves had promiſed, the ſeveral tribes, in diſtinct bodies, coming forth to meet him, as alſo the Senate in their robes of ſtate, with mighty droves of women and children, ranged in claſſes according to their ſex and age; and all along where he was to paſs, a ſucceſſive variety of plays and ſhews, and ſcenes of public rejoicing, were prepared, with all the parade attending a triumph. Elated with ſuch reception, and as if crowned with victory from this

general servitude, he repaired to the Capitol, paid his vows and oblations, and thenceforth abandoned himself to the full bent of all his furious passions; for though he had hitherto but poorly controuled them, yet his reverence to his mother, however weak it were, had till then checked their violence.

It was a usual diversion of his, and long allowed him, to drive a chariot drawn by four horses; nor less scandalous was his passion for singing to the harp, as he was wont when he supped, in a theatrical gesture and habit: 'An employment, which he alledged
' to have been commonly practised by Kings and
' Heroes of old; that the same was celebrated in
' the songs of the poets, and even performed to
' the honour of the Gods; for thus were music and
' singing sacred to Apollo, and thus represented,
' with the same dress and instrument, not only
' in the cities of Greece, but even in the Roman
' Temples, stood that sublime and oracular Deity.'
Neither could this his bent be restrained: So that Seneca and Burrhus, left he should have persisted in both, judged it advisable to indulge him in one. Thus a piece of ground, in the Vatican, was inclosed with a wall, that he might there exert his dexterity in racing and the discipline of steeds; without being exposed, as in a public shew to the promiscuous crowd. But, in a short time, he even sought to be publickly seen, and invited to the sight the Roman populace, who failed not to magnify him with abundant encomiums; for the vulgar is ever longing after public diversions and ever delighted with the same inclination in the Prince. Moreover, such open prostitution and forfeiture of all shame did not, as his ministers expected, produce in him any satiety, but contrariwise fresh eagerness: As he imagined too that, by bringing many under such debasement, he should remove his own, he introduced, as actors, into the Theatre, several
who

who were descended from illustrious families, but through indigence become venal, men whose names (as they are now no more) I repeat not with their story; a consideration which I judge due to the dignity of their ancestors; seeing too, that upon his head the iniquities recoil, who, rather than they should not transgress, gave them money for transgressing. He likewise engaged several Roman Knights (men well known) to undertake parts in theatrical representations by excessive rewards; unless it be thought that pay from one who has authority to command, carries with it the power of compulsion.

Nevertheless, that he might not as yet debase himself in the common Theatre, he instituted a sort of plays called *Juvenales*; and for celebrating these names were given in from all quarters. Here no man's quality and blood, nor his age, nor the public figure and offices which any of them had borne, excused them from personating the port and buffoonry of the Greek and Roman mimics, even in the obscene gesticulation of their bodies and the effeminate cadences of their voice: Even Ladies of illustrious quality came also to devise unseemly revellings So that, in the grove planted by Augustus round the lake where the naval combat was exhibited, tabernacles were erected and booths were built, where wine and dainties were exposed to sale, with whatever incites to sensuality and wantonness. To promote the debauch, money was given to the innocent as well as the voluptuous, to be wasted alike in riot, by the former from awe of Nero, by the latter from ostentation of vice. From this source arose a monstrous increase of all pollution and enormities; and though our manners had been long since corrupted, yet never were they more debauched and pervaded by any inundation of vice and depravity, than by this shocking sink of lewdness. Modesty is a thing hard to be secured even by the most virtuous management and restraints; much less is modesty, or chastity, or any honest endowment, to be preserved amidst scenes of impurity, where vices are engaged in a contention to outvie each other.

At length, Nero could forbear no longer, but mounted the Stage and took the harp, trying the strings with awful attention, and studying his part. About him stood his companions; a Cohort too of the guards were arrived, with many Tribunes and Centurions; as also Burrhus the Præfect, praising Nero and grieving for him. At this time likewise was first enrolled the body of Roman Knights entituled *Augustani*, young men distinguished by the bloom of their years, and strength of body, all professed profligates, some from the bent of nature, the rest in hopes of preferment. These attended nights and days, wholly employed in clapping the Emperor and sounding his applauses. They extolled his person and voice by epithets peculiar to the Gods, as if only from their zeal for virtue they sought splendor and honour.

The Emperor, however, that he might not be only renowned for the accomplishments of a player, studied to excel also in Poetry, having drawn about him several who had a genius for poesy, though not yet noted for their poems. These were wont to sit down in concert with the Prince, and connect together such lines as they had severally brought, or such as they found already composed, piecing out with supplements of their own all his effusions, however lame and crude: This is apparent from the very composition of these poems, which flow with no uniformity of stile or genius, like the productions of one man. He used, besides, to bestow some time after meals upon hearing the reasonings of Philosophers; and while each maintained his own sect, and contradicted the rest, they all exposed their endless broils: Nay, some of them were
fond

fond of being seen, with their ſtern aſpect and accent, amidſt the royal exceſſes and recreations of
Nero.

About the ſame time, from a conteſt altogether
trivial, there aroſe a horrid ſlaughter between two of
our Italian Colonies, Nuceria and Pompeium, at the
celebration of a combat of Gladiators exhibited by
Livineius Regulus, whoſe expulſion from the Senate
I have before recounted. Now, as they teaſed and
rallied each other with the uſual gibes and petulance
of citizens, they proceeded to bitterneſs and invectives,
then to rage and vollies of ſtones, at length to a general encounter at arms. But to the Pompeian populace, who were the more powerful, the victory
remained, as in their territories too the revel was exhibited. Hence, numbers of thoſe of Nuceria were
borne to Rome with mangled and mutilated bodies;
and many arrived there with complaints and wailings, ſome for the death of their ſons, ſome for that
of their fathers. The cognizance of this affair was
by the Prince left to the Senate, by them to the
Conſuls, but returned again before the fathers, who
by a decree diſabled the Pompeians from meeting
in any ſuch popular concourſe for ten years, and
diſſolved for ever the fraternities which they had
inſtituted againſt the Law. Livineius and the other
incendiaries of the riot were doomed to exile.

Pedius Blæſus was alſo puniſhed with expulſion
from the Senate, at the ſuit of the Cyrenians, who
urged that he had robbed the treaſure of Æſculapius,
and in the inrolling of ſoldiers had been governed
by price and popularity. The ſame Cyrenians brought
a charge againſt Acilius Strabo, one who had been
inveſted with the Prætorian power, and ſent as an
arbitrator from the Emperor Claudius to adjuſt and
diſcriminate the territories formerly held by King
Apion, and by him bequeathed, together with his

whole

whole Kingdom, to the Roman people; for that the same had been usurped on every side by the borderers, who having thus enjoyed them a long while, derived a claim of right from encroachment and iniquity. Strabo, therefore, having adjudged the lands to the Romans and expulsed the invaders, much matter of popular hate against the arbitrator was thence administered to the Cyreneans. In answer to the charge the Senate said, 'That to them
' the tenor of his commission from Claudius was
' unknown, and they must consult the Prince.' Nero approved the arbitration of Strabo, but wrote back,
' That he would nevertheless relieve our confede-
' rates the Cyrenians, and yield them up the usurp-
' ed possessions.'

Thereafter followed the deaths of these illustrious Romans, Domitius Afer and Marcus Servilius, men, who, for the sublime dignities of the state which they had swayed, and for their own abounding eloquence, had flourished in signal credit. The first was renowned for a powerful Pleader, Servilius too for his long success at the bar, and afterwards for the History by him compiled of the Roman affairs, as also for the elegance and probity of his life, which received fresh lustre from the opposite behaviour of Afer, who in parts and genius was his equal, but far different in life and manners.

During the fourth Consulship of Nero with Cornelius Cossus for his colleague, Quinquennial Games were instituted at Rome, after the fashion of the prize-matches amongst the Greeks, and, like almost all new institutions, were variously represented. Some alledged, 'That Pompey too was censured
' by our ancestors, for having founded a permanent
' Theatre; till then, the public sports were wont
' to be exhibited from scenes occasionally erected
' for the solemnity, to last no longer, and to be
' seen from seats suddenly reared; or, if times more
' re-

' remote were confulted, the people would be found
' to have then beheld fuch reprefentations ftauding,
' left, had they been indulged with feats, they might
' have confumed whole days in amufements of the
' theatre. In truth, the primitive rule in reprefent-
' ing popular fhews would be preferved, were the
' fame ftill exhibited by the Prætors, and no Roman
' citizen whatever compelled to enter the public
' lifts. But, now, the ancient ufages of our coun-
' try, which had been long decaying piece-meal,
' were utterly obliterated by the prevalence of fo-
' reign fports and gratifications: Infomuch that at
' Rome might be feen, from all quarters, whatever
' was capable of being corrupted or of propagating
' corruption; the Roman youth deviated into fo-
' reign ftudies, frequented common wreftling-fchools,
' indulged floth, and purfued unnatural amours, fince
' they were influenced by the example and fupreme
' direction of Prince and Senate, who not only
' granted licence to a torrent of vice, but promot-
' ed it by authority and coercion. Romans of the
' firft rank, under colour of rehearfing their poems
' and harangues, defiled themfelves with the prac-
' tice of the ftage. What remained further, un-
' lefs they ftripped themfelves naked, and commenc-
' ing fencers, wielded the whirlebat, and, for mi-
' litary glory and arms, ftudied thefe theatrical fkir-
' mifhes for pay? Would the bands of Roman
' Knights, would thofe intituled *Auguftani*, more
' worthily fulfil their high office of judicature, by
' a nice ear in the modulations of mufic, and by
' applauding the foft fhakes and thrills of Nero's
' throat? Nights as well as days were beftowed
' upon the infamous revel, that no portion of time
' might remain for fkreening modefty and fhame;
' but in that huge affembly, blended at random,
' every libertine might dare to gratify by night what-
' ever his concupifcence prompted him to by day.'

Many others were even well pleased with this dissolute pastime, but disguised it however under venerable names. 'Our ancestors too, they alledged, 'had not abstained from the divertisement of public 'representations, which were exhibited in a manner 'suitable to the fortune and revenue of that time. 'Thus from Tuscany they procured players; from 'Thurium the diversion of racing; and after the 'conquest of Greece and Asia, the Roman sports 'were solemnized with greater elegance and accu- 'racy: Yet in a course of two hundred years, 'ever since the triumphs of Lucius Mummius, who 'first presented the Romans with these foreign shews, 'no Roman of ingenuous birth had debased himself 'to the business of the stage. Nay, public fruga- 'lity too had been consulted, by rearing a standing 'Theatre, much more than by erecting a great oc- 'casional edifice, at an immense expence, every 'year. Neither had the magistrates occasion, 'henceforth, to exhaust their private fortune, nor 'the people to importune the Magistrates for 'the exhibition of the prize combats of Greece, 'since by the Commonwealth all the expence was 'defrayed. Moreover, the prizes then gained by 'Poets and Orators, would prove incentives to the 'cultivation of genius; nor to any one of those 'who sat judges there, could it prove irksome to 'lend his ear to the rehearsal of generous produc- 'tions, and to recreations altogether lawful. A few 'nights spent upon this solemnity once in the course 'of five years, were rather assigned to diversion 'than to lewdness, during such a copious blaze of 'lights, that no sally of iniquity could possibly be 'concealed.' It is very true, that this revel escaped free from any signal act of dishonour; moreover, the popular contention and zeal for the several actors was so moderate, that it produced no sort of uproar. For though the Pantomimes were again restored to the stage, they were restrained from the

cele-

celebration of games which were held sacred. The prize of eloquence was borne away by none, but the victory was adjudged to Nero. The Grecian garb, worn at such solemnities by many, and generally railed at, waxed now into disuse.

During these transactions a Comet blazed, a phænomenon which, according to the persuasion of the vulgar, always portends a change of Kings. Hence, as if Nero had been already deposed, it became the topic of general inquiry, who should be chosen to succeed him, and, by the universal voice on this occasion, the name of Rubellius Plautus was resounded, one who by his mother inherited the nobility of the Julian race. He himself observed the reverend manners of our ancestors, severe in his dress, his house virtuous, regular, and devoted to retirement: But the more retired his apprehensions made him to be, the higher renown he acquired. The rumour was heightened by a flash of lightning, which was expounded with the like credulity and folly: For as Nero sat at meat in a villa called Sublaqueum, upon the banks of the Simbruine Lakes, lightning darted upon the repast, scattered the dishes, and overthrew the table; and as this casualty happened in the neighbourhood of Tivoli, from whence Plautus by his father's side originally sprang, the people believed him the man destined to Empire by the Deities. He was likewise favoured by many such whose ambition always hurrying, and for the most part deceiving them, engages them in novel pursuits fraught with ambiguity and danger. All this alarmed Nero, who therefore signified to Plautus by a letter, ' That he would do well to
' consult the tranquillity of Rome, and withdraw
' himself from the reach of those who malignantly
' defamed him. In Asia he had ancient possessions,
' where he might enjoy the bloom of his life free
' from all peril and the embroilments of state.' Upon this warning he retired thither, with Antistia his

wife and a few friends. In the course of these days, the inordinate propensity of Nero to unbounded voluptuousness involved him in much danger and infamy; for as he would needs swim in the source of the aqueduct which supplies the city, and derives its name from (Ancus) Marcius the founder, it was construed, that he had with an impure body polluted the sacred stream, and profaned the sanctity of the place; and a dangerous malady immediately ensuing, ascertained the resentment of the Deities.

Now Corbulo judged it proper, after the demolition of Artaxata, to improve the reigning terror, and to seize Tigranocerta; for that, having once taken it, whether he were to raze it or save it, he should either infuse fresh dread into the foe, or fill them with the fame of his clemency. Thus he marched towards it, but committed no hostilities, lest he should banish all hopes of pardon, nor yet receded from his usual discipline, as he knew it to be a nation addicted to sudden changes; and, as in encountering dangers, dull and spiritless; so, in feats of perfidiousness, dexterous and vigilant. The Barbarians took various courses according to their several humours. Some met him as supplicants; others abandoned their dwellings, and betook themselves to the recesses of the desart; several crept into caves, accompanied with whatever was dearest to them. The methods therefore taken by the Roman General were various as the occasion; to the supplicants he extended mercy; after the fugitives he ordered quick pursuits; but towards those who had hid themselves in dens, he was rigorously severe; for with faggots and brushes he filled the mouths and issues of the caverns, and set the same on fire. Then continuing his march along the confines of the Mardians, he was insulted by the prædatory bands of that people, exercised in continual robberies, and protected by their wild mountains against reprizals and invasions. But Corbulo, by pouring in the

Hibe-

Hiberians upon them, expofed them to devaftation and fword, and took vengeance of their infolent hoftilities, at the expence of the blood of foreigners.

But though neither he, nor his army, was any wife impaired by fighting, they were both fpent with continued travel and want, and reduced to combat hunger with the ufe of flefh alone. Add to thefe diftreffes, a fcorching fummer, extreme fcarcity of water, mighty marches; evils which were extenuated only by the exemplary patience of the General, who underwent more hardfhips than any common foldier. Thence they arrived in places that were cultivated, where the ripened harveft furnifhed grain for bread; and as here ftood two caftles whither the Armenians had flocked for fanctuary, one was taken at once by ftorm; the other, having repulfed the firft onfet, was by a fiege compelled to furrender. Corbulo paffed next to the country of the Taurantes, where he efcaped a fudden and threatening danger; for hard by his pavilion a Barbarian, armed with a dagger, was apprehended, one of no mean degree, who, upon the rack, unfolded the order of the confpiracy, owned himfelf the contriver, and difcovered his affociates, who, being all convicted, fuffered the juft doom of traitors, fnch who under the facred name and profeffion of peace and friendfhip were meditating guile and blood. Not long after, the Ambaffadors by him fent forward to Tigranocerta returned with tidings, that the inhabitants were bent upon fubmitting to the Roman authority, and their gates flood open to receive the Roman army. At the fame time they prefented him from the city with a golden crown, as a token of hofpitality and friendly reception; an acknowledgment which he accepted with all marks of honour, and in no one inftance infringed the property or privileges of the town, that thence they might perfevere in their allegiance, being left in full enjoyment of their eftate.

But the Royal citadel, which was garrisoned by a band of young men of resolute valour, was not mastered without blows. They even ventured upon a sally, and joining battle without the walls, were beaten back into their fortifications, whither, as our men forced an entrance after them, they were obliged at last to yield to the arms of the assailants. These enterprizes were the more easily accomplished, for that the Parthians were engaged the while in a war with the Hyrcanians, a people who had already sent an embassy to the Roman Emperor to intreat his alliance, representing it as a pledge of their friendship to Rome, that they had thus diverted the power of Vologeses. As these Ambassadors were returning, that they might not, by crossing the Euphrates, be intercepted by the stationary guards of the enemy, Corbulo furnished them with a convoy of soldiers, who conducted them as far as the coast of the

of Partha, they returned in safety to their native homes. Moreover, as Tiridates had passed through Media, and thence invaded the extreme parts of Armenia, Corbulo, having sent forward Verulanus his Lieutenant-General, with the auxiliary troops, advanced himself at the head of the Legions lightly equipped, and constraining the invader to retire

all hopes from pursuing the war; having likewise laid waste, with fire and slaughter, all those quarters which he had learnt were zealous for that King, and therefore disaffected to us, he had already assumed the complete possession and government of all Armenia, when Tigranes arrived, a Prince preferred by Nero to that crown. He was a Cappadocian, nobly descended, and grandson to King Archelaus; but from the former lot of his life, having passed many years at Rome in the quality of a hostage, his spirit was miserably debased, even to a degree of abjectness and servility; neither was he

now

now received into the sovereignty with general unanimity, as amongst several there still remained a lasting affection for the family of the Arsacides. However, as there were many who abominated the pride of the Parthians, they preferred the accepting of a King from the hands of the Romans. Upon the new Monarch too was bestowed a body of guards, namely, a thousand legionary soldiers, three Cohorts detached from our confederates, and two wings of horse, to support him in maintaining his new realm. Several portions, besides, of Armenia, were subjected to the neighbouring Kings, to Pharasmenes, to Polemon, Aristobulus, and Antiochus, according to the contiguity of the same to their respective dominions. Corbulo having completed this settlement, withdrew into Syria, a province assigned to him, upon the death of Venidius, the late Governor.

The same year, Laodicea, one of the capital cities of Asia, having been overthrown by an earthquake, rose again, by her own ability and means, into her former lustre, unassisted by any aid from us. But, in Italy, the ancient city of Puzzoli obtained from Nero the prerogative and title of a Colony. All the Veterans then dismissed were ingrafted amongst the inhabitants of Tarentum and Antium, yet cured not the defect and thinness of people there; for many of these new-comers straggled away to their old haunts in the provinces, where, during their term of service, they had quartered; being, besides, never accustomed to engage in wedlock, or to rear children, they lived without families, and died without posterity. For Colonies were not now established as of old, when intire Legions were transplanted thither, with their officers, Tribunes, and Centurions, and all the soldiers in their distinct classes; so as they might from ancient acquaintance and unanimity fall naturally into the form of a commonweal; but a medley of men,

not

not known to each other, now thrown together, without any ruler to manage them, without mutual affection to unite them, and all detached from different companies, like so many individuals suddenly amassed from so many different races of men, were rather a crowd than a Colony.

The election of Prætors followed, a transaction wont to be subject to the pleasure of the Senate; but as this proceeded with unusual vehemence and caballing, the Prince settled the contention, by preferring to the command of a Legion the three candidates who exceeded the stated number. He also exalted the dignity of the Fathers, by ordaining, that, ' whoever should appeal from the stated judges ' to the Senate, should be exposed to the hazard ' of forfeiting the same sum of money as did those ' who appealed to the Emperor.' For hitherto this was left at large and free from all penalty. At the close of the year Vibius Secundus, a Roman Knight, was, upon the accusation of the Moors, condemned for public extortion, and expelled Italy; for he escaped a severer doom by the prevailing credit and opulence of Vibius Crispus, his brother.

During the Consulship of Cæsonius Pætus and Petronius Turpilianus we suffered a cruel slaughter in Britain. In truth, as Avitus the Governor had done no more there than (what I have already observed) just maintained our former conquests, so his successor Veranius, having only in some light incursions ravaged the territories of the Silures, was intercepted by death from any further prosecution of the war; a man indeed of high reputation during his life, for severe virtue and manners; but by the stile of his last will, his servile ambition and court to power became notorious; for after manifold flatteries bestowed upon Nero, he added, ' that he ' should have completely subjected that province ' to his obedience, had his own life been prolonged ' for two years. After him, Suetonius Paulinus obtained the government of Britain, a competitor with Corbulo in the science of war, and in the voice of the populace, who to every man of renown are sure to create a rival. He hoped too, by subduing that fierce enemy, to reap equal glory to that which the other derived from the recovery of Armenia: He therefore prepared to fall upon the isle of Anglesea, powerful in inhabitants, and a common refuge to the revolters and fugitives. He built, for that 'end, boats with broad flat bottoms, the easier to approach a shore full of shallows and uncertain landings; upon these the foot were embarked; the horse followed partly by fording, partly by swimming.

On the opposite shore stood the enemy's army, compact with men and arms: amongst them were women running franticly to and fro, resembling the wild transports of furies; dismally clad in funereal apparel, their hair disheveled, and torches in their hands. Round the host also appeared their Priests the Druids, with their hands lifted up to heaven, uttering bitter and direful imprecations; and from the strangeness of the spectacle, struck the spirit of the Roman soldiers with great dismay; insomuch, that, as if all their limbs had been benumbed, they stood motionless, with their bodies exposed, like marks, to wounds and darts, till, by the repeated exhortations of the General, as well as by mutual incitements from one another, they were at last roused to shake off the scandalous terror inspired by a band of raving women and fanatic priests; and thus advancing their ensigns, they discomfited all that resisted, and involved them in their own fires. A garrison was thereafter established over the vanquished, and the groves cut down by them dedicated in detestable superstitions; for there they sacrificed captives, and, in order to discover the will of the Gods, consulted the entrails of men;

prac-

practices of cruelty by them accounted holy. While Suetonius was thus employed, tidings were brought him of the sudden revolt of the province.

Præsutagus, the late King of the Icenians, a Prince long renowned for his opulence and grandeur, had by will left the Emperor joint heir with his own two daughters; as by such a signal instance of loyalty, he judged he should purchase a sure protection to his Kingdom and family against all injury and violence. A scheme which produced an effect so intirely contrary, that his realm was ravaged by the Centurions, and his house by slaves; as if both his house and realm had been the just spoils of war. First of all Boudicea his wife underwent the ignominious violence of stripes, and his daughters that of constupration; and, as though the entire region had been bequeathed to the plunderers, all the principal Icenians were spoiled of their ancient possessions, and the Royal relations of the late King were kept and treated as slaves. Enraged by all this contumelious tyranny, and dreading oppressions still more severe, since they were thus reduced into a province, they flew unanimously to arms, having animated the Trinobantes to join in the revolt, as well as all others who were not yet broken by the yoke of servitude, and had secretly conspired to recover their original liberty. Their most implacable enmity was towards the Veterans, lately translated to the Colony of Camalodunum; for these new guests had thrust them out of their houses, exterminated them from their native lands, and treated them with the vile titles of captives and slaves. These outrages too of the Veterans were abetted by the common soldiers from their similitude of life and inclination, and in hopes of enjoying the same licentious situation. Moreover, the Temple built and dedicated to the deified Claudius was by them regarded as the bulwark of a domination established over them without end.

end. Besides that the Priests, culled out for ministering in the Temple, under the cloak of Religion, devoured their whole substance. Neither did it appear an arduous undertaking to extirpate a Colony no wise secured by fortifications; a provision little minded by our Commanders, who had consulted accommodation and pleasure antecedently to advantage and security.

During these transactions, the statue of victory at Camalodunum, without any visible violence, tumbled down with her face turned round; as if by it she betokened her yielding to the enemy. There were women too who, transported with oracular fury, chanted destruction to be at hand. In the place where they assembled for the business of the public, the accent and tumultuous murmurs of strangers were heard; their Theatre ecchoed with dismal howlings, and, in the lakes formed by the tides resisting the Thames, a representation was seen of a Colony overthrown. The sea too appeared all dyed with blood, and at the departure of the tide, phantoms of human bodies appeared left behind upon the strand. From which omens, as the Britons derived matter of hope and joy, so did the Veterans matter of heaviness and fear. But, because Suetonius was at a great distance, they sought succours from Catus Decianus, Procurator of the province, who yet sent them no more than two hundred men, nor these completely armed; and, in the Colony itself, was but a small handful of soldiers. The Veterans not only relied upon the shelter and strength of the Temple, but were frustrated in their measures by such as were secret accomplices in the revolt; hence they had neither secured themselves by a ditch or pallisade, nor removed their women and old men, reserving only those of youth and vigour for their defence. So that, utterly unprepared, and as void of circumspection as if full peace had reigned, they were beset and cut off

by

by a vaft hoft of Barbarians. In truth, every thing in the Colony yielded to inftant violence, and was razed or burnt; only the Temple, whither the foldiers were retired in a body, ftood a two days fiege, and was then taken by ftorm. Moreover, Petilius Cerialis, Commander of the ninth Legion, as he advanced to relieve his friends, was met and encountered by the victorious Britons, his Legion routed, and all his infantry flain. Cerialis, with the horfe, efcaped to the Camp, and there defended himfelf in his entrenchments. Catus the Procurator, terrified with this ruin and flaughter, and with the univerfal hate of the province, which by his rapacious avarice he had driven into hoftility, fled over into Gaul.

But Suetonius, with marvellous bravery, marched through the heart of the enemy quite to London, a city in truth not diftinguifhed with the title of a Colony, but highly famed for the vaft conflux of traders, and her abundant commerce and plenty. Here he was deliberating about fettling his head quarters in this place, and chufing it for the feat and centre of the war; but reflecting upon the thin number of his foldiers, and well warned by the temerity of Petilius fo fignally chaftized, he refolved to abandon it, and, with the lofs of one town, to fave the whole province. Nor could the tears and wailings of numbers imploring his protection divert him from ordering the fignal for departure to be founded. Into part of his forces he affumed all thofe who would accompany him; whoever ftaid behind, whether detained by the weaknefs of their fex, by the unwieldinefs of old age, or by the charms of the place, fell, without exception, by the rage of the enemy. The like flaughter befell the municipal city of Verulamium. For the Barbarians, who were charmed with plunder, but cold and daftardly in other exploits of war, omitted to attack forts and garrifons; but where-ever there was abundant booty,

booty, eafy to be feized by the fpoiler, dangerous to be defended by the owner, thither they carried their animofity and arms. In the feveral places which I have mentioned, it appeared that feventy thoufand fouls had perifhed, all Romans, or the confederates of Rome; for the enemy neither made, nor fold, nor exchanged prifoners, nor obferved any other law of war; but upon all exercifed mortal fury, by prefent killing, gibbetting, burning, and crucifying with the defperate eagernefs and precipitation of men, who were fure of undergoing a terrible doom, and refolved, by anticipated vengeance, to fpill the blood of others before their own were fpilt.

Suetonius had already an army of nigh ten thoufand men; namely, the fourteenth Legion, with the Veterans of the twentieth, and auxiliaries from the quarters next adjoining; fo that relinquifhing all further delay, he prepared for encountering the enemy in battle, and chofe a place which ftretched out before into a hollow and narrow vale, with fteep fides, and was behind girt in with wood. He was thoroughly apprized, that in the front only the whole forces of the enemy were to be expected, and that the fpace between was a plain bottom, where no ftratagems nor ambufhes were to be dreaded: He therefore drew up the Legionary foldiers into clofe ranks, fuftained them with the foldiery lightly armed, and on each wing placed the cavalry. The Britifh army were every where exulting and bounding in great feparate bands, fome of horfe, fome of foot, and exhibited in all a multitude fo vaft as hitherto was not parallelled. They were even animated by a fpirit fo confident and fierce, that with them they had alfo brought their wives, to be fpectators of their victory, and ftowed them in their waggons, which they had placed round the extremity of the camp.

Boudicea was carried about in a chariot, where before her fat her two daughters. Traverfing the field,

field, from nation to nation, she to all declared,
' That it was, in truth, usual to the Britons to war
' under the conduct of women; yet, upon this oc-
' casion, she assumed not the authority of one de-
' scended from such mighty ancestors; nor aimed
' to revenge the loss of her Kingdom, and that of
' her Royal opulence basely plundered; but she
' then appeared upon the same foot with one of the
' vulgar, and sought vengeance for the oppression
' of public liberty, for the stripes inflicted upon her
' person, for the defilement of her virgin daughters.
' To such height was the wild fury and concupis-
' cence of the Romans advanced, that neither the
' persons of individuals, nor even old age, nor even
' tender maidens could escape their rage and con-
' tamination. The incensed Deities were however
' ready to aid the just sword of vengeance; by it a
' Legion, which dared to tempt an engagement,
' had already fallen; the rest skulked behind the
' entrenchments of their camp, or were devising on
' every side which way to fly: nor would they be
' able to bear even the uproar and shouts of so many
' thousand men, how much less their impetuous
' onset and vengeful arms. If the Britons would
' survey the number of men under arms; if they
' would well weigh the affecting causes of the war;
' they would find, that in that battle they must re-
' main utterly victorious, or utterly perish. Such
' was the firm purpose of her who was a woman.
' The men, if they pleased, might still enjoy life
' and bondage.'

Neither was Suetonius silent at a juncture so pe-
rillous, and though he confided in the bravery of his
men, yet failed not to join to it the force of exhortations mixed with entreaties, ' to despise the sa-
' vage din and clamour of the Barbarians, with
' all their impotent menaces. In that great host
' were to be seen more weak women than vigorous
' men,

'men, an unwarlike hoſt, deſtitute of arms, and
' diſpoſed to inſtant flight, as ſoon as they came to
' experience again the ſame victorious bravery and
' ſteel which by ſo many defeats they had proved.
' Even in an army compoſed of many Legions,
' the glory of diſcomfiting the foe retrained always
' to a few; hence it would redound to their pe-
' culiar glory, that though but a ſmall band, they
' ſhould reap all the renown which could accrue to
' a great and complete army. They were only to
' keep condenſed in their ranks, and, having firſt
' diſcharged their darts, cloſe in, and with the na-
' vels of their ſhields and edge of their ſwords
' purſue the defeat and ſlaughter. Of the ſpoil they
' muſt have no thought, ſince after victory, to their
' ſhare of courſe would fall ſpoil, and honour; and
' all things."

Every part of the General's ſpeech was followed
by ſuch ſignal ardour in his men, with ſuch prompt-
neſs had all the old ſoldiers, men long inured to all
the arts and events of battle, already aſſumed a proper poſture for wielding and darting their javelins,
that Suetonius, as certain of the iſſue, gave the ſignal for onſet.

Pirſt of all, the Legion kept their ground immove-
able, and ſtill ſheltered themſelves, as with a bulwark, within the natural ſtreights of the place, till
the enemy had advanced within arrow ſhot, and ex-
hauſted all their darts. Upon this advantage, they
ruſhed out upon them, as it were with the force and
keenneſs of a wedge; equal was the impetuoſity of
the auxiliaries: The horſe too, advancing with a
battlement of pikes, utterly broke and overthrew
whatever quarters of the foe exerted any reſiſtance
and ſtrength; for all the reſt turned their backs,
but found it difficult to eſcape; the incloſure made
by their own carriages had obſtructed their flight.
Such too was the fury of the ſoldiers, that they ſpared

not

not even the lives of women; nay, the very beafts escaped not, but were pierced with darts, and ferved to fwell the mighty heaps of the dead. Signal was the glory that day gained, and equal to the victories of the ancient Romans; for there are authors who record, that of the Britons were flain almoft eighty thoufand, of our men about four hundred, with not many more wounded. Boudicca ended her life by poifon. Poenius Poftumus too, Camp-Marfhal to the fecond Legion, upon tidings of the exploits and fuccefs of the fourteenth and twentieth, as he had defrauded his own of equal honour, and, contrary to the laws of military duty, difobeyed the orders of his General, ran himfelf through with his fword.

The whole army was thereafter drawn together, and kept the field under tents, in order to finifh the remains of the war. Their forces were moreover augmented by Nero, who fent them from Germany two thoufand Legionary foldiers, eight Cohorts of auxiliaries, and a thoufand horfe. By their arrival the ninth Legion was fupplied with a Legionary recruit; the auxiliary Cohorts and wings of the cavalry were pofted in new winter quarters; and thus, which ever of the feveral nations appeared hoftile or fufpicious, were fubjected to the devaftations of fire and fword. But famine, above all other calamities, afflicted the foe, who had neglected to cultivate the ground; and, as thofe of every age were bent upon the war, they had defigned to appropriate our ftores to their own ufe. Befides, that this people, by nature wonderfully ftubborn, were become more backward to peace, from the behaviour of Julius Clafficianus, who was come as fucceffor to Catus, and, being at variance with Suetonius, obftructed the public good to gratify private pique. Thus he had every-where publifhed, 'That another Governor 'was to be expected, who, free from the wrath of
' an

' an enemy, free from the arrogance of a conqueror,
' would by merciful meafures enfure the fubmiffion
' of the province.' At the fame time he tranfmit-
ed advice to Rome, 'That unlefs a fucceffor were
' fent to Suetonius, there never would be an end of
' war;' and, while he charged all the difafters of
that General upon bafenefs of conduct, he afcribed
all his conquefts and fuccefs to the aufpicious fortune of the Republic.

Hence Polycletus, one of the imperial freedmen,
was difpatched to infpect the condition of Britain;
a project from which Nero conceived mighty hopes,
that by the authority of his domeftic, private amity
between the Governor and Procurator would not
only be effected, but the hoftile fpirits of the revolted Barbarians reconciled to peace. Nor was Polycletus backward to the employment, thus far at
leaft, that having travelled through Italy and Gaul,
and oppreffed both with his enormous train, thence
croffing the channel, he marched in fuch awful ftate,
that even to our own foldiers he became a terror:
But to the enemy he proved an object of derifion;
for as amongft them popular liberty even then reigned, they were hitherto utter ftrangers to the power
of manumifed bondmen. They were likewife a-
mazed, that a General and army, who had finifhed
fo formidable a war, fhould themfelves be fubfer-
vient to flaves. The whole affair, however, was reported to the Emperor in a favourable light; fo that
Suetonius was continued in the government. But
after having ftranded a few gallies, and loft the men
who rowed them, as if this accident had been a
proof that the war ftill fubfifted, he was ordered to
refign his army to Petronius Turplianus, who had
juft ended his Confulfhip; a Commander who, as
he neither offered to the foe any act of hoftility,
nor from them received any infult, beftowed upon
fuch ftupid inaction the worthy appellation of Peace.

This same year were perpetrated at Rome two glaring iniquities, one by a Senator, the other by the desperate hand of a slave. Domitius Balbus had sustained the dignity of Prætor, and his wealth and childlesness, added to his exceeding age, exposed him to the machinations of villainy: Hence a will was forged in his name by Valerius Fabianus his kinsman, one nominated to public offices; who took into the combination Vincius Rufinus and Terentius Lentinus, both Roman Knights; with them were associated in the same cause Antonius Primus and Allnins Marcellus; Antonius a man of a prompt daring spirit; Marcellus signal in his descent, as on him devolved the lustre of his great grand-father Asinius Pollio; nor passed he himself for a despicable person in his own conduct, save that he believed poverty to be of all evils the heaviest and most severe. Fabianus therefore, in confederacy with those whom I have mentioned, and others of less note, sealed and witnessed the testament: A fraud of which they were convicted before the Senate. Thus Fabianus and Antonius, with Rufinus and Terentius, were all doomed to the penalties of the Cornelian law. In behalf of Marcellus, the illustrious memory of his ancestors, with the entreaties of Nero, prevailed, and procured him an exemption rather from punishment than infamy. The same day involved Pompeius Ælianus too in his doom, a young man once invested with the dignity of Quæstor, but now charged with being privy to the vile practices of Fabianus; thus he was interdicted Italy, as also the place of his nativity, Spain. Upon Valerius Ponticus was inflicted the like ignominious sentence; for that he had arraigned the delinquents at the tribunal of the Prætor, on purpose to save them from being impleaded before the Governor of Rome, and would have eluded the punishment through the false glosses of law; nay at last

last had meditated their escape by manifest collusion and double dealing. To the decree of penalties therefore the Senate added, 'That whoever should 'take a price for such vile employment, or whoso-'ever should procure it at a price, should be in-'volved in the same penalty with one publicly con-'demned for calumny.'

Not long after Pedanius Secundus, Governor of Rome, was murdered by a slave of his own, either upon refusing him his liberty, for which he had bargained at a certain price, or that he was enraged by a jealous passion for a pathic, and could not bear his Lord for a rival. Now, since according to the strict institutions of antiquity, the whole family of slaves, who upon such occasion abode under the same roof, must inevitably be adjudged to the pains of death; such was the uproar and conflux of the populace, zealous to save so many innocent lives, that it proceeded even to sedition. In the Senate itself there were different opinions, some were for the popular side, against such excessive rigour; while many would admit no innovation or abatement. Of these last was Caius Cassius, who, leaving the question then under debate, reasoned in this manner:

'Many times have I assisted, Conscript Fathers, 'in this august assembly, when new decrees of Se-'nate have been demanded, contrary to the laws and 'establishments of our fore-fathers, without setting 'myself to oppose such demands; not from any 'doubt that, in transactions of every kind, the pro-'visions made of old were not more judicious and 'upright, and whenever they were changed, for 'the worse they were changed. But I forbore, lest 'I should seem, from an immoderate fondness for 'primitive rules, to magnify my own zeal; besides, 'whatever weight I may have, I judged ought not 'to be forfeited, by engaging in frequent opposi-'tions, but to be reserved in full vigour against any 'emergent

' emergent conjuncture, when the Commonwealth
' should stand in need of council; a conjuncture
' which this very day has produced. A Senator of
' Consular rank is murdered in his own house by the
' treachery of one of his own slaves; a treachery
' which was by none of the rest prevented, by none
' of them disclosed, although over their heads was
' hanging still in full force the decree of Senate,
' which denounced to the whole domestic tribe the
' pains of death. In the name of the Gods, ascer-
' tain by a decree the desired impunity. But then,
' what security will any man derive from his dignity,
' when even the Government of Rome secured not
' him who possessed it? Who will be protected by
' the number of his slaves, when a band of four
' hundred afforded no protection to Pedanius Se-
' cundus? To which of us will our domestics,
' upon any occasion, administer aid, when they re-
' gard not our lives, even where for their neglect
' capital terrors threaten theirs? or has, in truth,
' what some without blushing feign, the murderer
' only taken vengeance for injuries received? Had
' this slave any dispute about his paternal patrimony?
' or had he inherited from his progenitors the bond-
' man his path? Let us even declare that his
' Lord was rightfully killed. Though it be strange
' we should hunt after arguments in an affair de-
' termined by our wiser ancestors! yet suppose the
' question were now first to be decided; still do you
' believe that a vindictive slave could desperately de-
' sign to kill his Lord, yet not a menacing word fall
' from him? was nothing rashly uttered by him?
' Be it so, that he effectually hid his bloody purpose;
' be it so, that he prepared the bloody instrument
' in the midst of his fellows, all ignorant of his ends;
' but still could he pass through the guard of slaves
' at the chamber door, open those doors, bring in a
' light, perpetrate the assassination, unknown to
' them

' them all? Many murderous designs are prevented
' by our slaves; and while they make such discove-
' ries, though we are but individuals, we can live
' safely amongst many, and owe our security to their
' care; or if at last we must perish by them, the
' blood of many traitors shall atone for ours. By
' our anceſtors the spirit of their slaves was al-
' ways suspected, even of such as were born in their
' private territories, nay, in their houses, and had
' with their milk sucked in a tenderness for their
' Lords. And since we are come to entertain in
' our families nations of slaves inured to their nati-
' onal rites widely different from ours, and addicted
' to strange Religions, or observing none; it is im-
' possible to curb such a promiscuous rabble, with-
' out the intervention of exemplary terrors. But
' with the guilty some innocents must perish. Yes;
' and so it is in an army, which, after a shameful
' rout are punished with decimation, where to be
' bastinadoed to death is often the lot of the faultless
' and brave. Somewhat there is grievous and un-
' just in every great exertion of justice, where private
' sufferings are compensated by public utility.'

This judgment of Cassius, which no particular Senator durst venture to combat, was yet opposed by the dissenting murmurs of such as thus uttered their compassion for those involved in it, for their number, for the age of some, for the sex of others, for the undoubted innocence of most. It was how-ever carried by the party who adjudged all to the pains of death. A judgement which yet it was impossible to execute; for the populace were flocked tumultuously together, and threatening to fall on with stones and firebrands. Nero therefore teprimanded the people by an edict, and with lines of soldiers secured all the way through which the condemned were led to execution. Cingonius Varro had moved, that the freedmen too, who abode under the same roof, should be for ever expelled Italy; but this was prohibited by the Prince, who urged, ' That 'since the rigorous usage of antiquity had not been 'mollified by mercy, it ought not to be heightened ' by cruelty.'

During the same Consuls, Tarquitius Priscus was, at the suit of the Bithynians, condemned for public rapine, to the infinite gratification of the fathers, who well remembered that by him had been accused Statilius Taurus, his own Proconsul in Africa. Moreover, a general poll was taken, and a general rate imposed throughout both the Gauls; an employment executed by Quintus Volusius, Sextius Africanus, and Trebellius Maximus, and, in it, much contention arose between Volusius and Africanus, two men who were competitors in nobility and rank; for Trebellius, while in this their strife he was neglected by both, they jointly contributed to render him superior to either.

The same year, Memmius Regulus finished his days, a man for his eminent authority and firmness of mind in signal estimation; and, as far as the lustre of a citizen is not darkened by the shade and high station of the Emperor, the distinction which he bore was splendid and sublime; insomuch that, when Nero was once under the pressure of sickness, and the flatterers about him were lamenting, ' that, ' if the illness proved fatal, there must be an end of ' the Empire with that of his life;' he replied, ' That to the Republic there would still remain a ' certain refuge.' And, as they then asked, 'In ' whom chiefly,' he added, ' Memmius Regulus.' Yet Regulus preserved his life after all this, under the protection of his own quiet spirit; besides that he derived his quality from a recent stock, and was no wise obnoxious for his wealth. This year too Nero instituted an Athletic school, and to the Knights and Senators, for their exercises there, presented anointing oil, according to the wanton usages of the revelling Greeks.

In the Consulship of Publius Marius and Lucius Asinius, the Prætor, Antistius, whose arbitrary administration, in the Tribuneship of the people I have remembered, framed a Poem full of invectives against the Prince, and exposed it to a numerous assembly, then banquetting in the house of Ostorius Scapula. Hence he was arraigned upon the Law of violated Majesty, by Cossutianus Capito, who, at the request of Tigellinus his father-in-law, had acquired the dignity of Senator. This Law, after a long disuse, was upon this occasion first revived, though it was believed, that thence the doom of Antistius was not so much intended, as matter of renown to the Emperor; for that, when the Senate had capitally condemned him, Cæsar meant, by interposing his Tribunitial power, to save him from the pains of death. Now, as the evidence delivered by Ostorius was, that he had heard nothing at all of the imputed crime, the contrary testimony of other witnesses was credited, and Junius Marullus, Consul elect, voted that 'The accused should be divested of his Prætorship, 'and executed according to rigour of antiquity.' The rest too were concurring with the same vote, when Pætus Thrasea, after much honourable commendation of Nero, and many bitter reproaches upon Antistius, argued, 'That whatever severity 'the guilt of the person accused might merit, 'yet an adequate measure of punishment was not 'what they were now to adjudge, under a Prince so 'excellent, and while the Senate in its decisions was 'under no controul. Halters and executioners were 'terrors long since abolished; moreover by the 'laws penal sentences were already prescribed, in 'conformity to which, punishments might be pro- 'nounced without bringing the judges under the 'imputation of cruelty, or the times under that of 'infamy. What therefore remained but to sen- 'tence his estate to confiscation, and him to exile

' in an island? whence the longer he protracted his
' guilty life, the greater private misery he must en-
' dure himself, however a singular example of public
' clemency.'

The freedom of Thrasea broke the bondage which hung upon the minds of others; so that after the Consul had given leave to divide by discession *; all but a few went readily into the motion of Thrasea. Of these few was Vitellius, most abandoned to strains of flattery, one whose custom it was to be carping at every upright man, and awed into silence by every reply; a conduct usual to slavish spirits. The Consuls however not daring to give the last sanction to the decree of Senate, wrote the Emperor an account of their unanimity; and the account affected him, insomuch that he hesitated a while, between shame and resentment; at last he returned an answer, ' That Antistius, unprovoked by any in-
' jury, had uttered many grievous aspersions upon
' the Prince; and, for these aspersions proper ven-
' geance had been required from the Senate. Neither
' would it have been more than just judgment, to
' have ordained a punishment suitable to the enor-
' mous measure of the iniquity. For himself, as he
' would have certainly opposed any rigorous doom,
' if such they had decreed, he would no wise frus-
' trate their mercy and moderation.' Determine
' therefore they might, as to them seemed best; nay,
' from him they had full leave to pronounce a sen-
' tence of acquittal.' By the recital of these ex-
pressions, with others in the like strain, his displeasure appeared notorious; yet neither did the Consuls vary the state of the question, nor Thrasea depart from his motion, nor any of the rest desert the
measures which by their assent they had approved.
Some would not, by a severer sentence, seem to ex-

* Namely, to go over to him whose vote they approved.

' pose

pose the Prince to popular malignity; many placed their safety in their numbers: Thrasea was governed by his wonted firmness of soul, and scorned to forfeit his illustrious renown.

For an offence much like the former, Fabricius Veiento was involved in a heavy prosecution; 'for that he had compiled a long train of invectives against Senators and Pontiffs, and inserted the same in the rolls, to which he had given the title of *Codicils*, or last will.' To this charge it was added by Talius Geminus his accuser, 'That he had made constant traffic of the Prince's bounty and favours, and turned into purchase and sale the right of occupying the great offices of the state;' an argument this that determined Nero to adjudge his cause in person. Veiento being convicted, the Emperor banished him from Italy, and doomed to the flames these his writings, which were universally sought and read; while it was difficult to find them, and dangerous to keep them; afterwards, from the freedom and impunity of possessing them, they sunk into neglect and oblivion.

But while the public evils waxed every day more poignant, the supports of the public became lessened, and Burrhus yielded to his last fate; nor is it certainly known whether by poison or a disease. The latter was imagined from hence, that a swelling which began in his throat increased inwardly by degrees, till by a total stoppage of respiration he died suffocated. Many asserted, that by the order of Nero, under appearance of applying a remedy, his palate and glands were fomented with some venomous medicine, and that Burrhus having perceived the deadly fraud, when the Prince came to visit him, turned his face and eyes another way, and to all his repeated inquiries about his health, returned no other answer but this, *I am well.* Great and permanent at Rome was the sense of his loss, as well

well through the memory of his own virtue, as from the characters of his successors, one innocent and heavy, the other black with all the most flagrant iniquities and defilements. For Nero had created two captains of the Prætorian guards, Fenius Rufus, in compliment to the populace, who loved him for his disinterested administration in the super-intendency of the public stores, as also Sofonius Tigellinus, purely from partiality to the inveterate lewdness and infamy of the man, for pollution and infamy were the characteristic of Tigellinus. Hence his superior sway over the spirit or Nero, as one assumed into power from an intimacy in all the secret sallies of his lust. Rufus was distinguished in the city and soldiery with popular estimation; a character which brought him under distaste with Nero.

The death of Burrhus quite overthrew the authority of Seneca, as righteous measures had no longer the same succours now the other champion of virtue was removed; and the heart of Nero was attached to men altogether wicked and depraved. These combined to assail Seneca with criminal imputations manifold; as, 'That he had already ac-
' cumulated wealth incredible, far surpassing the
' measure of a citizen, and was still accumulating
' more: that from the Emperor he was labouring
' to withdraw the veneration of the Roman people;
' nay, such were the charms of his gardens, such
' the magnificence of his seats, as if in them he
' aimed even to excel the Emperor. To himself
' alone he arrogated the praise and perfection of
' eloquence; and, ever since Nero became inspired
' with a passion for versifying, Seneca had employed
' himself, with unusual assiduity, in the same study:
' for, to the bodily recreations of the Prince, he
' had declared an open enmity, and hence disparag-
' ed his vigour and skill in the managing horses;
' hence turned his voice into mockery, whenever
' he

' he sung; all with this view, that in the whole
' Republic there should nothing occur signal or sub-
' lime, which was not by him introduced and de-
' vised. Surely Nero was passed the weakness of
' childhood, and arrived at his prime of youth: he
' ought now to depose his pedagogue, and trust only
' to the documents conveyed to him by tutors suf-
' ficiently famous, his own mighty ancestors.'

Seneca was not unapprized of the efforts of his
calumniators, the same being disclosed to him by
such as still retained some concern for truth and honour; but, as the Emperor manifested daily more
shyness and less affability, he besought an hour of
audience, and having obtained it, began thus:
' This is the fourteenth year since I was first af-
' signed to cultivate thy promising and princely
' spirit, Cæsar, and the eighth since thy advance-
' ment to the Empire. During this whole series of
' time, so mighty and so many are the honours and
' riches which thou hast showered down upon me,
' that to my abundant felicity nought is wanting
' but some bounds and moderation. To corrobo-
' rate this address, I shall quote great examples,
' and illustrious names, such as are adapted, not
' to my station and fortune, but to thine. Augus-
' tus, from whom thou art the fourth in descent,
' granted to Marcus Agrippa leave to retreat to
' Mitylene, and to Caius Mæcenas he allowed,
' even in Rome, a recess as complete as in any re-
' mote country he could have enjoyed; the former
' his companion in the war, the other long harrassed
' at Rome, with occupations manifold, both by him
' distinguished with such remuneration as were glo-
' rious, in truth, yet signally due to their transcen-
' dent worth and services. For myself, by what
' merit could I pretend to incite that boundless
' munificence of thine, other than mine own soli-
' tary studies, formed, if I may so speak, and nou-

I. 6. 'rished

'rished in obscurity? and even from them this glory
' is devolved upon me, that in the seasonings of
' literature I am thought to have initiated thy youth;
' a sublime reward alone for such slender service!
' but thou hast encompassed me about with an ac-
' cumulation of Imperial benignity and grace, be-
' yond all expression and limits, and with wealth
' without measure or end: insomuch that I often
' reason thus with myself, Am I, (one by rank no
' higher than a Knight, by birth no other than a
' foreigner) am I numbered with the Grandees of
' the Imperial city? Hath my new name thus blaz-
' ed forth amongst the illustrious Lords of Rome,
' men who justly boast a long train of hereditary
' honours? Where then is that Philosophic spirit,
' which professes to be satisfied with humble neces-
' saries? Is Seneca that man? He who thus incloses
' and adorns such spacious gardens; he who thus
' travels in pomp from seat to seat in the neigh-
' bourhood of Rome? Is it he who wallows in
' wealth, in ample possessions, in copious and ex-
' tensive usury? One plea only there is that occurs
' to my thoughts, that against thy donations it be-
' came not me to strive; but both of us have
' now discharged to the utmost measure this com-
' merce of liberality and duty; whatever the
' bounty of a Prince could confer upon his friend,
' whatever a friend could accept from the bounty
' of his Prince, thou hast already conferred, I have
' already accepted. Any further addition can only
' prove fresh fuel to the bitterness of envy, an ene-
' my which, like all other earthly things, lies, in
' truth, subdued under the weight of thy mighty
' grandeur, but fastens upon me with all its rage,
' and I stand in imminent need of succour. Thus,
' in the same manner, as were I weary and faint
' through the toil of journeying or of warfare, I
' should

' should supplicate for refreshment and rest; so in
' this long journey of life, old as I am, and no longer
' equal to the easiest trust, and lightest cares,
' and utterly unable to sustain the load and envy
' of my own over-grown riches, I seek assistance
' and support. Order the auditors of thy revenue
' to undertake the direction of my fortune, and to
' annex it to thy own. Nor shall I by this plunge
' myself into indigence and poverty, but having
' only surrendered that immense opulence, which
' exposes me to so much invidious splendor, I shall
' redeem all the time which is at present sequester-
' ed to the care of so many seats and gardens, and
' apply it to the repose and cultivation of my mind.
' To thee remains abundant strength and support,
' and thy rule is, by a long course of reigning,
' throughly established, thou mayst now spare thy
' ancient friends and councellors, and vouchsafe
' them a retreat to quiet and ease. To thy glory
' this also will redound, that to the highest estate
' thou hadst advanced such men as knew how to
' bear the lowest.'

To this speech Nero replied in this manner:
' That I am able thus instantly to combat these
' studied reasonings of thine, is a faculty which
' from thy benignity and care I first derived; for
' thou hast taught me, not only the art of acquit-
' ing myself promptly, where matters are prepared,
' but even in emergencies intirely unforeseen. It
' is true, my ancestor Augustus granted liberty to
' Agrippa and Mæcenas to retreat, after a life of
' many labours, to a life of ease; but at such a
' time of his age and establishment he granted it,
' that his authority was sufficient to sustain any
' concession which he could have made them, of
' what kind or importance soever: And he divested
' neither of them of the bounties and recompences
' which he had conferred upon them. In the perils
' of

' of war and of civil diſtraction they had merito-
' riouſly ſerved him; for in ſuch were the younger
' years of Auguſtus employed. Neither wouldſt
' thou, Seneca, have failed to have aſſiſted me with
' thy perſon and arms, if I had been engaged in
' war. What my different circumſtances required,
' thou haſt done. With wiſe rules, wholſome coun-
' ſel, and uſeful precepts, thou haſt cheriſhed my
' infancy, and ſince, my youth. In truth, the
' gifts and acquirements which I hold from thee,
' while my life remains, will never forſake me:
' whereas the acknowledgments which thou reap-
' eſt from me, thy gardens, ſeats, and rents, are
' all expoſed to uncertainty and diſaſters; and
' however copious they may appear, there are
' many inſtances of favourites, in worthy accomp-
' liſhments no wiſe equal to thee, yet diſtinguiſhed
' with larger poſſeſſions. I bluſh to quote freedmen,
' that are beheld more wealthy than thou. Hence
' too I am ſhamed that thou, who in dearneſs to
' me art beyond all others, doſt not yet in fortune
' ſurpaſs all. Thy age, moreover, ſtill retains ſound-
' neſs and vigour, is ſtill capable of managing thy
' revenues, and of enjoying them with pleaſure. For,
' myſelf, I am but yet in the dawn of Empire; un-
' leſs, perhaps, thou doſt account that my munifi-
' cence to thee has already exceeded that of Clau-
' dius to Vitellius, a man diſtinguiſhed with three
' Conſulſhips; when, in truth, all my bounty to-
' wards thee, cannot equal the opulence which
' Voluſius, by a long courſe of parſimony only,
' has acquired. I add that, if in any particular
' I deviate, through the frailty of my years, it is
' thou who doſt check and recover me: and, as
' thou haſt with good education embelliſhed my
' youth, thou doſt ſtill manage and controul it. It
' is not with thy moderation, if thou returneſt thy
' wealth, nor with thy receſs, if thou forſakeſt thy
' Prince,

'. Prince, that the tongues of men will be employ-
' ed; no, the treasure returned will by the univer-
' sal cry be ascribed to my rapaciousness, and thy
' retirement to the dread of my cruelty. But sup-
' pose this disinterestedness of thine meet with the
' highest strains of popular praise; yet surely upon
' a wise man it will reflect no honour, that to him-
' self he meditates glory from a proceeding, which
' upon his friend must bring infamy.' To all this
he added kisses and embracing, framed as he was
by nature, and by habit nurtured, to smother his
hate under hollow courtesy and blandishments. Seneca presented his thanks, which is the certa n issue
of every argument with one who possesses sovereignty. He changed, however, the methods and symptoms of his former power, flopped the usual conflux of such as attended to pay their court, avoided
a train of attendants, and his appearance abroad was
exceeding rare, as if by ill health, or the study of
philosophy, he were confined at home.

After the disgrace of Seneca, to depress the authority of Fenius Rufus became a short task, when the
crime charged upon him by his enemies was that
of his adherence to Agrippina. Tigellinus too, waxed
daily more mighty, and as he was persuaded that
his mischievous devices, in which alone his whole
sufficiency lay, would prove still more agreeable and
meritorious, if he could engage the Prince under
the ties of a confederacy in acts of blood, he dived
curiously into his secret fears; and having discovered that Plautus and Sylla were the men principally
dreaded, and thence both lately removed from Italy;
the former into Asia, the other into Narbon Gaul,
he urged upon Nero, ' the signal quality of the men,
' the nearness of their abode to great armies; Plau-
' tus in the neighbourhood of that in the East,
' Sylla of that in Germany. For himself, he har-
' boured not, like Burrhus, different hopes and
' views, but consulted purely the security of the
                                          ' Prince.

'Prince. But though his safety at Rome might be
' ensured and all conspiracies there obviated by
' prompt and temporary measures; yet, by what
' measures could remote insurrections be suppres-
' sed, and revolts in the confines of the Empire?
' the nations of Gaul, animated by the dictatorial
' name of Sylla, were already upon the wing for
' rebellion; nor were the several people of Asia
' less suspected of an attachment to the other, for
' the illustrious memory and renown of his grand-
' father Drusus. Sylla was likewise indigent, an
' especial incitement to resoluteness and enterprize;
' and he feigned sloth only till he spied an opportu-
' nity for some desperate attempt. Plautus was
' master of mighty wealth, nor so much as pre-
' tended a fondness for quiet, but even professed to
' admire the lives and examples of the ancient Ro-
' mans; nay, he had adopted the sect of the Stoics,
' with all their superciliousness and pride, a sect
' which prompts men to be turbulent and to choose
' a life full of action.' Without further deliberation
or delay, the murder of both was doomed. Sylla
was by assassins, who in six days arrived express at
Marseilles, dispatched as he sat down to meat, without previous apprehension or tidings. When his
head was presented to Nero, the sight moved him to
derision, ' as if it were unseasonably hoary, and
'' thence uncomely.'

The bloody sentence awarded against Plautus was
not so successfully concealed, for his life was of sensible concernment to many; moreover, from the
length of the way, and the passing of the sea, so
much time intervened, that public fame became
alarmed; and amongst the people an imagination
prevailed, that he had fled for sanctuary to Corbulo,
who then commanded mighty armies, a man who,
if men signal in name and innocence were to be
marked out for slaughter, stood in the first degree
of

of fear and jeopardy. Nay, it was divulged with the same credulity, 'That all Asia had taken arms 'to espouse the defence of the young nobleman; 'and that, as the soldiers dispatched to perpetrate 'the murder, were neither powerful in their num- 'ber, nor prompt in their inclinations, when they 'could not execute their orders, they also had of 'themselves joined in the revolt, and espoused the 'new cause.' These rumours, published by the wild breath of common fame, were readily credited by all the disaffected, and, through hate and disaffection, inlarged. Moreover, to Plautus were brought the counsel and admonitions of Lucius Antistius, his father-in-law, by a freedman of his own, who, speeded by a brisk wind, had out-sailed the fatal Centurion. The advice imported, 'That he should 'be sure to shun a dastardly death; he had yet lei- 'sure to escape, and could not fail of finding from 'the worthy and generous, compassion for a name 'so noble and distinguished. With himself he must 'associate the resolute and brave, nor ought he the 'while to slight any means of aid. If he had once 'repulsed the sixty soldiers (for so many were 'coming to the execution) he might then, while 'tidings were transmitting to Nero, while another 'band of men were advancing so vast a way, pro- 'secute a world of schemes, sufficient to lay the 'terrible foundations of a war. At worst he would 'either, by such measures, purchase honourable se- 'curity; at least, after a brave resistance, he had 'nought more dreadful to suffer, than he must suffer 'under a stupid acquiescence.'

But these considerations moved not Plautus; whether it were that being an exile, and destitute of arms, he foresaw no certain resource, or whether he were weary of perplexity and wavering hopes, or perhaps chiefly influenced by tenderness for his wife and children, to whom he imagined the Prince would

would prove the more reconcilable, when he found himself no wise incensed by any insurrection or alarms. There are those who relate, that the advices he received from his father-in-law were of a different strain, importing as if nothing sanguinary or capital threatened him. They add, ' That two Philoso-
' phers, Ceranus a Greek, and Musonius a Tuscan,
' had exhorted him to wait his death with unshaken
' intrepidity, as by it he would be disburdened of a
' life fraught with uncertainty and fears. Certain it
' is, the assassins found him in the middle of the day,
' naked and applying himself to the usual exercises
' of his body.' In this situation the Centurion butchered him, in the light of Pelago the Eunuch, who was by Nero set over the Centurion and his band, like the Royal minister of some tyrant, trusted with the command of his body-guards, and instruments of blood. The head of the slain was carried to Rome, and shewed to the Emperor. What he said when he saw it, I shall repeat in his very words. ' What is it,
  cried he, that withstands Nero, that he may not
' now discard all fear, and instantly set about solemniz-
' ing his nuptials with Poppæa, a solemnity hitherto
' deferred, because of the terrors arising from such
' men as this? may he not instantly divorce Octavia
' his wife? one easy, in truth, and modest in her
' conduct, but, still from the name of her Imperial
' father, and from the ardent zeal of the people to-
' wards her, a burden and eye-sore.' To the Senate he sent letters, but in them owned nothing of the assassination of Sylla and Plautus, yet alledged, that both were turbulent and seditious spirits, and what vehement solicitude it cost him to preserve the peace and stability of the Commonwealth. Hence, public processions and devotions were decreed to the Deities, and Sylla and Plautus degraded from the dignity of Senators. Strange mockery and insult, more provoking to the public, than its more substantial injuries!

Nero

Nero therefore having received the decree of Senate, and perceiving that all his wickedness and bloody cruelties passed for so many feats of renown, thrust Octavia forthwith from his bed, alledging,: ' that she was barren,' and then espoused Poppæa. This woman, who had been long the concubine of Nero, and both as her adulterer and her husband, ever ruled him implicitly, suborned a domestic of Octavia's to accuse her of criminal amours with a slave. For this end one Eucerus, a native of Alexandria, who excelled upon the flute, was impleaded as her gallant. Hence her maids were examined upon the rack; and though some of them, overcome by the fury of the torture, favoured the perfidions forgery, the major part persevered to vindicate the unspotted sanctimony of their Lady. Amongst these was one, who, while Tigellinus was vehemently urging a confession, returned him for answer, '. That the parts of Octavia which denoted her a ': woman, were purer than his mouth.' The result however was her removal from the palace, and her husband, under the mock-judgment of a legal divorcement, and for her appenage she was presented with the house of Burrhus, and with the possessions of Plautus, black and ill-boding donations. She was thereafter banished into Campania, and over her a guard of soldiers placed. From this cruel treatment there arose amongst the populace many mournful complaints, by them no wise smothered or disguised; since they are governed by a lower measure of circumspection, and, from the mediocrity of their lot, exposed to fewer perils. Whether, by these daring resentments of the people, Nero was alarmed, or moved by remorse for such black iniquity, he recalled Octavia his wife.

Hence the people in transports of joy ascended the Capitol, and now at last found occasion to accost the Deities with adoration and thanksgiving; overthrew
the

the ſtatues of Poppæa, but bore upon their ſhoulders the images of Octavia, bedecked them with freſh flowers, placed them in the great Forum, and in the ſeveral Temples They alſo burſt into ſtrains of praiſes to the Prince, and ſought to offer him in perſon their veneration and vows Already they were filling the palace with their multitude and acclamations, when ſuddenly ſome bands of the guards iſſued out upon them, and aſſailing them with blows, nay, threatening them with ſlaughter, repulſed and utterly diſperſed them. The diſorders too committed during the tumult, were repaired, to Poppæa her honour publicly reſtored, and her ſtatues replaced: But ſhe, ever implacable in her hate, was now become more implacable through fear, left either the fury of the populace ſhould break into outrages ſtill more terrible, or Nero be brought to change with the bent and inclination of the people. She therefore fell proſtrate at his knees, and ſaid, ‘ Her af-
‘ fairs were no longer in a ſituation to encourage
‘ her competition for the glory of his marriage,
‘ though dearer to her than life was that glory; her
‘ life itſelf was in extremity of danger from the fol-
‘ lowers and ſlaves of Octavia, a rabble who, hav-
‘ ing aſſumed the name of the people, in the midſt
‘ of peace, committed ſuch violences as were ſcarce
‘ produced by war. Againſt the Prince theſe arms
‘ were wielded, nor was aught wanting but a leader,
‘ a want which, when commotions were once raiſ-
‘ ed, was ever eaſy to be ſupplied. Octavia had
‘ no more to do, but to relinquiſh Campania, and
‘ advance to Rome itſelf; ſhe at whoſe nod even in
‘ her abſence inſurrections could be excited. For
‘ her own particular, with what tranſgreſſion was
‘ ſhe chargeable? in what inſtance had ſhe offended
‘ any individual? was ſhe from hence obnoxious,
‘ that to the houſe of the Cæſars ſhe would yield a
‘ genuine iſſue; when the Roman people rather af-
‘ fected.

' fected to see the offspring of an Ægyptian minstrel
' heir to the Imperial dignity? in a word, if this
' expedient best suited with the exigency of things,
' he ought to call home his Lady rather through
' choice than compulsion, or else to consult the se-
' enrity of himself and the state by just vengeance.
' It was true, the first tumult was dissipated by
' small force; but, if the people came utterly to de-
' spair of seeing Octavia any longer the wife of
' Nero, they themselves would not fail to give a
' proper bulband to Octavia.'

This discourse, artfully mixed and framed to produce both terror and wrath, had its effect upon Nero, and while he listened to it at once frightened and enraged him. But little had availed the fiction of Octavia's intrigue with her slaves, a fiction which was quite defeated by the testimony of her maids upon the rack. It was therefore agreed to procure some one who should own himself guilty with her, one against whom might be also feigned a plausible charge of meditating a revolution in the state; and such a proper instrument was judged Anicetus, who had accomplished the murder of his mother, and, as I have related, commanded the fleet at Misenum, a man held by the Emperor, just after that bloody service, in some slight favour, and thenceforth in heavier detestation; for Princes behold the ministers of their cruelties, as men whose looks reproach their guilty souls. Him therefore Nero summoned, and reminding him of his former exploit, ' Thou alone,
' said he, ' didst relieve me from the conspiracies of a
' mother; service of no less merit at present invites
' thee, if thou canst but discharge me effectually of
' an irksome and disaffected wife; nor in this task
' needest thou either strength or weapon; thou art
' only to acknowledge that thou hast been engaged
' with Octavia in adultery.' Nero promised him rewards of mighty value, though at first it was
necessary

'neceffary they should continue private, and unknown, as also, upon his mock condemnation, delectable retirements; but, in case of refusal, threatened him with present death. Anicetus, prompted by his own frantic spirit, and by the protection and impunity which had followed all his enormities past, carried his fictions even beyond his orders, and communicated, as secrets, all his fictions to his friends : a set of men whom the Prince had placed about him, as it were to aid him by their counsels in his designs. Then, as convicted by his own confession, he was banished into Sardinia, where he underwent a sort of exile far from necessitous or miserable, and died at last by the lot of nature.

Now Nero issued an edict, ‘That Octavia, in ‘ hopes of engaging the fleet in her conspiracy, had ‘ thence corrupted Anicetus the admiral; and, forgetting that he had but just before accused her of barrenness, he added, ‘that, conscious of her secret ‘ lusts, she had always forced abortion; and that all ‘ these her crimes were by him fully detected.’ Thus he commanded her to be shut up in an island, that of Pandateria.

Never exile filled the hearts of the beholders with more affecting compassion. Some still remembered to have seen Agrippina doomed to the like fate; the more recent sufferings of Julia were likewise recalled to mind, the first banished by Tiberius, the other by Claudius. But these Ladies had arrived at maturity of years, had enjoyed some seasons of felicity, tasted some share of delight, and, by reviewing their once happier fortune, their pangs, from instant cruelty, were abated. To Octavia the first day of her nuptials served for a funeral day; she was brought under a roof where all must appear dismal and sad, where her unhappy father was snatched away by poison, and instantly afterwards her brother by the same cruel

cruel means: Next, though a wife, she was subjected to the ascendancy of a slave. Then her husband espoused Poppæa; a marriage threatening nothing less than destruction to his legitimate wife. Lastly, she suffered the imputation of a crime more piercing than the most cruel death whatsoever. Add to all this, a tender girl, in the twentieth year of her age, encompassed with an host of soldiers and Centurions, already bereft of life, through the sad presages of impending evils, yet not surrendered to the quiet rest of death.'

After the interval of a few days, she was formally doomed to die, though to prevent it, she descended to alledge, ' That she owned herself in ' a state of widowhood, and claimed no other prerogative than of being only the Emperor's sister. ' She pleaded their common ancestors, who bore ' the dear and favourite name of *Germanicus*:' at length she even invoked the name of Agrippina; she said, ' That had Agrippina lived, she should, ' in truth, have endured a lot of wedlock sufficiently unhappy, but still such a one as would never ' have ended in a bloody doom.' Forthwith she was tied down with bonds, and the veins over all her limbs were opened; but, as her blood was chilled through fear, and issued slowly, the execution was completed by stifling her in the steam of a boiling bath. This cruelty was followed by another yet more crying and brutal; her head being cut off and carried to Rome, Poppæa chose to entertain herself with the tragical spectacle. For this execution the Senate decreed gifts and oblations to the Temples; a circumstance which I insert with design that whoever shall, from me or any other Writer, learn the events of those calamitous times, may hold it for granted, that as often as ever sentences of murder and banishment were pronounced by the Prince, so often were thanksgivings by the fathers paid to the Deities;

Deities; and the very same ordinances, which of old were monuments of public prosperity, served now for testimonies of public havock and ruin. And yet I shall not fail to recount every decree of Senate, which either proved a new flight of flattery, or only the dregs of excessive tameness and servitude.

This year was fatal to Doryphorus and Pallas, two Imperial freedmen of most conspicuous note, both believed to have perished by poison, the former, for thwarthing the marriage with Poppæa, and Pallas, for that by his great age he detained from the Emperor his inestimable wealth. Against Seneca, Romanus had secretly laboured a charge of being an associate with Caius Piso, but was himself encountered by Seneca with more vigour for the same crime.* Hence a source of much dread to Piso; and against Nero there arose a conspiracy, mighty indeed, and menacing, but abortive and unprosperous.

THE ANNALS OF TACITUS.

BOOK XV.

The SUMMARY.

Vologeses *King of Parthia invades Armenia, but is opposed by* Corbulo *with great prudence and spirit.* Cæsennius Pætus *sent by* Nero *to command in Armenia. His rashness, vanity, and disgraceful concessions to the enemy.* Corbulo *relieves him.* Poppæa *bears a daughter to* Nero. *Deputies from Parthia to sue for holding the sovereignty of Armenia, return without success, and the conduct of that war committed to* Corbulo, *who again enters Armenia, terrifies the Parthians into a treaty, obliges them to lay down their arms, and* Tiridates *to lay his crown at the feet of* Nero's *statue, never to resume it more without the Emperor's consent.* Nero *sings in the public Theatre at* Naples. *His excesses in all pollution and cruelty.* Rome *consumed by fire;* Nero *suspected as the author of it. He falsly charges it upon the* Christians, *and destroys them by many wanton and merciless*

merciless torments. A conspiracy formed against him; its progress, detection, and the many illustrious lives sacrificed for it, with the boundless public flattery then arising from private sufferings and sorrow.

DURING these transactions, Vologeses King of the Parthians, having learnt the exploits of Corbulo, that Tigranes, an alien born, was by him established King of Armenia, from whence his brother Tiridates had been ignominiously expulsed, was in himself bent to revenge the despite done to the Monarchy of the Arsacides; but revolving again upon the mighty power of the Romans, and awed with reverence for the constant league between the two Empires, was perplexed and divided between interfering passions; for he was a Prince by nature addicted to lingering, and then particularly retarded by the revolt of the Hyrcanians (a very potent nation) and by the long series of wars that followed it. In this suspense he was roused by the tidings of a fresh insult, for that Tigranes having passed the limits of Armenia, had wasted the territories of the Adiabenians, a bordering people, with more lasting and extensive spoil than by robbers was wont to be committed: an outrage which the chiefs of these nations underwent with painful regret, ' that they were sunk into such
' abject scorn as to be over-run not in truth by the
' prowess of any Roman leader, but by the inso-
' lent arms of an hostage to Rome, one there kept
' for so many years amongst his fellow-slaves.' The anguish of Vologeses was inflamed by Monobazus, in whose hands lay the government of the Adiabenians, and who pressed to know ' what military
' succours were there to secure them, and from
' what quarter to be sought? The fate of Armenia
' was already determined, the adjacent regions
' were about to be swallowed up; and unless they
' were

'were defended by the Parthians, they themselves
' would soon consider, that bondage from the Ro-
' mans proved always much lighter to such as sub-
', mitted to mercy, than to those who flaid to be
' subdued.' Tiridates too, who was a fugitive
from his kingdom, affected Vologeses yet more
grievously, whether he beheld the silent distress of
his brother, or heard his respectful complainings.
For the deprived Prince was wont to alledge, ', that
' mighty empires were not to be sustained by sloth
'. and inaction; the vigour of men and arms was to
' be exerted. In sovereign fortune, those measures
'. were ever most righteous, which proved most
'. successful. To those in a private station belonged
' the narrow domestic ambition of preserving their
' own; to struggle for the possessions of others was
' renown truly monarchical.'

Vologeses, therefore, stimulated by all these considerations, assembled a council, and placing Tiridates next to himself, began thus: ' This Prince,
' begotten by the same father with myself, I invest-
' ed with the possession of Armenia, since to me,
' in regard of primogeniture, it was his lot to
' yield the sovereignty of Parthia; and thus he be-
' came what we account the third sovereign of our
' blood; for Pacorus already occupied the realm
' of Media. By this means I seemed to have hap-
' pily settled our family, and provided against the
' ancient hate and competition of brothers. This
' the Romans oppose, and though they never in-
' fringed the peace with any felicity to themselves,
' they now again openly break it, doubtless to their
' own bane and confusion. I am far from deny-
'. ing, that rather by arguments than arms would
' I choose to preserve the acquisition of my ances-
' tors. If I have been blameable in my delays, I
' will redouble my vigour. Your glory is unsul-
' lied, your force undiminished; to this praise you
have

' have also added that of moderation, a virtue never
' to be slighted by the most elevated amongst men,
' and is held by the Gods themselves in high esti-
' mation.' As soon as he had thus spoke, upon
the head of Tiridates he set the royal diadem; to
Moneses, a noble Parthian, he delivered a complete
band of stout horse, which according, to the custom
of monarchy, always attended the person of the
king; to these he added a body of auxiliary Adiabenians, and commanded that General ' to force
' Tigranes from Armenia.' He purposed himself the
while to drop his contest with the Hyrcanians, to
amass all his forces in the heart of Parthia, and reserving to his own conduct the main stress of the
war, to advance, and threaten a descent into the
Roman provinces.

Corbulo, as soon as by certain intelligence he had
learnt all these proceedings, sent two legions to succour Triganes, under the command of Verulanus
Severus and Vettius Bolanus, with secret injunctions, ' rather to study delays than to act with dis-
' patch.' The truth was, Corbulo aimed more at
keeping a war on foot, than pushing it to a conclusion; besides he had written to Nero, ' That in
' order to defend Armenia, another General was
' necessary; for that Syria, now threatened with
' a terrible tempest from Vologeses, was thence ex-
' posed to more vehement danger.' In the mean
while he disposed the remaining legions along the
banks of the Euphrates, suddenly raised a body of
militia out of the natives of the province; at all the
passes he posted guards to obstruct the inroads of
the enemy; and because that region is scanty of
water, over the several fountains forts were erected,
and some springs he buried under hills of sand.

While Corbulo was thus busied in measures for
securing Syria, Moneses advanced towards Armenia
with rapid marches, as by them he meant to out-
run the report of his coming: but he found Ti-

granes

granes neither void of intelligence, nor in a negligent situation; for that Prince had possessed himself of Tigranocerta, a city of great strength in the multitude of its defenders, and the mightiness of its walls; add, that the Nicephorus, a river of no small breadth, environed great part of the wall, and round the rest, where the defence of the river was not trusted, a vast trench was drawn; within it too was a garrison of soldiers, and stores of provision before laid up. In bringing in these provisions some few soldiers, having out of greediness straggled too far, fell into the hands of the swift and unexpected foe; but by this mishap of theirs, the minds of the rest became filled with resentment, rather than with dismay; neither have the Parthians any bravery to venture a close attack upon a place besieged: it was but a few scattering arrows that they shot, nor thence at all dismayed the besieged, but only baffled themselves. The Adiabenians, when with ladders and engines of battery, they began to approach the walls, were easily driven back, and by an immediate sally of our men put to the slaughter.

Corbulo, however, though all his proceedings prospered, judging it wisdom to moderate the career of his good fortune, dispatched embassadors to Vologeses to expostulate with him upon his hostile conduct, ' That he had with violence, and war fallen ' upon a Roman province; that his forces besieged ' a king who was a friend and confederate of Rome; ' nay, besieged the Roman cohorts themselves;' and to warn him, ' that either he must abandon ' the siege, or Corbulo too would instantly march ' and encamp upon the territories of the enemy.' Caspeiius the Centurion, who was delegated to execute this embassy, reached the king at the city of Nisibis, thirty seven miles distant from Tigranocerta, and there delivered his message with great sternness.

ness: It was, in truth, long since the political drift of Vologeses, and thoroughly rivetted in his heart, to avoid engaging with the arms of Rome; neither did his present enterprizes advance with any measure of success; fruitless and vain had been the siege of Tigranocerta; Tigranes sat secure and strong in men and provisions; they who had undertaken to storm the walls, were utterly routed; two legions were sent to the relief of Armenia; the remaining legions covered Syria, nay stood ready for an offensive war, and to invade the dominions of Parthia; his whole cavalry, through scarcity of forage, were miserably enfeebled; for such an infinite flight of locusts had fallen, as utterly devoured the whole crop of the earth and every green thing: smothering, however, his dread, and assuming a guise of moderation, he returned for answer, 'That he ' would send embassadors to Rome to sue to Cæsar ' for a concession of the kingdom of Armenia, and ' to corroborate the peace between them:' and instantly commanding Monesses to relinquish the siege of Tigranocerta, he departed himself homewards again.

These quick changes were by many extolled, as
' events altogether honourable, purely atchieved
' by the menaces of Corbulo, and the dismay of
' the King.' Others explained the whole ' into a
' secret compact between them, that the war being
' dropped on both sides, and Vologeses withdraw-
' ing from Armenia, Tigranes too should depart
' that kingdom. Upon what motives else was the
' Roman army led out of Tigranocerta? Why, in
' a time of inaction, were those places abandoned,
' which during war were strenuously defended?
' Had the troops found, in the remotest parts of
' Cappadocia, more commodious winter quarters,
' under huts suddenly raised, than in the capital of
' a kingdom just before carefully kept and protect-
' ed?

' ed?' Without all doubt, the war was therefore
' fufpended, that upon fome other commander than
' Corbulo the lot might fall of, meeting Vologefes
' in the field; nor would Corbulo expofe to new
' rifques that renown and glory which for fo many
' years he had been acquiring:' for, as I have
already obferved, he had demanded that a General
fhould be fent for the particular defence of Armenia,
and heard that Cæfennius Pætus was approaching
with that character. Cæfennius was, in truth, already arrived, and the forces fo divided, that under
the command of Pætus were to remain the fourth
legion and the twelfth, to which was added the
fifth, lately called thither from Mœfia, as alfo the
auxiliaries from Pontus, Galatia, and Cappadocia;
with Corbulo were to continue the third, fixth,
and tenth legions, and what forces formerly belonged to Syria. All other particulars they were to
poffefs in common, or to fhare, juft as the public
fervice required. But as Corbulo could not bear a
competitor, fo Pætus, to whom it was doubtlefs
abundant glory if in merit he were reckoned the
fecond, difparaged all the atchievements of Corbulo;
he affirmed, ' that in all his exploits nothing of
' hoftile blood was fpilled, nothing of fpoil was
' taken; and all the boafted praife of maftering
' and affaulting cities was merely nominal and
' affumed: for himfelf he would impofe upon the
' vanquifhed tribute and laws, and inftead of the
' prefent fhadow of a king, fubject them at once to
' the jurifdiction of Rome.'

At this very juncture, the embaffadors of Vologefes, the fame whom I have mentioned to have
been fent to the Prince, returned unfuccefsful. Hence
the Parthians proceeded to open war, nor did Pætus
decline it; but with two legions, the fourth and
twelfth, the former then commanded by Famifula-
nus Vectonianus, the other by Calvifius Sabinus,

he entered Armenia, and a sad presage accompanied his entrance; for in passing over the Euphrates, which he crossed upon a bridge, the horse which carried the Consular ornaments became frightened without any apparent cause, and starting back again, got clear away: moreover, as they were fortifying their quarters against winter, a victim which stood by the works, before the same were above half finished, broke violently through, leaped over the pale, and fled; the javelins too of our men blazed with spontaneous fire, a prodigy which appeared the more signal, for that with javelins and such weapons missive their enemies the Parthians always fight.

But all these omens were contemned by Fætus, who, before his winter encampment was yet sufficiently fortified, without preparing any the least magazine of grain, hurried the army over the mountain Taurus, ' to recover, as he said, the city of ' Tigranocerta, and lay waste the several regions ' which Corbulo had spared:' and it is true that he took certain castles, somewhat of glory too he won, and somewhat of plunder, if he had either possessed his glory with moderation, or his plunder with care: but while with long marches he overran countries which could not possibly be maintained, what provisions he had pillaged became corrupted and spoiled, and the winter was just overtaking him, so that he led back the army to their quarters; there he composed letters to Nero in a pompous stile, as if the war had been already concluded; but as to any available performances, his letters were empty and vain.

Corbulo the while sat down upon the banks of the Euphrates, a station which he had never neglected; he now particularly multiplied the guards which defended it: and that the enemy's troops, who with great ostentation and numbers were prancing over the opposite plains, might create no obstruction ftruction to his laying a bridge over the river, he faftened together with great beams certain veffels of vaft bulk; upon them he reared large towers, and fteering this armed float to and fro upon the ftream, did thence with engines of battery annoy and diffipate the Barbarians, upon whom by this means were poured volleys of ftones and darts, at a greater diftance than could be equalled by the flight of arrows by them returned: thereafter the bridge was extended quite over; the oppofite hills were immediately poffeffed by the confederate cohorts, and upon them the legions next pitched their camp; all which was executed with fuch celerity, and fuch a formidable difplay of forces, that the Parthians intirely abandoned their difpofitions for invading Syria, and turned all their hopes and efforts towards Armenia.

There abode Pætus, in fuch utter ignorance of the impending tempeft that he ftill kept the fifth legion at fo great a diftance as Pontus, and had weakened the reft by allowing the foldiers without reftriction leave to be abfent: in this fituation he received the news that Vologefes advanced with a mighty hoft, breathing terror and vengeance; forthwith he called to him the twelfth legion; but this very thing, from whence he hoped the reputation of having augmented his army, betrayed their thinnefs: yet they ftill might have maintained their camp, and by protracting the war have baffled all the efforts of the Parthians, if in the fpirit of Pætus there had been any firmnefs, either in adhering to his own counfel, or to the counfels of others; but whenever by officers of experience he feemed fixed in his meafures againft fuch preffing dangers, prefently after, that he might not feem to want the judgment of any man, he lapfed into courfes which were different, and always worfe. At this very juncture he wilfully departed out of the entrenchments

ments which inclosed their winter quarters, and uttering brave words, ' that in order to repulse the
' foe, to him was committed neither ditch nor pale,
' but the bodies and arms of men;' he led forth the
legions like one who would needs encounter the
Parthians in battle; but having lost a centurion
and a few private men, whom he had sent forward
to view the enemy's forces, he returned to his camp
in great haste and affright: yet seeing Vologeses
had pursued his advantage with no remarkable ardour, Pætus became once more infatuated with
vain confidence, and upon the next summit of mount
Taurus placed three thousand select infantry, to repulse the king from passing it; he likewise committed a particular part of the plain to the troops of
Pannonia, which were the strength of his cavalry:
his wife and son he shut up in a castle named Arsamosata, and for garrisoning the castle gave them
a band of five hundred men. Thus he dispersed
his army, who, had they been in a body, might with
more vigour have sustained the shock of a roving
and inconstant enemy: nay, it is said that he was
with great difficulty induced to transmit to Corbulo
any account of the enemy's distressing him; neither
did Corbulo make much dispatch, that the more
the danger increased, the greater praise he might
reap from bringing relief: he gave orders, however,
to make ready a body of succours consisting of three
thousand legionary soldiers (one from each of the
three legions) of eight hundred horse, and an equal
number of foot detached from the cohorts.

Vologeses, though he was advised that Pætus
beset the roads on every hand, here with his infantry, there with his horse, yet no wise varied his
design or his march, but with a violent onset, and
ostentation of terrors, quite dismayed and drove away
the Pannonian troops; the legionary foot posted
upon Taurus he utterly overthrew, and found re-

siftance

sistance from one centurion only, namely, Tarquitius Crescens, who had the bravery to defend a tower in which he kept garrison; he even made frequent sallies, and such of the Barbarians who ventured to approach he slew, till at last he was assaulted and overwhelmed by volleys of flaming matter. Such of the infantry as escaped unhurt, betook themselves to wild and remote deserts, and the wounded recovered the camp: there they published, ' the signal bravery of the Parthian king, the mul- ' titudes and barbarity of the several nations his ' followers,' and, through the impulse of their own fears, magnified excessively whatever inspired them; all which was swallowed with ready credulity by the rest, who were themselves possessed by the same terrors: nor in truth did the General make any efforts to repel this torrent of adversity; he had already deserted all the duties of war, and again dispatched more entreaties to Corbulo, ' to come ' with speed, and save the Roman Ensigns and Ea- ' gles; to save the name and remains of an unhappy ' army, who with himself would, while their lives ' remained, honour their deliverer with perfect faith ' and gratitude.'

Corbulo was no wise daunted, and, leaving part of his forces in Syria to maintain the posts which he had fortified upon the Euphrates, began the shortest route, where no hazard was incurred of lacking provisions; first through Comagena; then through Cappadocia, and thence into Armenia. There accompanied his army, besides other implements usual in war, a huge train of camels loaded with grain, thence to repel famine as well as the foe. The first that he met of those who were routed was Pactius, a Centurion of principal rank; after him came several common soldiers, who, while they strove to cover the shame of their flight each by a different excuse, were by Corbulo admonished

K 6. ' to

'to return to their colours, and try the mercy of
Pætus: for his particular, he owned himself implacable to all who in battle came not off victorious.' At the same time he addressed himself to his own legions, from rank to rank persuading and exhorting, reminded them of their exploits and victories past, and to their present view exhibited a scene of fresh glory; ' Not now the villages and cities of the Armenians were to be possessed as the recompence of their services and hardships, but the Roman camp to be saved, and in it two Roman legions. If every private soldier were, for saving the life of a citizen, distinguished with the lustre of a Civic Crown publicly presented by the hand of his General, how much more signal and extensive must be the renown, when the lives preserved, and they who preserve them, were thus equally numerous?' By these and the like stimulations they became fired with alacrity for the common cause; besides some were prompted by personal incitements, even the distresses and dangers in which their brothers, or their companions and kinsmen, were involved; so that they sped their march night and day without intermission.

Hence the more vehemently did Vologeses press the besieged, now assaulting the entrenchment of the legions, then the castle in which were guarded those who from the tenderness of their sex and years were unfit for the roughness and toils of war; and he pushed these his assaults much more closely than was usual to the Parthians, in hopes by such designed temerity to tempt out the enemy to a battle; but they, with all these insults, could scarce be dragged out of their tents, at most only endeavoured to maintain their works, part of them submitting to the orders and restrictions of their General, others resigned to their own cowardice, as men who stupidly waited for deliverance from
Corbulo;

Corbulo; or if the power of the assailants in the mean while prevailed, they had already provided themselves with examples to follow, namely, the behaviour of two old Roman armies overthrown, one at Caudium in Italy, the other at Numantia in Spain; 'for that neither were the Samnites (a
' single Italian state) nor were the Spaniards, either
' of them masters of forces comparable to those of
' the Parthians, a mighty empire, rival with that
' of Rome; nay, those same ancients, so very brave
' and stubborn, and so much extolled, as often as
' fortune forsook them, were ever supple enough to
' consult self-preservation.' By the temper of the army, thus abandoned to despair, the General was constrained to write to Vologeses; yet the first letter which he sent contained nothing of supplicancy or abasement, but was conceived in a strain of expostulation and complaint, ' That for the kingdom of
' Armenia he should thus exercise the violences of
' enmity and war; a country ever subject to the
' Roman jurisdiction, or to a king appointed by
' the Emperor of Rome. Peace was, in truth,
' alike advantageous to the Parthians and to the
' Romans; neither ought he to view only the pre-
' sent situation of things, but remember that against
' two legions he was come at the head of the whole
' power of his kingdom, while to the Romans re-
' mained, for the support of the war, all the rest of
' the globe.'

Vologeses, without entering at all into the merit of the war, in answer to the representation wrote back, ' That he must wait the coming of his bro-
' thers Pacorus and Tiridates, as to them was re-
' served the appointment of a place and time for
' adjusting such measures concerning Armenia, as
' became their own high character and the gran-
' deur of the Arsacides; at the same time too,
' they would determine how to deal with the Ro-
' man

"man legions." Pætus again difpatched a meffage, and defired a conference with the king, who, in his own ftead, deputed Vafaces, his general of horfe. At this interview Pætus urged examples, and reprefented: " fuch Roman Captains as Lucullus " and Pompey, and fince fome of the Cæfars, ac- " quiring and beftowing the realm of Armenia." Vafaces alledged, ' That indeed the name and fha- " dow of holding and conferring it refted in us Ro- " mans, but in the Parthians the effential power." After much mutual conteftation, Monobazus the Adiabenian was the next day joined with them, as a witnefs to their ftipulations, and between them it was agreed, ' That the legions fhould be releafed " from the leaguer, all the Roman troops utterly " depart the territories of Armenia, all their for- " treffes and ftores be delivered up to the Parthians. " Then after complete performance of thefe con- " ceffions, Vologefes fhould have free privilege to " fend embaffadors to Nero.'

In the mean time Pætus laid a bridge over the river Arfanias, which flowed along his camp, under pretext of his preparing to march off that way; but it was in reality a work enjoined him by the Parthians, as a monument and confeffion of their victory, fince to them only it was of ufe; for our men took a different route. All this difgrace was heightened by public rumour, which added, that ' the legions had paffed like captives under a gal- ' lows,' with many other difaftrous circumftances, fuch as are wont to accompany diftrefs; and it is true, that of fuch ignominious treatment fome fem- blance was adminiftered by the infulting behaviour of the Armenians, who, before the Roman army was yet difcamped, entered their works, hefet all the avenues and thoroughfares, fingled out their own captive flaves, diftinguifhed their loft beafts, and ref- cued both: they even ftripped the Romans of

their

'their cloaths,' and seized their arms, while the poor soldiers only trembled and delivered, thus to cut off all provocation and excuse of involving them in a battle! Vologeses raised a pompous heap of all the arms and bodies of the slain, by it to manifest our overthrow, but forbore beholding the scandalous flight of the legions, from whence he aimed at acquiring the applause of moderation, when he had just before satiated his pride: he passed the river Arsanias mounted upon an elephant, as did all that were near the king in blood or favour, by the vigour of their horses; for a report had spread that the bridge, by the fraud of the builders, would certainly sink under any considerable pressure; though they who ventured over it, experienced it to be a strong and secure fabric.

For the rest, it was notorious that the beleagured army were to the last provided with such abundant supplies of grain, that they even set fire to their storehouses; and it was by Corbulo recounted, ' That the Parthians, on the contrary, were desti-
' tute of provisions, and their forage entirely con-
' sumed, so that they were about to have forsaken
' the leaguer; neither was he himself above three
' days march distant with his forces;' he even added, ' That Pætus covenanted, under the tye of
' an oath solemnly taken under the sacred Eagles,
' in the presence of those whom the king had sent
' to witness it, That no Roman should enter Ar-
' menia, till by the arrival of letters from Nero it
' were known whether he consented to the peace:'
but though such imputations were to pass only for infamy aggravated, yet the subsequent conduct of Pætus and his army is liable to no ambiguity, that in one day they travelled the space of forty miles, that the wounded were every where dropped and forsaken, and that no less infamous was the flight and dismay of those fugitives, than if they had turned

ed their backs and run in the day of battle. Upon the banks of the Euphrates Corbulo with his forces met them, but without such a display of flying colours and glittering arms as might seem to upbraid their different and melancholy plight; sorrowful were his several bands, and in commiseration for the heavy lot of their fellow-soldiers, could not refrain from a flood of tears; scarce were they able to exchange their salutations for weeping: all competition about superior bravery was vanished, as well as all ambition for glory; for these are the passions of happy and prosperous men! here compassion only prevailed, and the lower the men the stronger their compassion.

Between the two leaders there followed a brief conference, Corbulo lamenting, ' That so much
' travel had been fruitlessly bestowed, when the war
' might have been finished with the utter flight of
' the Parthians.' The other replied, ' That the
' affairs of Armenia remained perfectly as they
' were. Let us, said he, turn about our Eagles,
' and invade it in concert, enfeebled as it is by
' the departure of Vologeses.' Corbulo alledged,
' That from the Emperor he had no such orders:
' he had already passed out of his province, from
' no other inducement than to deliver the distressed
' legions; and as it was altogether uncertain where
' the next efforts of the Parthians would fall, he
' would retire back into Syria : even thus they had
' cause to invoke the deity of happy fortune, that
' the foot, which were so miserably spent with
' great marches, might be able to come up with
' the Parthian horse, which were altogether fresh
' and untired, and in travelling easily over those
' smooth plains, were sure to out-march them.'
Pætus therefore withdrew to Cappadocia, and there wintered; but to Corbulo a message arrived from Vologeses, ' To withdraw his several garrisons from
' beyond

' beyond the Euphrates, and let the river remain,
' as formerly, the common boundary.' Corbulo
too infifted, ' That all the Parthian garrifons
' fhould evacuate Armenia;' and at laft the king
complied. Moreover, all the fortifications raifed
by Corbulo on the other fide Euphrates were demolifhed, and by both the king and Corbulo the
Armenians were left to their own difpofal and controulment.

But at Rome the while, they were erecting trophies of victory over the Parthians, and raifing triumphal arches upon the mount of the Capitol; folemnities decreed by the Senate while the war was
yet in its height, nor even now difcontinued, as
popular fhew was only ftudied, in defiance of conviction and fact; nay, Nero, in order to difguife
all folicitude from affairs abroad, ordered the flores
of grain, which from time to time was diftributed
amongft the populace, but now corrupted with
ftalenefs, to be thrown into the Tiber, in oftentation of the public fecurity and plenty of provifions:
it is certain their price became nothing raifed, notwithftanding that almoft two hundred veffels thus
loaded were by a violent ftorm funk in the very
harbour, and a hundred more, already arrived in
the Tiber, were confumed by an accidental fire.
Thereafter he committed the direction of the public
revenue to three Senators of Confular dignity, Lucius Pifo, Ducennius Geminus, and Pompeius Paullinus, inveighing againft the Princes his anceftors,
' for that through the profufenefs of their expence
' and difburfements they had exceeded their annual receipts; whereas by himfelf the Common-
' wealth was yearly prefented with more than a
' million of crowns.'

There prevailed in thofe days a peftilent abufe,
practifed by men afpiring and childlefs, who, whenever the election of magiftrates, or the allotment
of

of provinces, was at hand, provided themselves with sons by fraudulent adoptions; then when in common with real fathers they had obtained Prætorships and provincial Governments, they instantly dismissed such as they had occasionally adopted. Hence those who were genuine fathers betook themselves with mighty indignation to the Senate: there, they represented their own ' inherent right
' from nature, their many toils and paternal cares
' bestowed in education and rearing, in opposition
' to the fraud, selfish devices, and facility of these
' adoptions hastily made, and suddenly dissolved.
' To such as were childless, it was abundant com-
' pensation, that with much security, and exempt
' from all anxiety and charge, they could arrive at
' public distinction and honours, and find every
' advantage in the state easy and open to their
' wishes. For themselves, the preference ensured
' to them by the law, and by them tediously ex-
' pected, vanished in mockery, while every man
' had it in his option to become a parent without
' parental tenderness and solicitude, and fatherless
' again without the lamentation and anguish of a
' parent, and by the collusive ceremony of a mo-
' ment, arrived at equal emoluments with natural
' fathers, by them so long pursued.' This produced a decree of Senate, ' That in the pursuit of
' any public employment whatsoever no feigned
' adoption should have influence, nor yet avail in
' claiming estates by will.'

What followed was the accusation and trial of Claudius Timarchus of Crete, who, besides other excesses common to the grandees of all provinces, elated with overgrown wealth, and thence wantonly prompted to domineer over their inferiors, had uttered an expression which imported great scandal and contumely upon the Senate; as he had often declared, that ' it lay in his power, whether the

' Proconsuls

"Proconsuls who had obtained the government of
"Crete, should receive for their administration 'the
"public thanks;' an occasion which Pætus Thra-
"sea sought to improve to the benefit of the public;
"so that after he had delivered his vote, namely,
"That the accused should be banished from Crete,'
"he added the following speech: 'It is a truth con-
"firmed by experience, Conscript Fathers, that re-
"nowned laws and wholesome precedents are by
"upright patriots derived from the transgressions and
"delinquency of others: thus was the Cincian
"law produced by the licentious behaviour of the
"Orators, the Julian ordinances by the caballings
"and efforts of the candidates for public prefer-
"ments, and the institutions of Calpurnius the
"Tribune by the rapaciousness of the magistrates;
"for guilt is ever antecedent to punishment, and
"later than the offence comes the correction. To
"quell, therefore, this fresh insolence of the Provin-
"cials, let us take measures worthy of the good
"faith, worthy of the magnanimity of the Romans,
"such as may no wise infringe the protection due
"to our confederates, nor yet leave room for any
"Roman to depend for his estimation upon other
"judgment than that of his fellow-citizens. Of
"old, indeed, not Prætors and Consuls only, and
"men in office, were sent into the provinces; but
"private persons, invested with no magistracy, were
"also sent to inspect the state of those provinces
"in general, and to report what they judged meet
"concerning the civil observance of every particu-
"lar; and by the judgment of single inspectors na-
"tions were awed: but now we court foreigners,
"and flatter them; and as at the beck of some one
"of them thanks are decreed to our magistrates,
"from the same motive too. but with more facility,
"is their accusation decreed: nay, let such accusa-
"tions be still decreed; to the Provincials let there
'always

'always continue a privilege of making, in such
'instances, an oftentation of their power; but let
'their false and groundless applause, their com-
'mendations extorted by importunity and prayers,
'be restrained with the same rigour as the efforts
'of malice, as the ravages of cruelty. Into hea-
'vier defaults we often fall, while we labour to
'oblige, than when we are not afraid to offend.
'There are even certain virtues subject to popular
'hate, such as a severity never to be shaken, and
'a soul impregnable against all insinuation and
'courtship. Hence the administration of our Ma-
'gistrates abroad is generally best at the begin-
'ing, but relaxes in the close, while in the sub-
'missive manner of candidates for honours at home
'we solicit favourable suffrages from the provin-
'cials. Now if this depraved custom be effectually
'suppressed, the provinces will be ruled with more
'impartiality, with greater firmness and resolution;
'for as by the terror of the law against extortion
'and rapine, the force of avarice in the governors
'is broken, so by abolishing the usage of giving
'them public thanks, the court by them paid to
'the provinces is to be restrained.'

Great was the applause and universal the assent that accompanied this proposition from Thrasea, which yet could not be reduced into a decree, since the Consuls insisted that the same was foreign from the question first moved; but afterwards, at the motion of the Prince, it was ordained, 'That to
'the general council of the provinces no man
'should have leave to propose a deputation to
'the Senate for public thanks to any Prætorian or
'Proconsular Governor whatsoever; and that no
'man should be allowed to execute such a deputa-
'tion.' During the same Consuls the Athletic Aca-
demy was by a blast of lightning burnt to ruins, and in it the brazen statue of Nero melted to a shape-
less

lefs mafs. Campania too, the noble city which from Pompey takes its name, was in a great meafure overturned by an earthquake; and this year died Lælia the Veftal virgin, into whofe place was affumed Cornelia, of the Coffian family.

In the Confulfhip of Memmius Regulus and Verginius Rufus, a daughter was by Poppæa born to Nero, and filled him with more than mortal joy, infomuch that he named her *Augufta*, and upon Poppæa conferred the fame title. The place of her birth was the Colony of Antium, where he himfelf was born. The Senate had before folemnly recommended to the Gods the pregnant womb of Poppæa, and for her delivery undertaken public vows: now many more were added, and the whole amply fulfilled: days of devotion and proceffions were alfo fubjoined; a temple was decreed to ' Fecundity, with Athletic fports in imitation of
' thofe which were peculiar to Antium; moreover
' that in the throne of Jupiter Capitolinus fhould
' be placed golden images of the Fortunes;. and
' that at Antium, in honour to the Claudian and
' Domitian families, Circenfian games fhould be
' celebrated, as at the fuburbs Bovillæ they were
' in diftinction to the Julian race:' but all thefe proved fleeting memorials; for within four months the infant expired; from whence arofe frefh fallies of flattery; fince deification was voted to her, with
' divine worfhip, a tabernacle, chapel, and prieft:' for the Emperor, as he had rejoiced, fo he forrowed beyond all meafure. It was a particular univerfally obferved, that when juft upon the delivery of Poppæa the Senate in a body flocked with congratulations to Antium, Thrafea was by Nero reftrained from accompanying them; a contumely which, though it foreboded his impending deftruction, he yet received with a fpirit perfectly undifmayed. It was reported that Nero afterwards
vaunted

vaunted to Seneca his own clemency and reconciliation to Thrasea, and that to Nero in return Seneca expressed his gladness and thanks. Hence fresh glory accrued to these illustrious patriots, and by it higher obnoxiousness and danger.

During these transactions there arrived, in the beginning of spring, embassadors from the Parthians, charged with overtures from Vologeses their king, and with letters in the same strain, that he now voluntarily relinquished ' all his former measures so of‐
' ten contested about the enjoyment of Armenia,
' since, the Gods, though they were the sovereign
' arbitrators between potent states, and had yielded
' the possession of it to the Parthians, yet so yielded
' it that thence ignominy devolved upon the Romans. He had lately held Tigranes blocked up,
' in a siege, then Pætus and the legions; and when
' it was in his power to have destroyed them, it
' was his choice to dismiss them unhurt. He had
' sufficiently displayed his forces and might, and
' exhibited too a glaring proof of his moderation.
' Neither would his brother Tiridates refuse coming
' to Rome, there to receive the Armenian diadem;
' but that as he was a Magian, the character of his
' priesthood with-held him; he was ready, how‐
' ever, to address himself to the Roman ensigns,
' and to the images of Cæsar, and there, in pre‐
' sence of the legions, receive the solemn investiture
' of the kingdom.'

When these letters of Vologeses were read, so opposite to the account transmitted by Pætus, as if things remained entirely in the same situation; the Centurion, who had arrived with the embassadors, was asked, ' In what condition stood the
' kingdom of Armenia? he answered, ' that all
' the Romans were to a man withdrawn from
' thence:' and as hence was understood the scorn offered by the Barbarians thus suing for a country
which

which they had already seized, Nero held a consultation with the principal Grandees, whether to
engage in a perilous war, or prefer an infamous
peace; nor was there any hesitation in resolving
upon war; and to Corbulo, who by the experience
of so many years knew both the soldiery and the
enemy, the supreme command was committed, left
through the temerity and unskilfulness of any other,
more faults and disgrace might be incurred; for
of Pætus and his conduct they were sorely ashamed:
the embassadors were therefore dismissed unsuccess-
ful, but distinguished with presents, thence to raise
hopes that, were Tiridates to bring his own supplications, he would not supplicate in vain. To
Sestius was given the administration of Syria, and
to Corbulo were granted all the military forces there,
which were also increased by the addition of the fifteenth legion, led by Marcus Celsus, from Pannonia:
directions were likewise written to the Kings and
Tetrarchs in the East, to the Deputies and Superin-
tendents, and to the several Proprætors, who ruled
the neighbouring provinces, 'to pay entire obedi-
' ence to the orders of Corbulo,' who was thus
trusted with much the same extensive authority
which the Roman people had conferred upon Pompey in his expedition against the pirates. Upon the
return of Pætus to Rome, while he was dreading a
more rigorous treatment, Nero deemed it sufficient
to lash him with railleries in this manner, " I par-
' don you, said he, instantly, left, with that strange
' propensity to fear, you might pine away, were
' your anxiety ever so little protracted.'

Now when Corbulo had removed into Syria the
fourth, and twelfth legions, which, from the loss
of all their bravest men, and the consternation of
the rest, were judged little qualified for feats of
war, he drew from that province the sixth legion
and the third, a body of men fresh and undiminished,
hardened

hardened by variety of military toils, and accustomed to prosperous exploits, and led them to Armenia: to them he added the fifth, which being quartered in Pontus had escaped the late defeat. Moreover, the soldiers of the fifteenth legion lately arrived, and some chosen bands from Illyrium and Ægypt, with all the auxiliary troops of horse and companies of foot, as also the succours from the confederate kings, were drawn together at Melitene, as from thence he had concerted their passing the Euphrates. He then purified the army by the usual solemnity of Lustration, and in a stated assembly animated them with a speech: in it he made a glorious display ' of the auspicious sway and invincible fortune ' of Cæsar; of the signal exploits by himself atchieved;' and upon the simple conduct of Pætus he cast ' whatever contumelies or disasters had been ' sustained.' These things he delivered with great spirit and authority, which in a military man like him, carried all the force of eloquence.

He took next the same route which of old was passed by Lucullus, having removed whatever impediments in so long a course of years had closed up the way; neither did he discountenance the embassadors who were approaching from Tiridates and Vologeses with overtures of peace; but to confer with them appointed certain Centurions, whom he furnished with instructions no wise harsh, namely, ' That as yet the contest was not risen ' to such height as that nothing could determine ' it but the decision of the sword. The Roman ' arms had in many instances been prosperous, in ' some the Parthian; whence a lesson might be ' drawn against arrogance and presumption in either. ' It moreover concerned the interest of Tiridates to ' possess a kingdom untouched by the ravages of ' war, by accepting it as the 'gift of the Romans: ' more substantially too would Vologeses study the

' ad-

' advantage of the people of Parthia by an alliance
' with the Romans, than by involving both in mu-
' tual damages and mischief. It was well known
' what terrible revolts were then rending the bowels
' of his Monarchy, as also what fierce and unruly
' nations he governed. To the Roman Emperor,
' on the contrary, there continued in all his domi-
' nions a steady peace, and only the weight of that
' single war.' To enforce his reasoning, he immediately subjoined the terrors of the sword, drove
from their seats the Grandees of Armenia, who
were the first revolters from us, razed their castles,
and filled with equal dismay the inhabitants of the
mountains and those of the vales, the warriors and
the unwarlike.

The hame of Corbulo was held in no distaste,
much less in hostile hate, even amongst the Barbarians; hence they believed his counsel worthy to be
trusted. Vologeses, therefore, who was never violent for a general war with the Romans, now sought
a truce for certain of his Governments. Tiridates
demanded a day and place for a conference; and
a time near at hand was appointed: for the place,
as the Barbarians chose that where they had lately
besieged Pætus and the Legions, from a fond remembrance of their more propitious atchievements
there, the same was not declined by Corbulo,
that from the different face of his own fortune,
his glory might be augmented. Yet neither suffered
he the disgrace of Pætus there to be blackened with
any fresh reproach; a tenderness chiefly manifest
from hence, that he ordered the son of Pætus, one
of his own Tribunes, to march at the head of some
companies and commit to sepulchres the ghostly remains of that unfortunate field. Upon the day stipulated, Tiberius Alexander an illustrious Roman
Knight, one sent with Corbulo as an assistant and
inspector in the measures of the war, and with

him Vivianus Annius, son-in-law to Corbulo, one under the age of a Senator, but set over the fifth Legion in the room of its own commander, entered together into the camp of Tiridates, as a compliment of honour, and that, possessed of such hostages, he might fear no guile. Then the King and the General took each twenty horse and proceeded to the interview. At the sight of Corbulo, the King leaped first from his horse, nor was Corbulo slow to return the courtesy, and both on foot interchanged their right hands.

Thence the Roman Captain proceeded to applaud the young Prince, 'that, renouncing all desperate mea-
' sures, he had adopted such as were wholesome and se-
' cure.' Tiridates, after a long display ' of the splen-
' dor of his race, pursued the rest of his discourse with sufficient modesty and condescension; ' That
' he would travel to Rome and present a new subject
' of glory to Cæsar, a prince of the Arsacides his sup-
' plicant, at a season when no public distress impaired
' the affairs of Parthia.' It was then agreed that before the image of Cæsar he should resign the Royal Diadem, never to resume it more, except from the hand of Nero; thus ended the conference with a mutual kiss. Then, after an interval of a few days, the two armies met with mighty pomp and ostentation on both sides: There stood the Parthian horse, ranged into troops, and distinguished by the standards of their several nations; here were posted the battalions of the Legions, their Eagles glittering, their Ensigns displayed, with the figures of the deified Emperors exhibited like Deities in a Temple. In the center was placed a tribunal, which supported a chair of state, as did the chair a statue of Nero: To this Tiridates approached, and having, according to form, slain certain victims, pulled the Diadem from his head and laid it at the feet of the statue.

Great

Great upon this occasion were the emotions in the minds of all men; and the greater as they had still before their eyes the late overthrow, at least the late liege of the Roman armies: 'But now in- 'tirely inverted were the operations of fortune; 'Tiridates was departing for Rome, exposed as a 'spectacle to the nations, under a character how 'little below that of a captive?'

Corbulo, to all his glory, added actions of com- plaisance and a sumptuous banquet; during which the King, as often as any usage of ours, new to him, occurred, was assiduous to know what the same might mean; why a Centurion advertised the General, when the watch was first set? why when meals were ended the trumpet sounded? why the fuel upon the altar reared before the Augural port was kindled with a torch? All which Corbulo ex- plained, and heightening all beyond just bounds, struck him with admiration of the ancient institu- tions of the Romans. The next day, Tiridates besought 'so much time, before he undertook so 'long a journey, as might suffice to visit his brothers 'and his mother;' and, for an hostage, delivered up his daughter, and writ a supplicant letter to Nero.

Thus he departed, and found Pacorus in Media, and at Ecbatana Vologeses, who, in truth, was far from neglecting the concerns of this his brother: For by a special embassy he had desired of Corbulo, 'That Tiridates might bear no visible semblance 'of slavery: nor be obliged to surrender his sword; 'nor be debarred from the distinction of embracing 'the Governors of Provinces; nor stand waiting 'at their gates for admittance; and that in Rome, 'the same honour should be paid him as to the Con- 'suls was paid.' In truth, that Prince, inured to the pride which prevails among foreigners, was a stranger to the maxims of us Romans, who study the energy of Empire, and overlook the shadows and empty forms.

The same year, Cæsar conferred upon those nations of the Alps who inhabit the sea coast, the rights and immunities of Latium: To the Roman Knights he assigned places in the Circus before the seats of the populace; for till that time they sat there without discrimination, as the sanctions of the Roscian law were only confined to the fourteen rows in the Theatre. On this year too was exhibited a combat of Gladiators equally magnificent with the former; but many Ladies of illustrious quality, and many Senators, by entering the lists, infamously stained themselves.

In the Consulship of Caius Lecanius and Marcus Licinius, Nero became every day more transported with a passion for mounting the public stage, and entertaining the promiscuous multitude; for hitherto he had only sung in the assemblies intituled *Juvenalia*, which were restrained to particular houses and gardens; places which he despised, as not sufficiently celebrated, and too confined for a voice so signal as his. At Rome, however, he dared not to begin, but chose Naples, the same being a Greek city, ' where having made his first essay, he would pass ' thence over to Greece, and there having, by vic- ' tory in song gained the prize-crowns, ever so ' highly renowned and held sacred of old, he could ' not fail of attracting with heightened applause ' the hearts of the Roman citizens.' To this entertainment crowded all the rabble of Neapolitans, with numbers from the neighbouring cities and colonies, excited by the rumour and curiosity of the spectacle; besides such as followed the Emperor, either in compliment to him, or about private affairs of their own: Nay, with these entered several bands of soldiers, and all together thronged the Theatre; where an accident befel, which, in the opinion of

many,

many, was sad and presaging; but with Nero it passed for a providential event, and betokened the tutelage of his guardian Deities: The Theatre, when the audience who filled it were retired, tumbled to the ground, but as not a soul was in it, none were hurt by its ruins. For this deliverance Nero celebrated the benignity of the Gods in songs of thanksgiving purposely composed, as also the story and description of the recent contingency. Then in his route to pass the Adriatic, he rested a while at Beneventum, where by Vatinius was presented a splendid shew of Gladiators: This Vatinius was one of the many baleful monsters that haunted the court, and one of the foremost, originally bred in a shoemaker's stall, in his person hideous and distorted, addicted to sneering and drollery, and at first admitted merely as a buffoon; thence, by lying accusations against every worthy man, he had arrived to such high consideration, that in favour, in opulence, and in power to injure and destroy, he even surpassed the other implements of mischief.

Nero, during the course of this solemnity, though he attended it assiduously, forbore not however, even in the midst of his diversion and pleasures, to pursue feats of blood; since, in those very days of festivity, Torquatus Silanus was forced to die, for that, besides the ancient splendor of the Junian family, he was great grandson to the deified Augustus. Against him the accusers had orders to object, ' his
' great prodigality and bounties; and that other
' resource and views he had none remaining, save
' only in a public revolution. Nay, already he
' kept about him men with the stile of principal
' Secretaries, of Chancellors, of Treasurers, names
' and offices of Imperial grandeur, which he thus
' aspired to, and even personated.' Immediately all his freedmen, in any degree of intimacy with their master, were cast into bonds, and hurried to

the dungeon. Torquatus, seeing his impending condemnation, opened the veins of both his arms, and expired; an event which was followed, according to the custom, with a speech from Nero; ' That 'however guilty the criminal had been, how justly 'soever he had despaired of acquitting himself by 'any defence, his life had still been spared, had he 'staid for the clemency of his Judge.'

Nero having deferred his voyage to Greece for reasons which were not known, soon after re-visited Rome, his head busied with many imaginations, all smothered at first, about shewing himself to the Provinces in the east, especially to Ægypt: At last this project became the subject of a public edict In it he declared, that ' his absence would not be of ' long continuance, and the Commonwealth, in ' all its parts, would continue the while in the same ' perfect quiet and prosperity;' then for the success of that journey, he betook himself in devotion to the Capitol. While he was there, paying his oblations to the several Deities, as he entered amongst others into the Temple of Vesta, he became seized with a sudden and prevailing horror, which shook him in every joint; whether the awe of the Goddess struck him with dismay; or whether, from the remembrance of his foulness and crimes, he was ever haunted by terrors, it is certain that he droped his project, making many asseverations, ' That ' lighter with him were all his pursuits than his ' passion for his Country: He had seen the sorrow-' ful looks of the Roman citizens, he still heard ' their secret complainings, that he would venture ' upon such mighty travels, when, in truth, they ' could never bear even his shortest excursions from ' Rome; as they were accustomed to be revived ' under all disasters by the joyful sight of the ' Prince.' Hence it was that as in private consan-' guinities and friendship, dearest in affection w r
' the

' the nearest in blood, so over himself above all
' considerations availed that of the Roman people;
' and when they would thus retain him, it behoved
' him to obey.' These and the like declarations of
his were well pleasing to the populace, from their
propensity to the revels and diversions, and from
another motive, ever the most prevalent of all, the
scarcity of provisions apprehended in his absence.
The Senate and Grandees were in suspense whether
he were to be esteemed a more raging tyrant at
Rome, or remote from Rome; and thence, according to the genius of all great and affecting fears,
they believed what happened to be the worst that
could happen.

Nero himself, in order to gain a reputation of
delighting, above all places, in Rome, banquetted
frequently in the public places and great squares,
and used the whole city as his own house. But as
particularly signal for luxury and popular observation was the feast prepared by Tigellinus, I shall
here, for an example, recount its order and state,
that henceforth I may not be obliged to a frequent
recital of the like enormous prodigalities. For this
purpose he built, in the lake of Agrippa, a large
vessel which contained the banquet, and was itself
drawn by other vessels with oars: The vessels were
embellished with diversified ornaments of gold and
ivory, and rowed by bands of Pathics, ranged according to their seniority and pre-eminence in the
science of unnatural prostitutions. From divers
regions he had procured variety of wild-fowl, and
wild beasts for venison, with sea-fish as far as the
Ocean. Upon the borders and angles of the lake
stood brothels filled with Ladies of illustrious rank;
over-against them professed harlots were exposed,
completely naked. Now every-where were beheld obscene postures and agitations; and as soon as
darkness spread all the neighbouring groves and
circumjacent

circumjacent dwellings refounded to each other with the joyful fymphony of mufic and fongs, and appeared all illuminated with a blaze of lights. For Nero's part, he wallowed in all forts of defilements, natural and unnatural: He, in truth, had then left no kind of abomination untried, which could ferve to finifh his vilenefs, had he not, in a few days after, perfonated a woman, and been given in marriage, with all the forms and folemnity of genuine nuptials, to one of this contaminated herd, a Pathic named Pythagoras: Over the Roman Emperor, as over a bride, was caft the facred nuptial veil; the Augurs were feen in form folemnizing the efpoufals, the portion of the bride was openly paid, the bridal bed difplayed, the nuptial torches kindled, and, in fine, to view was expofed whatever, even in natural commerce with women, is buried under the fhades of night.

There followed a dreadful calamity, but whether merely fortuitous, or by the execrable contrivance of the Prince, is not determined; for both are by authors afferted: But of all the evils which ever befel this city by the rage of fire, this was the moft deftructive and tragical. It arofe in that part of the Circus which is contiguous to mount Palatine and mount Cœlius, where beginning amongft fhops, in which were kept fuch goods as are proper to feed the fury of fire, it grew inftantly outragious; and being alfo aided by frefh force from the wind, it devoured the whole extent of the Circus. For neither were particular houfes fecured by any inclofures, nor the Temples by their Walls, and it had nothing to encounter capable of obftructing its violence; but the flame fpreading every way, with terrible impetuofity, invaded firft the flat regions of the city, then mounted to the higher, and again ravaging the lower, fuch was its amazing velocity as to fruftrate all relief, and its havock was felt before

fore any measures to oppose it could be tried. Besides, the city was obnoxious to conflagrations from the disposition of its building, with long narrow alleys, winding like labyrinths to and fro, and streets void of all regularity, as was the fashion of old Rome. Add to all this, the shrieks and wailings of women under woe and dismay, the helpless condition of the young and tender, that of the aged and infirm, with the confusion of such as strove only to provide for themselves, interfering with those who laboured to assist others, these dragging the weak and unweildy, those waiting for the like help; some running, others lingering. From all which various efforts there arose only mutual interruption and universal embarrassment; and while they chiefly regarded the danger that pursued them behind, they often found themselves suddenly beset before, and on every side; or if they had first escaped into the quarters adjoining, these too were already seized by the devouring flames; even the parts which they believed quite remote and exempt, were discovered to be under the same affecting calamity. At last, utterly perplexed what they had best shun, or where to seek sanctuary, they filled with their multitude the streets and ways, and lay along in the open fields. Some there were who, in despair for the loss of their whole substance, and even bereft of daily sustenance, others who through tenderness for their relations, whom they had not been able to snatch from the flames, suffered themselves to perish in them, though they had full scope and opportuity to escape. Neither durst any man offer to marr the progress of the fire: Such were the repeated menaces of many who openly forbid all attempts to extinguish it; and as there were others who, in the face of the public, heightened it by volleys of lighted firebrands, with loud declarations, " that they had one to authorize them ;' whether it were a device a device for the more licentious exercife of plunder, or whether in reality they had fuch orders.

Nero was at that juncture fojourning at Antium, but never offered to return to the city, till he heard that the fire was advancing to that quarter of his houfe which filled the fpace between the Palace and the Gardens of Mæcenas: Nor, even upon his arrival, could its rage be ftaid, but, in fpight of oppofition, it devoured houfes and palace, and every thing round about. For the relief, however, of the forlorn people, thus vagabond and bereft of their dwellings, he laid open the field of Mars and all the great edifices erected by Agrippa, and called his monuments; he even prefented them the ufe of his own Gardens. He likewife reared hafty tabernacles for the reception of the deftitute multitude: from Oftia too and the neighbouring cities, by his orders, were brought all forts of houfhold implements and neceffaries; and the price of grain reduced to three fefterces the meafure. All which bounties of his, however popular, were beftowed in vain, without any gratitude returned; becaufe a rumour had flown abroad, ' That, during the ' very time when Rome was under the fury of con- ' fuming flames, he entered his domeftic Theatre, ' and chanted the deftruction of Troy, likening the ' prefent defolation to the tragical calamities of ' antiquity.'

At length, on the fixth day, the conflagration was ftayed, at the foot of mount Efquiline, by levelling with the ground an infinite number of buildings, and making a mighty void; fo that the raging devaftation, hitherto uninterrupted, might find nothing to encounter but open fields and empty air. Scarce had the late confternation ceafed, when a new and no trivial alarm recurred; for the fire broke out with frefh outrage, but in places more wide and spacious; hence fewer lives were destroyed: But more Temples were here overthrown, and more sumptuous Porticos, such as were appropriated to public diversion and festivity. This conflagration too was subject to the greater measure of infamy, for that it rose in the possessions of Tigellinus, in the Amylian fields; whence it was conjectured, that Nero was thus aiming at the glory of building a new city, and calling it by his name. For of the fourteen quarters into which Rome is divided, four were still standing entire, three lay in utter ruins; and in the seven others, there remained only here and there a few shadows of houses miserably shattered and half consumed.

Easy it were not to recount the number of the houses, squares, palaces, and temples which were lost: But foremost in antiquity and primitive rites were the following edifices; that dedicated by Servius Tullius to the Moon; the Temple and great Altar consecrated by Evander the Arcadian to Hercules, then a living Deity, and present in person; the Chapel vowed by Romulus to Jupiter the Stayer; the Court of Numa, with the Temple of Vesta, and in it the tutelar Gods peculiar to the Romans; all now consumed to ruins. In the same fate were involved the treasures acquired and accumulated by so many victories; the beautiful productions of Greek artists, ancient writings of celebrated authors, and till then preserved perfectly intire, which, though many of them were still remembered by aged men, yet even upon the restoration of the city with such mighty lustre and embellishments, could never be retrieved nor supplied. There were those who observed, that on the eighteenth of July the fire began, the same day on which the Gauls, called Senones, having taken and spoiled the city, burnt it to the ground: Others were so curious in their cal-

L. 6.   culations,

culation, as to reckon the juſt number of years, months, and days between the two conflagrations*.

For the reſt; Nero appropriated to himſelf the ruins of his native country, and upon them founded a palace, one where profuſion of gold and precious ſtones raiſed not the chief admiration, ſince theſe were ſtale and uſual ornaments, ſuch as from diffuſive luxury were become long common: But the principal ſurprize aroſe from the ſpacious glades, and large artificial lakes. In imitation of vaſt wilderneſſes, here ſtood thick woods and ſhades; there lay ample lawns, avenues, and open views. The projectors and comptrollers of this plan were Severus and Celer, two men of ſuch temerity and enterprizing talents, as to attempt to remove by art the everlaſting obſtacles of nature, and to baffle, in vain experiments, all the Emperor's power: For they had undertaken to ſink a navigable canal from the lake Avernus to the mouth of the Tiber, over a dry and deſert ſhore, or through ſteep intervening mountains: Yet in all that way, they could not have encountered any ſource of moiſture for ſupplying water, ſave only the marſh Pomptina; the reſt was every where a ſucceſſion of rocks, or a ſoil parched and untractable: Or, had it ever been poſſible to have broke through all obſtruction, intolerable had been the toil, and the end incompetent. Nero however, zealous for atchieving feats which were deemed incredible, exerted all his might to perforate the mountains adjoining to Avernus; and to this day remain the traces of his romantic and abortive ambition.

The remainder of the old foundations, which his own court covered not, was aſſigned for houſes;

---

* I doubt the text here is faulty. Perhaps it ought to be read, as it is in one of the Manuſcripts, 'Between the foundation of the city, and both conflagrations. *Inter conditam urbem & utraque incendia.*'

nor were thefe placed, as after it was burnt by the Gauls, at random and ftraggling; but the ftreets were delineated regularly, fpacious, and ftraight; the height of the buildings was reftrained to a certain ftandard; the courts were widened; and to all the great houfes which ftood by themfelves, for fecuring their fronts, large Porticos were added: Thefe Porticos Nero engaged to rear at his own expence, and then to deliver to each proprietor the fquares about them, difcharged of all rubbifh. He moreover affigned donatives proportioned to every man's rank and fubftance; and fet a day for payment, on condition that againft that day their feveral houfes or palaces were finifhed. He appointed the marfhes of Oftia for a receptacle of the ruins, and that with thefe the veffels which had conveyed grain up the Tiber, fhould return laden back; that the new buildings fhould be raifed to a certain height from the foundation, without rafters or boards; that they fhould be arched and partitioned with ftone from the quarries of Gabii or Alba, the fame being proof againft the violence of fire: That over the common fpiings, which were licentioufly diverted and wafted by private hands, overfeers fhould be placed, to provide for their flowing in greater abundance into the public cifterns, and for fupplying a greater number of places: That every houfekeeper fhould furnifh his yard with fome machine proper to extinguifh fire; neither fhould there be any more a common intermediate wall between houfe and houfe, but within its own independent walls every houfe fhould be inclofed. Thefe regulations, which importing the general benefit of the citizens, were popularly received, derived alfo much beauty and decoration upon the new city: Yet fome there were who believed the ancient form and ftructure more conducing to health; as from the narrownefs of the ftreets, and the height of the building, the

rays

rays of the fun were hardly felt or admitted; whereas now, fo fpacious was the breadth of the ftreets, and fo utterly deftitute of all fhade, that the heat fcorched with unabated rage.

Thus far the provifions made were the refult of counfels purely human. The Gods are next accofted with expiations, and recourfe had to the Sibyl's Books. By admonition from them, to Vulcan, Ceres, and Proferpina, fupplicatory facrifices were made, and Juno atoned by the devotion of Matrons, firft folemnized in the Capitol, then upon the next fhore, where by water drawn from the fea the Temple and Image of the Goddefs were befprinkled, and her feaft and wake were celebrated by Ladies who had hufbands. But not all the relief that could come from man, not all the bounties that the Prince could beftow, nor all the atonements which could be prefented to the Gods, availed to acquit Nero from the hideous charge, which was ftill univerfally believed, that by him the conflagration was authorized. Hence, to fupprefs the prevailing rumour, he transferred the guilt upon fictitious criminals, and fubjected to moft exquifite tortures, and doomed to executions fingularly cruel thofe people who, for their deteftable crimes, were already in truth univerfally abhorred, and known to the vulgar by the name of *Chriftians*. The founder of this name was Chrift, one who in the reign of Tiberius fuffered death as a criminal under Pontius Pilate, Imperial Procurator of Judæa, and, for a while, the peftilent fuperftition was quelled, but revived again and fpread, not only over Judæa, where this evil was firft broached, but even through Rome, the great gulph into which, from every quarter of the earth, there are torrents for ever flowing of all that is hideous and abominable amongft men; nay, in it the filthy glut of iniquity never fails to find popular reverence and diftinction. Firft therefore were feized fuch as freely

owned

owned their fect, then a vast multitude by them difcovered; and all were convicted, not fo much for the imputed crime of burning Rome, as for their hate and enmity to human kind. To their death and torture were added the aggravations of cruel derifion and fport; for either they were difguifed in the fkins of favage beafts, and expofed to expire by the teeth of devouring dogs; or they were hoifted up alive, and nailed to croffes; or wrapt in combuftible veftments, and fet up as torches, that, when the day fet, they might be kindled to illuminate the night. For prefenting this tragical fpectacle, Nero had lent his own gardens, and exhibited at the fame time the public diverfion of the Circus, fometimes driving a chariot in perfon, and at intervals ftanding as a fpectator amongft the vulgar in the habit of a charioteer. Hence it proceeded, that towards the miferable fufferers, however guilty and juftly deferving the moft exemplary death, popular commiferation arofe, as for people who, with no view to the Utility of the State, but only to gratify the bloody fpirit of one man, were doomed to perifh.

In the mean time, in order to fupply his prodigality with money, all Italy was pillaged, the Provinces were fqueezed and defolated; fo were the feveral nations our confederates, and all thofe cities which have the title of free. In this general fpoil, even the Gods were involved, their Temples in the City plundered, and from thence all the treafures of gold conveyed, which the Roman people, in every age of their ftate, either as monuments of triumphs celebrated or of vows fulfilled, had folemnly confecrated, both in their times of profperity, and in feafons of public peril Through Greece and Afia, in truth, the Deities were not only defpoiled of their gifts and oblations, but even of their Statues and Images; for into thefe Provinces, and with this commiffion, had been fent Acratus his freedman,

man, and Secundus Carinas, the former a prompt inftrument to execute any iniquity, however black and flagrant; the other a man practifed in the Greek learning, which however funk no deeper than his lips, and with virtuous acquirements he had never formed his foul. Of Seneca it was reported; ‘ That ‘ to avert from himfelf the odium and imputation ‘ of this facrilege, he had befought Nero for leave ‘ to retire to a feat of his own, remote from Rome, ‘ but was refufed, and thence feigning an indifpo- ‘ fition in his nerves, confined himfelf to his cham- ‘ ber.’ It is by fome authors recorded, ‘ That a ‘ freedman of his, named Cleonicus, had, by the ‘ command of Nero, prepared poifon for his maf- ‘ ter, who efcaped it either from the difcovery made ‘ by the freedman, or from the caution infpired by ‘ his own inceffant apprehenfions; while with a ‘ diet exceeding fimple he fupported an abftemious ‘ life, fatisfying the call of hunger by wild fruit ‘ from the woods, and of thirft by a draught from ‘ the brook.’

About the fame time a body of Gladiators, who were kept at the city of Præncfte, laboured an efcape and revolt; and though by the diligence of the foldiers who guarded them they were maftered and fuppreffed, the people were already in bufy murmurs reviving the terror of Spartacus and the public miferies of old; fond as they ever are of agitations and novelty, yet ever frightened by them. Nor was it long after this that a fatal difafter befel the fleet, from no encounter in war; for fcarce ever was known a time of fuch profound peace: But Nero had ordered the gallies to return to the coaft of Campania at a limited day, without any allowance made for the changes and cafualties of the deep; fo that the pilots, even while the fea raged, fteered from the port of Formia, and, by a violent tempeft from the South, while they ftruggled to double the

Cape

Cape of Misenum, were driven upon the shore of Cuma, where many gallies of three banks of oars, and a number of smaller vessels, were wrecked.

In the close of the year, the heads and mouths of the people were filled with a long rote of prodigies, as so many heralds of impending calamities. At no time had thunder roared, or lightning shot with such fierceness and frequency, besides the appearance of a Comet, an omen ever expiated by Nero with the effusion of illustrious blood. In the streets and roads were found exposed several monstrous births with double heads, some of the human species, some of brutes; as also from the bellies of victims some such were taken, when for the sacrifice custom required beasts that are pregnant: And in the territory of Placentia, by the side of the public way, was brought forth a calf with its head growing upon its leg, a prodigy which, according to the interpretation returned by the Soothsayers, boded, 'That for human kind another head was 'preparing, but one which would never arrive at 'strength, or remain concealed; for that this which 'presaged it, had lain repressed in the womb, and 'then issued into the world close by the public road.'

Silius Nerva and Atticus Vestinus commenced Consuls, during the progress of a conspiracy so vigorous, that to the same moment it owed its beginning and advancement. In it Senators, Knights, soldiers, and even women, had engaged with a spirit of eagerness and competition; such was their detestation of Nero, and equally strong their zeal for Caius Piso. This Patrician, a descendant of the Calpurnian house, and by the nobleness of his paternal blood allied to many illustrious families, was, for his own virtue, or for qualities that resembled virtues, held amongst the populace in signal applause: for as he was a master of eloquence, he employed it in the patronage and defence of his fellow-

fellow-citizens; be was generous to his friends and acquaintance; and even toward such as were unknown to him, complaisant in his language and address: He possessed, with these advantages, others that were fortuitous, tallness of person and a graceful countenance; but strictness of life and manners he never practised, nor observed restraints in his pleasures; the ways of delicacy he ever indulged, as also those of magnificence, sometimes the excesses of luxury. Many too there were who approved this his conduct, such who, in a general prevalence of debauchery, would not have the supreme head confined in his morals, nor strictly severe.

It was from no ambition or pursuit of his that the birth of the conspiracy sprung; and yet I could not easily recount who he was that first concerted it, nor who animated a design which was by such a number espoused. That Subrius Flavius Tribune of a Prætorian Cohort, and Sulpicius Asper the Centurion, were the keenest champions in it, the spirit and constancy with which they encountered death, do abundantly evince. Lucan the Poet, and Plautius Lateranus, Consul elect, concurred from ardent animosity and hate; the former stimulated by persoual provocation, for that Nero had obstructed the fame of his Poems, and, from a ridiculous emulation, forbid their publication. Lateranus was piqued by no injury done to himself, but f om sincere affection to the Republic became an accomplice. But there were two men, Flavius Scevinus and Afranius Quinctianus, both Senators, who by engaging in an enterprize so great and daring, and even claiming to be foremost in the execution, departed from the constant character of their lives; for Scevinus had a soul drowned in sensuality, and thence led a stupid life devoted to sleep and sloth: Quinctianus was infamous for unnatural prostitution;

tion; and having been by Nero expofed in a virulent Satire, to revenge the indignity he confpired.

Now as all thefe, as well in conferences with one another as amongft their friends, were ever difplaying, 'the inhuman cruelties of the Prince, 'the condition of the Empire, threatened with in- 'ftant diffolution, and the neceffity of fubftitut- 'ing in his place fome one capable of relieving 'the afflicted ftate;' they drew into the combination Tullius Senecio, Cervarius Proculus, Vulcatus Araricus, Julius Tugurinus, Munatius, Gratus, Antonius Natalis, and Martius Feftus, all Roman Knights. Of thefe Senecio, who had lived in fingular intimacy with Nero, and preferved even then the face of favour, was thence the more encompaffed with dread and danger. To Natalis all the fecret purpofes in the heart of Pifo were open without referve: fecret views governed the reft, and they fought their own intereft in a change. Of the men of the fword, befides Subrius and Sulpicius, the officers already mentioned, there were affumed as accomplices, Granius Silvanus and Statius Proximus, Tribunes of the Prætorian bands, with the Centurions Maximus Scaurus, and Venetus Paullus. But, as their main ftrength and dependence, they confidered Fenius Rufus, Captain of the Imperial Guards, a man for life and eftimation in fignal credit and popularity, one who expofed himfelf to daily perils from the hate and perfecution of Tigellinus his colleague, who by the recommendations of a cruel fpirit, and manners altogether impure, had gained a fuperior afcendancy in the heart of the Prince, and, labouring to deftroy him by forged crimes, had often well nigh effected his deftruction, by alarming Nero with the views and difcontents of Rufus; 'as one who had been en- 'gaged in a criminal commerce with Agrippina, 'and, in anguifh and refentment for her untimely
'end,

'end, was bent upon vengeance.' As soon therefore as the conspirators had, from the frequent discourse of the Captain, received full conviction that he too had embraced their party, they proceeded more resolutely to debate about the time and place of the assassination. It was reported, 'That Subrius
'Flavius had undertaken to make the first onset,
'and assail Nero, either while he was chanting in
'the Theatre, or scouring from place to place in
'his drunken revels by night, unattended by his
'guards.' In the latter project an incitement from solitude; in the former, even the great conflux of people, all witnesses of an exploit so glorious, had roused his soul to a purpose so full of nobleness and merit, had not a solicitude to execute it with impunity restrained him; a consideration which, in all grand enterprizes, is ever unseasonable and fatal.

In the mean time, while they were hesitating and protracting the issue of their hopes and fears, a certain woman, named Epicharis, applied herself to rouse the conspirators; though it was a perfect mystery by what means she came at all apprized of the conspiracy (for till then she had never shewn any regard to aught that was worthy or honourable) at last she became impatient of their slowness, and retiring to Campania, employed all her industry and skill to alienate the hearts of the chief officers in the fleet riding at Misenum; and, to engage them in the design, she began in the following manner. In that fleet Volusius Proculus had the command of a thousand marines, one of the ministers of blood employed to dispatch the mother of Nero, and, in his own opinion, not distinguished with promotion equal to the mighty and meritorious murder. As this officer, whether from old acquaintance with Epicharis, or a friendship newly contracted, recounted to her 'his signal services to Nero, and how fruit-
'less they had been bestowed,' and as he subjoined

joined 'bitter complaints with a settled resolution
'of taking vengeance whenever opportunity arose,'
she conceived hopes that he might be engaged himself in the design, and to it conciliate many others.
Nor of small moment was the aid and concurrence
of the fleet, and frequent were the opportunities of
exerting it, as Nero took singular delight in sailing
often about the coasts of Misenum and Puzzoli.
Epicharis therefore, in answer to Proculus, urged
many reasonings, with a detail of all the crying cruelties committed by the Prince; she added, 'That
' to the Senate, nothing remained to be done to-
' wards accomplishing his fall; only it was already
' determined to what pains the tyrant must be
' doomed for destroying the Roman state. What
' therefore was to be expected from Proculus, but
' that he should assume the task with zeal, associate
' in the cause all the bravest soldiers; and then
' depend upon a recompence worthy of such sub-
' lime service.' From him, however, she concealed
the names of the conspirators: hence it was that
even when he had betrayed to Nero her whole discourse, his discovery availed nothing. For when
Epicharis was summoned, and confronted with the
informer, as his charge against her was supported
by no witnesses, she found it easy to refute and
baffle him. After all, she was detained in prison, because Nero vehemently suspected that these matters were not the more false for not being proved
to be true.

Notwithstanding the silence of Epicharis, the
conspirators, who were thoroughly alarmed with the
dread of a discovery, came to a result to hasten the
assassination, and to do it at Baiæ in a villa belonging to Piso, whither the Emperor often resorted,
charmed with the loveliness of the place, and there
wont to bathe and banquet, remote from his guards
and the other incumbrances of Imperial state. But

in this, Piso would by no means concur: he alledged
'the general abhorrence which must ensue, were
'the inviolable rites of the table, were the Gods of
'hospitality, defiled by the blood of a Prince, how-
'ever vile he were: hence it were more adviseable
'to dispatch him at Rome, in that same detested
'house which with the spoils of the unhappy citi-
'zens he had reared; or rather they ought, in the
'face of the public, to execute a deed which for
'the benefit of the public they had undertaken.'
Thus he reasoned openly amongst the conspirators,
but his heart was influenced by secret jealousy, as
he dreaded Lucius Silanus, a man of transcendent
quality, and, by the tuition of Caius Cassius, by
whom he was bred, ennobled with accomplishments
proper for every the most resplendent dignity; lest
Silanus might seize the vacant sovereignty for himself, as he would be sure of instant assistance from
all such as were clear of the conspiracy, and from
all those who should prove affected with compassion
for Nero, as for one traiterously slain. There were
many who believed, that 'Piso likewise distrusted
'the lively and turbulent spirit of the Consul Ves-
'tinus, whether he might not be prompted to re-
'store liberty and the ancient government, or else,
'procuring some other than Piso to be chosen Em-
'peror, turn the Republic into a gift of his own
'bestowing.' For in the conspiracy he had no share,
though Nero afterwards, under the imputation of
this very crime, doomed him an innocent sacrifice
to satiate his own inveterate rancour.

At length they agreed to perpetrate their designs
upon the anniversary sacred to Ceres, and always
solemnized with the Circensian games; for that
the Emperor, who otherwise came seldom abroad,
but remained shut up in his apartments or gardens,
was yet wont to frequent the diversions of the Circus, where, during the gaiety and pleasures of the
sports,

sports, access to him was more readily obtained. The scheme of their plot they contrived on this wise: 'Lateranus, in the posture of a supplicant, and 'feigning to implore relief in his domestic affairs, 'was to fall at the Prince's feet, and, while he ap-'prehended no such attempt, throw him down, 'and, as Lateranus was of a daring spirit and huge 'in stature, hold him fixt to the place. While he 'lay thus pressed and entangled, the Tribunes, Cen-'turions, and all the rest, according as they felt 'themselves prompted by present impulse and mag-'nanimity, were instantly to rush in and slay him. 'That Scevinus should be the foremost to strike,' was a task by himself earnestly claimed; for from the Temple of Health in Etruria, or, as others have recorded, from that of Fortune in the city of Fe-reutum, he had brought away a dagger, and carried it constantly about him, as a weapon consecrated to the perpetration of a deed of mighty moment. It was moreover concluded, 'That Piso should wait 'the event in the Temple of Ceres, and be thence 'brought forth by Fenius, Captain of the Guards, 'and the other conspirators, and conducted to the 'camp; moreover, in order to attract the affections 'of the populace, Antonia, daughter of the late 'emperor Claudius, was to accompany him.' A particular recorded by Caius Plinius; for myself, I was determined to suppress no circumstance in what way soever delivered; however marvellous and inconsistent it may seem, that either Antonia should contribute her name, and risque her life, to promote a scheme, to herself altogether fruitless and vain; or that Piso, a man universally known to have been passionately fond of his wife, should engage to marry another; were it not that, of all the passions which actuate the heart of man, the lust of reigning is the most vehement and flaming.

But,

But, wonderful it was, in a combination so numerous, so variously framed, amongst those of every condition, different in rank, in quality, sex, and age, many wealthy, many poor, all things should be buried in such faithful secrecy, till from the family of Scevinus the traiterous discovery first arose. The day before that of the designed assassination he had been engaged in a long conference with Antonius Natalis, and immediately, upon returning home, sealed his will; then unsheathing the dagger mentioned above, he complained that it had lain so long neglected till it was become blunt, ordered it to be grinded into an edge, and the point to be accurately sharpened. The charge of this he committed to Milichus, one of his freedmen, and next betook himself to a repast more gaudy and profuse than ordinary. His favourite slaves he presented with their liberty, others with sums of money; upon his countenance too there hung clouds and melancholy; and it was apparent that his mind laboured with some grand design, though he counterfeited cheerfulness by many starts of discourse upon as many subjects. At last, he directed the same Milichus to prepare bandages for wounds and applications for stopping blood; whether the freedman were in truth already privy to the conspiracy, and had hitherto persevered in fidelity, or whether he were utterly in the dark, and then first, as several authors have written, gathered from consequences his sudden suspicion; for when the freedman, still acted by the base spirit of a slave, revolved with himself the recompence to be expected from proving a traitor to his master, and at the same time beheld, as already his own, immense wealth and potent sway; he renounced at once every tie of faith, all tenderness for his Lord, and all remembrance of liberty by him generously bestowed. In truth, besides his own mercenary motives, he had taken
counsel

counsel of his wife, a woman's counsel and the worst; for she was ever urging him with the dreadful peril of hiding treason, 'That many freedmen, many 'slaves, had beheld, as well as he, the same things, 'and of no availment would prove the silence of 'one; and yet only by one, whoever he were who '·first discovered, would all the rewards be reaped.'

Milichus, therefore, at the first dawn of day, went straight to the Gardens of Servilius, where Nero then abode, and, being refused admittance, declared that he brought 'mighty and horrible dis- 'coveries,' with such earnestness, that he was conducted by the porters to Epaphroditus, a freedman of Nero's, and by him forthwith to Nero himself. To him he represented, 'what formidable conspi- 'racies were concerted, what mortal danger was 'just impending,' with all the circumstances which he had heard, with whatever from his own observation he conjectured, and even shewing the dagger destined to destroy him, desired the criminal to be instantly produced. Scevinus was by the soldiers haled hastily thither, and proceeding to his defence, answered, 'That for the dagger with which he 'was charged, it was a relique left him by his fore- 'fathers, ever held sacred in their family, by him- 'self always kept in his chamber, and from thence 'traiterously conveyed away by his freedman.' New 'wills he had often made, and sealed them, with- 'out observing any distinction of days. Frequently 'before this he had bestowed upon his slaves li- 'berty and largesses, lately with the greater libera- 'lity, for that his fortune being reduced, and his 'creditors importunate, he distrusted his power of 'gratifying his domestics by legacies. A generous 'table he had ever kept, and ever indulged himself 'in a life of ease and pleasure, such as by the rigid 'censures of manners, was but little approved. 'Dresses for wounds, he had ordered none; but,

VOL. II.   M   ' as

'as all the other imputations objected by his freed-
'man were manifestly impotent and vain, he had
'invented and added a charge of treason, such as
'might enable him to be at once witness and accu-
'ser.' His words he enforced with an undaunted
spirit; he even charged the accuser, as 'a fellow
'altogether pestilent and traiterous, and his testi-
'mony incompetent,' with a voice and countenance
so intrepid, that the informer must have been baffled, but for his wife. She advertised him, that
'with Scevinus, Antonius Natalis had held a long
'conversation and exceeding secret, and that both
'were close confidents of Caius Piso.'

Natalis therefore was called, and both were examined, but apart, concerning 'the particulars,
'and the subject of that conversation.' As their
answers varied, cause of suspicion arose, and they
were thrown into irons; but the sight of the rack,
and the menaces of torture, neither could bear.
Natalis however was foremost to confess, as better
acquainted with the whole order and progress of the
conspiracy, and withal more expert in impeaching:
First, he discovered how far Piso was concerned,
afterwards to him he added Seneca; whether he had
indeed acted as an inter-agent between him and
Piso, or whether he only did it to purchase the favour of Nero, who, in ardent hate to Seneca, was
daily hunting after all sorts of devices to destroy
him. Now Scevinus, having learnt that by Natalis
a confession was made, yielded to the same imbe-
cility of spirit; or perhaps, he believed that already
the confederacy was, in every particular, disclosed,
and from his own silence no emolument to be expected. Hence he declared all the other accomplices. Of these Lucan and Quinctianus, and Senecio, persisted long in denying the charge; but at
length, by a promise of their exemption from punishment, they suffered themselves to be corrupted;
then,

then, to atone for their late flowness, they named their dearest friends. Lucan informed against Attilla, his own mother, Quinctianus against Glicius Gallus, and Senecio against Annius Pollio.

Nero the while recollected that, upon the evidence of Volusius Proculus, Epicharis was holden in custody, and, supposing that the tender body of a woman could never endure the rage of the rack, ordered her to be crushed and mangled with variety of torments. But neither the fury of stripes, nor of fire, nor of the torturers, who tore her with the more vehemence, left, with all their dexterity and efforts in cruelty, they should be at last scorned and baffled by a woman, could at all vanquish her. She still utterly denied every particular objected: this was the issue of the torture the first day, and by her its violence was despised. The day following, as she was returning to suffer a repetition of the same outrageous torments, and reconducted in a chair (for all her members being rent and disjointed, she could not support herself) with the girdle that bound her breasts she framed a noose for her neck, and tying it to the canopy of the chair, hung upon it with all the weight of her body, and thence dislodged the slender remains of life. Behind her she left an example the more signal and heroick, for that a woman who was once a slave, should, upon an occasion so trying and important, undergo torture and death to protect such to whom she had no tye of kindred or friendship, nay, such as she scarce knew; when men, men born free, when Roman Knights, and Senators of Rome, without once feeling the torture, betrayed, without exception, every one the dearest pledges which he had in friendship and blood. For Lucan too and Senecio, and Quinctianus, never ceased making discoveries, and were still naming more accomplices; a detail which was incessantly adding to the affright and dismay of

Nero;

Nero; though he had, with guards redoubled, fenced himself in; nay, as if he meant to have imprisoned Rome itself; upon the walls, all round, bands of soldiers were posted: even the sea and the Tiber were garrisoned. Moreover, parties of foot and horse were perpetually ranged every-where, in the public squares, in private houses, even through the circumjacent territory and neighbouring municipal towns. But with both horse and foot, there were Germans intermixed; for in them, as they were foreigners, the Prince chiefly confided. Thenceforth, the accused were haled in whole droves, numbers after numbers, without intermission, towards his tribunal, and lay in miserable expectation, at the gates of his Garden. When they had entered, in order to be successively heard, if it appeared, ' that they had ever been seen gay or smiling with ' any of the conspirators, or happened to speak to ' them, though fortuitously, or to meet them, how- ' ever unexpectedly, or to have been common guests ' at the same table, or sat together at some public ' shew;' all this, or any part of it, was imputed as guilt and treason. Besides the cruel scrutiny made by Nero and Tigellinus, violent were the questions and imputations urged by Fenius Rufus, who had as yet escaped all information, and, to beget a persuasion that he had been an utter stranger to the plot, manifested himself now stern and outrageous against his own associates. Nay, it was he that frustrated the bold purpose of Subrius Flavius, who, while he attended, and demanded by signs, whether he should draw his sabre, and, even in the heat of the inquest, perpetrate the assassination, was by contrary signs from Rufus forbid, and his ardor checked, when already his hand grasped the hilt.

There were those who, when the conspiracy was first betrayed, while Milichus was yet under examination, while Scevinus wavered, exhorted Piso
' to

' to proceed directly to the Camp, or mount the
' Roſtrum, and try the affections of the people and
' ſoldiery; for if once his accomplices were openly
' aſſembled to maintain his efforts, thoſe too who
' were not engaged, would certainly follow; and,
' when the commotion was once begun, mighty
' would be the public noiſe and alarm; an incident
' which, in all new attempts, is of infinite avail-
' ment: Neither was Nero provided to reſiſt the
' ſhock. With terrors that come ſudden and un-
' foreſeen, even brave men were daunted; how
' little then was it to be apprehended that that
' Comedian, guarded forſooth by Tigellinus with
' his hoſt of harlots, would dare to riſque a conflict
' of arms? Many deſigns there were, which, though
' to daſtardly ſpirits they appeared arduous and im-
' poſſible, were yet accompliſhed by trying to ac-
' compliſh them. In ſuch a mixt multitude, en-
' gaged in the plot, or privy to it, it was vain to
' expect conſtant faith and ſecrecy; or that the
' minds of all would be proof againſt temptation,
' and their bodies againſt pain. To the force of
' recompences and tortures nothing was impene-
' trable; nay, there would ſoon arrive men, who
' would commit to bonds Piſo himſelf, and at length
' ſubject him to a contumelious death. But with
' how much more glory and renown would he fall,
' while he eſpouſed the Commonwealth, bravely
' invoking aid, and rouſing champions for public
' Liberty; while, even though the ſoldiers failed
' him, though the people forſook him, he ſtill per-
' ſiſted, and, by loſing his life, approved his death
' worthy of his anceſtors, glorious to his poſterity?'
But upon Piſo theſe reaſonings had no influence.
After he had appeared for a ſmall ſpace abroad, he
retired to privacy at home, and was preparing his
mind to encounter a deliberate death, when at his
houſe arrived a band of ſoldiers, all young men,

either

either in years or service, purposely called by Nero, who dreaded the old soldiers, as tinctured with partiality for the conspirators. Then it was, that causeing the veins in both his arms to be broached, he expired. He left a will full of noisome flattery to Nero, thus framed in tenderness to his wife, a woman of vicious conduct, void of every recommendation save the beauty of her person, one whom he had ravished from her husband, a friend of his own, his name Domitius Sillius, and hers Arria Galla; and both concurred, he by his passiveness, she by her wantonness, to blaze the dishonour of Piso.

The next death added by Nero to this, was that of Plautius Lateranus, Consul elect, and inflicted with such precipitation, that he would not allow him to pay the last embraces to his children, nor that short interval wont to be indulged to the condemned, for choosing their own death. Instantly he was dragged to the place allotted for the execution of slaves, and there by the hand of Statius the Tribune slaughtered. He died full of exemplary firmness and invincible silence, nor once upbraiding the Tribune with an equal participation in the conspiracy. The bloody doom of Seneca followed, to the infinite joy of the Prince, from no proof that he had of his engagement in the plot, but to satiate his own cruelty, that the raging sword might perpetrate what had been by poison unsuccessfully attempted. For Natalis only had named him; but concerning him could discover no more than thus much, ' That he had been by Piso sent
' to visit Seneca, then indisposed, to complain in
' his name, that he himself was refused admit-
' tance; and withal to represent, that it would be
' better if they maintained their friendship in free
' and familiar intercourse; that to this Seneca re-
' plied, That the maintaining of frequent conver-
' sations

'sations and interviews by themselves was conducing to the service of neither, but upon the safety of Piso his own security rested.' Granius Silvanus, Tribune of a Prætorian Cohort, was ordered to represent all this to Seneca, and to demand of him, whether he owned the words of Natalis, and his own answers. Seneca had that very day, either from chance or foresight, returned from Campania, and rested at a villa of his, four miles from Rome: Thither arrived the Tribune in the evening, beset the villa with his men, and to him as he sat at table with Paulina his wife, and two friends, delivered his orders from the Emperor.

Seneca replied, 'That Natalis had, in truth, been sent to him, and in the name of Piso complained, that the latter was debarred from visiting him; a complaint which he had answered by excuses taken from his bodily disorder and desire of quiet; but still he never had any motive to declare, that to his own security he preferred the safety of a private man. A genius addicted to flatter, he never had, as no man better knew than Nero, who from Seneca had felt more frequent proofs of freedom than servility.' When this his answer was by the Tribune reported to Nero, in presence of Poppæa and Tigellinus, who were assistants to the raging tyrant, and composed his cabinet-council, he asked, whether Seneca were determined upon a voluntary death? The Tribune averred, 'That he had manifested no one symptom of fear, and neither in his words nor looks was aught of anguish to be discovered.' Hence he was commanded to return directly, and carry him the denunciation of death. Fabius Rusticus writes, 'That the Tribune took not now the same road which he came, but wheeling aside to Fenius, Captain of the guards, and disclosing the emperor's orders, demanded whether he should obey 'him,

'him, was by him admonished to pursue them.' Such was the fatal spiritlessness and timidity of all the conspirators! Silvanus too was one, and yet contributing to multiply the same bloody iniquities which he had conspired to avenge. He avoided however seeing Seneca, and delivering in person the sad message, but sent in a Centurion to apprize him of 'his final doom.'

The denunciation no wise dismayed Seneca, who called calmly for his will, and as this was prohibited by the Centurion, turning to his friends, he told them, ' That since he was disabled from a grate-
' ful requital of their benefits, he bequeathed them
' that which alone was now left him, yet some-
' thing more glorious and amiable than all the rest,
' the pattern of his life; if they retained the im-
' pressions and resemblance of this, they would
thence reap the applause of virtuous manners, as
' well as that of persevering in their friendship.' He withal repressed their tears, sometimes with gentle reasoning, sometimes in the stile of authority and correction, and strove to recover them to resolution and constancy. ' Where he often asked, where
' were now all the documents of philosophy, where
' that philosophical principle, for so many years pre-
' meditated, against the sudden encounter of calami-
' ties? For to whom was unknown the bloody nature
' of Nero? Nor, after the butchering of his mother,
' and the murdering of his brother, did aught remain
' to consummate his cruelty, but to add to theirs the
' slaughter of his nursing father and instructor.'

Having uttered these and the like reasonings, directed to the company in general, he embraced his wife; an affecting object, which somewhat abated his firmness, and softened him into anxiety for her future lot; he pressed and besought her to moderate her sorrow, to beware of perpetuating such ' a dis-
' mal passion; but to bear the death of her husband
' by

'by contemplating his life spent in a steady course
'of virtue, and to support his loss by all worthy
'consolations.' Paullina, on the contrary, urged
her purpose to die with him, and called for the
aid of a minister of death. Upon this declaration,
Seneca would not bereave her of so much glory;
such besides was his fondness for her, that he was
loth to leave one by himself beloved above all things,
exposed to insults and injuries: 'I had laid before
'thee, said he, the delights and solacements of
'living; thou preferrest the renown of dying; I
'shall not envy thee the honour of the example.
'Between us let us equally share the fortitude of
'an end to brave, but greater will be the splendor.
'of thy particular fall.' Presently after this conversation, both had the veins of their arms opened
at the same instant. Seneca was aged, his body
cold, and extenuated by feeble diet, so that the issues of his blood were exceeding flow; hence he
caused to be cut the veins also of his legs and those
about the joints of his knees. As he was succumbing under many grievous agonies, he persuaded
her to retire into another chamber, lest his own sufferings might vanquish the resolution of his wife,
or he himself, by beholding her pangs, lapse into
weakness and impatience; and his eloquence flowing even to the last moment of his life, he called
for his scribes, and to them dictated many things,
which being already published in his own words,
and common, I forbear to rehearse in any words
of mine.

Towards Paullina, Nero bore no personal hate,
and, to avoid feeding the public abhorrence of
his cruelty, ordered her death to be prevented.
Hence, at the persuasion of the soldiers, her domestic slaves and freedmen bound up her arms, and
staid the blood; but whether with her own concurrence is uncertain. For as the populace in

their cenfure are rather prone to malignancy, there were fome who believed, ' that, while fhe feared ' the wrath of Nero as implacable, fhe aimed at ' the applaufe of dying with her hufband; but, ' as foon as gentler hopes occurred, fhe became van- ' quifhed with the fweetnefs and allurements of ' life:' to which it is certain, fhe added but a fmall portion of years, ever retaining for the memory of her hufband a reverence worthy of all praife; her face too, and all her limbs, were ftill covered with fuch deadly palenefs, that it was notorious the principles of life had been in a great meafure exhaufted. Seneca, the while, afflicted with the tedious protraction of life, and the flow advances of death, befought Statius Annæus, one long proved by him for faith in friendfhip and fkill in medicine, to bring him a draught of the poifon, which a great while ago he had laid up in ftore, the fame fort which is ufed at Athens to difpatch fuch as are by the public judgment condemned: This he fwallowed, but in vain; for already all his limbs were chilled, all his juices ftagnated and impenetrable to the rapidity of poifon; he therefore had recourfe to a hot bath, from whence he befprinkled fuch of his flaves as flood neareft, adding, that ' of this liquor ' he made a libation to Jupiter the deliverer.' From thence he was conveyed into a ftove, and fuffocated with the fteam. His corps was burnt without any funeral folemnity; for thus in his will he had enjoined, even then, when in the plenitude of his opulence and authority, he had provided for his deccafe and obfequies.

A rumour there was, that Subrius Flavius, in a fecret confultation with the Centurions, and even with the privacy of Seneca, had determined, that, as foon as by the aid of Pifo, Nero was flain, Pifo too fhould be difpatched, and the Empire transfered to Seneca, as one exempt from all reproach, and only 'for the fame and refplendency of his virtues preferred to the fupreme dignity.' Nay, even the words faid to have been by Flavius then uttered, became current, ' That it would nothing avail towards abolifhing the public contumely, to depofe a Minftrel, if to the vacant purple a Tragedian fucceeded.' For as Nero was wont to fing to the harp, fo was Pifo to chant in the accent and drefs of tragedy.

Now neither could the fhare of the foldiers in the confpiracy be kept longer a myftery; fuch was the temptation and eagernefs of the difcoverers to betray Fenius Rufus, whom they could not bear both for an accomplice and inquifitor. Hence it was, that in the examination of Scevinus, while Rufus urged him to a full confeffion, with much vehemence and many menaces, the other fmiled, and told him, ' that in all the particulars of the plot, no man was more knowing than himfelf;' he even exhorted him, ' to make fuitable returns of gratitude to fo good a Prince.' To refute the charge, Fenius had not a fyllable to utter, nor yet would acquiefce in filence, but faultering and perplexed in his fpeech, expofed notorioufly his inward difmay. At the fame time the reft, chiefly Cervarius Proculus, a Roman Knight, combining with all their might to convict him, one Caffius a foldier, who for his fignal ftrength of body was appointed to attend the trials, laid hold upon him by the Emperor's order, and caft him into bonds.

In the detection made by the fame men, Subrius Flavius the Tribune was next fatally involved. At firft he aimed at a defence, and pleaded ' the diverfity of his profeffion and manners from thofe of the confpirators; for that, never for the execution of an attempt fo great and daring, would he, who is a man of arms, have leagued with fuch as were refigned to effeminacy, and never ' bore

'bore any.' But at last, finding himself pushed with questions and circumstances, he aspired to the glory of confession; and in answer to Nero, who asked him from what provocations he had slighted the obligation of his oath; 'I abhorred thee, said he, though, amongst all thy soldiery, none was more faithful and affectionate than I, as long as thou didst merit affection. With thy own detestable crimes my abhorrence of thee began, after thou hadst become the murderer of thy mother, the murderer of thy wife, a Charioteer, a Comedian, and the Incendiary that set fire to Rome.' I have repeated his very words; for they were not divulged abroad, like those of Seneca: nor less worthy to be known were the sentiments of a man of the sword, which, however artless and unpolite, are vigorous and brave. It is apparent, that this whole conspiracy had afforded nothing, which proved more bitter and pungent than this to the ears of Nero, who was abandoned to every black iniquity, but unaccustomed and too imperious to be upbraided afterwards with his flagitious doings. The execution of Flavius was committed to the Tribune Veinus Niger, and in the next field, by his direction, was digged a funeral trench, which Flavius derided, 'as too straight and shallow;' and, applying to the guard of soldiers, 'This, says he, is not so much as according to the laws of discipline.' Being admonished by the Tribune to extend his neck valiantly, 'I wish, replied he, thou mayst strike with equal valour.' In truth, Niger was totally overcome by a violent trembling, and hardly at two blows beheaded him; hence, to magnify his own cruelty, he boasted to Nero, that in putting him to death, he designedly employed more strokes than one.

The next example of constancy and fortitude was administered by Sulpicius Asper the Centurion, who,

who, in anfwer to the queftion urged by Nero, why he had confpired to kill him, faid in few words, ' Other relief there was none againft thy number- ' lefs and raging enormities;' and immediately underwent his prefcribed doom. Nor did the other Centurions deviate in bravery and fpirit, but gallantly faced death, and fuffered its pains In Fenius Rufus equal magnanimity was not found; nay, fuch and fo permanent were his unmanly lamentations and anguifh, that even in his laft will he bewailed himfelf. Great was the expectation which Nero was foftering, that Veftinus the Conful would prove likewife involved in the treafon, as he efteemed him a man of a violent fpirit, and prompted by virulent hate and difaffection. But to Veftinus the confpirators had imparted none of their counfels, fome influenced by ftale perfonal diftaftes, many becaufe they believed him a man altogether precipitate and untractable. But that which begot in Nero his enmity to Veftinus, was an intimate fellowfhip between them; from thence the latter throughly knew and fcorned the vile cowardly heart of the Prince, and the Prince dreaded the haughty and vehement temper of his friend, by whom he had been frequently infulted with poignant and difdainful farcafms, which, whenever they are feafoned with much truth, never fail to leave behind them a bitter and vengeful remembrance. A recent provocation had likewife occurred, Veftinus had taken to wife Statilia Meffalina, though he was aware that amongft her other gallants, Cæfar too was one.

When therefore there appeared no accufer to charge him, no crime to be charged, Nero, fince he could not fatiate his rancour, under the title and guife of a Judge, flew to the violence of a Tyrant. Againft him he difpatched Gerelanus the Tribune, at the head of five hundred men, with

orders,

orders, 'To obviate the attempts and machinations
'of the Conful, to take poffeffion of his houfe fo
'much refembling a citadel, and to fubdue his do-
'meftic band of chofen youths:' for the dwelling
of Veftinus overlooked the great Forum, and he
always kept a number of beautiful flaves, all of an
age. He had that day difcharged all the functions
of Conful; he was afterwards celebrating a banquet
at home, void of all fear, or perhaps, by the gaiety
of feafting, feeking to hide his fears, when the foldiers entered. They told him, the Tribune had
fent them to bring him; nor delayed he a jot, but
rofe from table, and in one and the fame moment
the hafty tragedy was begun and finifhed: he was
fhut up in a chamber, the phyfician attended, his
veins were cut, and, while yet full of life, and
his ftrength unabated, he was conveyed into a bag-
nio and fmothered with hot water; nor under all
this deadly denunciation and procefs did a fyllable
efcape him, importing the leaft regret or felf-com-
miferation. In the mean time, the whole company
who fupped with him were enclofed with a Guard,
nor releafed till the night was far fpent. Nero,
after he had reprefented to himfelf the confternation
of men, who from the joy of a feaft, were waiting
for their mortal doom, and had even made himfelf
fport with their fears, declared at laft, 'That they
'had undergone penalty fufficient for their Con-
'fular fupper.'

The next bloody fentence he pronounced, was
againft Lucan the Poet. He, while his blood if-
fued in ftreams, perceiving his feet and hands to,
grow cold and ftiffen, and life to retire by little and
little from the extremities, while his heart was ftill
beating with vital warmth, and his faculties no wife
impaired, recollected fome lines of his own, which
defcribed a wounded foldier expiring in a manner
that refembled this: The lines themfelves he re-
hearfed,

hearsed, and they were the last words he ever uttered. Thereafter Senecio, and Quinctianus, and Scevinus, suffered the violence of their fate, but with a spirit far different from the former effeminacy and voluptuousness of their lives. Anon too were executed the residue of the conspirators, without aught memorable done or expressed by them.

Now, when Rome was filled with deaths, and corses, and funerals, so was the Capitol with victims. One man had lost a son, one a brother, this a friend, that a kinsman; all fallen by the fury of the sword; and every man paid his public thanksgiving to the Gods, adorned his house with laurel, fell prostrate at the Emperor's feet, embraced his knees, and worried his right hand with kisses. He, who believed all this to be a sincere manifestation of joy, rewarded Antonius Natalis and Cervarius Proculus with pardon for their early confession and discovery. Upon Milichus was accumulated abundant wealth and recompence, and he assumed a Greek name, signifying *Protector*. Granius Sylvanus, one of the conspiring Tribunes, though he was acquitted, fell by his own hand. Statius Proximus, another, frustrated the Prince's pardon by vainly engaging afterwards in another offence, and dying for it. Of their commands next were bereft the following Tribunes, Pompeius, Cornelius Martialis, Flavius Nepos, and Statius Domitius, for no charge as if towards the Emperor they bore any malevolence, but only that they were dreaded by him. To Nonius Priscus, to Glitius Gallus, and Annius Pollio, all obnoxious from their friendship to Seneca, and rather calumniated than convicted, banishment was adjudged. Antonia Flacilla accompanied Priscus her exiled husband; and Gallus too was attended by his wife Egnatia Maximilla, a couple at first possessed of wealth mighty and unimpaired, afterwards dispossessed of all, and from both these

these different fortunes their glory was augmented. Into banishment too was driven Rufius Crispinus; a punishment for which the conspiracy furnished a pretence; but the real cause was the antipathy of Nero, and his crime, to have been once the husband of Poppæa. Upon Virginius and Musonius Rufus, their own signal renown drew the severity of expulsion: They had both engaged the affections of the Roman youth; Virginius by lectures of Eloquence, Musonius by reasonings upon the precepts of Philosophy. Cluvidienus Quietus, Julius Agrippa, Blitius Catulinus, Petronius Priscus, and Julius Altinus, as if a host had been formed of criminals convict, and their doom and numbers displayed, were all at once condemned to be transported into the Islands of the Ægean sea. Cæsonius Maximus, and Cadicia the wife of Scevinus, were exterminated Italy, and, only by suffering the punishment of crimes, learnt that ever they had been charged as criminals. The information against Atilla, the mother of Lucan, was dissembled, and, without being cleared, she escaped unpunished.

Nero having accomplished all these matters, assembled the soldiery, entertained them with a speech, distributed amongst them a largess of fifty crowns a man; and whereas hitherto they had been supplied with grain at the established rate, he allowed it them thenceforth without payment. Then, as if he had been about to recount to the Senate the feats and event of a war, he ordered the fathers to assemble. Upon Petronius Turpilianus the Consular, upon Cocceius Nerva, Prætor elect, and upon Tigellinus, Captain of the Prætorian Guards, he conferred the ornaments and distinction of triumph. Nay, to such notable eminence did he raise Tigellinus and Nerva, that, besides their triumphal Statues erected in the Forum, he would needs have their images placed likewise in the palace. To Nym-

Nymphidius he granted the Consular decorations; a man concerning whom, since his name now first occurs, I shall here recite a few particulars; for he too will have his share in the bloody calamities and vicissitudes of Rome. He was born of a manumised slave, who having a comely person, had prostituted the same to the domestics of the Emperors, bond and free, without distinction; hence he boasted himself the son of Caligula, seeing, like him, he happened to be tall of stature, and of a countenance stern and terrible. Or, perhaps, it is likely that Caligula, who was addicted to the embraces of harlots, had also descended to gallantries with the mother of Nymphidius.

Nero having thus assembled the fathers, and delivered a discourse concerning the late transactions, addressed an edict to the people upon the same subject, and published from records the several evidences against the condemned conspirators, as also their own confessions. He was, indeed, sorely reproached by a rumour current amongst the populace, ' That merely to satiate his malice, or out of ' base fear, he had sacrificed guiltless and illustrious ' men.' Yet, that there was a real conspiracy, concerted and grown to maturity, and at last detected and crushed, was no matter of doubt to such as were then curious to be truly informed, and even acknowledged by those of the conspirators, who, after the fall of Nero, returned from banishment to Rome. Now in the Senate, where every particular, the more sensibly he was pierced with anguish, the more fawnings and congratulations he expressed, Salienus Clemens fell upon Junius Gallio, already terrified with the death of Seneca his brother, and then a supplicant for his own life, charging Gallio with the character of ' a parricide ' and a public enemy,' till the fathers unanimously awed and restrained him. They advised him, ' That
' he

' he would not seem to take an advantage of the
' public calamities to gratify his own personal
' animosity; and since, through the clemency of
' the Prince, all matters were composed, or all
' faults cancelled, he would not revive staid pro-
' ceedings, nor open a new source of cruelty.'

And now it was decreed that ' public thanks-
' givings and oblations should be paid to all the
' Deities, and peculiar honours to the Sun, the
' God, who possessing an ancient Chapel in the
' Circus, the place intended for the perpetration of
' the parricide, had exposed to light the dark con-
' trivances of the conspirators; that the Circensian
' Games, exhibited to Ceres, should be solemnized
' with an extraordinary accession of horses and cha-
' riots; that the month of April should thence-
' forth bear the name of Nero, and to the Goddess
' *Salus* a Temple be erected in the place whence
' Scevinus had brought the dagger.' The dagger itself was by Nero dedicated in the Capitol, and inscribed, *To Jove the avenger* (*Jupiter Vindex*) words
which at that time were not minded. ' But, upon
the revolt of Julius Vindex, which afterwards happened, from them was then drawn a happy augury
and presage of approaching vengeance. In the
Journals of the Senate, I find that Cerialis Anicius,
Consul elect, when it came to his vote, proposed,
' That a Temple should with all speed be raised,
' at the charge of the state, and consecrated to
' the deified Nero;' a motion which he really meant
in compliment, as to one who soared above the
highest lot of mortality, and was entitled to celestial worship from men: but from whence too was
inferred an omen of his hastening fate, since to
Princes divine honours are never paid till they have
finally forsaken all commerce with men.

THE
ANNALS
OF
TACITUS.

BOOK XVI.

The SUMMARY.

False hopes of mighty Treasures in Africa, and thence the vanity, and wild prodigality of Nero. *He contends for the public prize at the Quinquennial Games. The death of* Poppæa, *and her royal funeral.* C. Cassius *and* L. Silanus *banished; the latter murdered, with several others. An uncommon tempest in Campania.* Anteius *and* Ostorius *doomed to die; as also* Mella, Crispinus, *and* Petronius. Thrasea Fætus *obnoxious to* Nero *for his distinguished virtue; thence accused and marked for destruction; as also* Bareas Soranus, *and his daughter* Servilia. *Her signal defence and tenderness towards her father. The remarkable behaviour and end of* Thrasea.

FORTUNE thereafter exposed Nero to public derision, through the intoxication of his own vanity, and the wild promises made him by Cesellius Bassus a Carthaginian, one of a restless

and

and chimerical spirit, who from the impulse of a nocturnal dream gathered certain high hopes, and sure of success, sailed to Rome, where, having by money procured access to the Prince, he set forth, ‘ That in his lands was discovered a cave of enor‑
‘ mous profundity, where lay immense store of
‘ gold, never reduced into form or coin, but in rude
‘ and ponderous lumps, such as were used by the
‘ ancients; that indeed the antiquity of the place
‘ was apparent in the structure and ruins, as here
‘ appeared heaps of huge massy bricks, there pil‑
‘ lars still erect; and all this wealth had for so many
‘ ages lain buried and reserved to multiply the riches
‘ and felicities of the present reign. For the rest,
‘ what could be learnt from conjecture was, that
‘ Dido the Phœnician, she who fled from Tyre, having
‘ founded Carthage, had buried this treasure, lest
‘ her new people might be debauched by excessive
‘ opulence, and become vicious and ungovernable;
‘ or lest the Princes of Numidia, who upon other
‘ accounts bore her malevolence, might from the
‘ ardent thirst of gold be instigated to make war
‘ upon her.’

This struck Nero, who little weighing the credibility of the account, or the faith and veracity of him that brought it, nor so much as dispatching inspectors to examine whether the particulars represented were true, heightened yet more the rumour of the discovery; and, as if it had been so much certain spoil already acquired, he sent over some to transport it to Rome, nay, to accelerate its arrival, furnished them with light galleys manned by sets of chosen and expert rowers. Nor did any other subject employ the conversation of the public at that time, while with the credulous multitude it passed for true, but from men of discernment met a different censure. And as the Quinquennial Games happened then for the second time to be in a course of celebration, the Poets and Orators, in their panegyrics upon the Prince, borrowed from thence their chief themes; 'for that ' the earth was no longer satisfied with yielding only ' her wonted bounties of fruits and grain, or gold, ' incorporated with other ore, but teemed in his ' reign with productions altogether new; and to ' him the Gods presented treasures already stored;' with many other fictions abounding in pompous eloquence, nor less remarkable for servile debasement and flattery, secure as they were of his prompt faith to believe whatever they could feign.

In the mean time, he rioted in prodigality without all measure, from these fantastical hopes, and utterly consumed his ancient treasures, as if others in their stead now spontaneously accrued, sufficient to supply him in a course of profusion for many years. Nay, out of this imaginary fund he was already distributing largesses; and the vain expectation of great riches became one of the causes of public poverty. When Bassus had perforated and hollowed all his grounds, with many adjacent fields, for a great compass round, hunting from place to place after the promised cave, which now he averred to be here, then to be there, attended not only with a number of soldiers, but by a multitude of boors employed as labourers in that work; he at last renounced his phrenzy, and wondering that his dreams had never proved false before, and that this was the first time he felt their delusion, discharged himself by a voluntary death from the agonies of shame and dread. Some authors say, that he was thrown into prison, and anon released, but his fortune seized in the room of this treasure Royal.

During the prosecution of this affair, as the time was at hand for disputing the prizes in the Quinquennial Games, the Senate, in order to avert in some degree the disgrace which Nero must incur by appearing a competitor there, offered to assert to him by decree 'the victory in Song;' nay even to adjudge him 'the crown of Eloquence;' meaning by such distinction from the fathers to throw a veil over his Theatrical debasement. But Nero declared, 'That he needed not the interposition 'and partiality of the Senate, nor any authority 'of theirs, since he himself was a match for all 'his competitors, and would only by the equitable 'determination of the Judges, purchase the just 'praise and recompence of his skill.' He then presented himself publicly, but first upon the Stage peculiar to the festival, and there rehearsed a Poem of his own composing; but anon, upon the clamour and importunity of the vulgar herd, 'that he would 'display to the public the whole fruits of his studies' (for this was the phrase which they used) he entered the Great Theatre and practised a sedulous obedience to all the laws of the Harp, such as not to sit down however fatigued, not to wipe the sweat from his face, save only with the vestment he wore, thence to keep dry his mouth and nose. In conclusion, bowing the knee and with his hands lifted up, paying veneration to the multitude, he awaited with fictitious awe the determination of his Judges. In truth, the commonalty of Rome, ever wont to humour and encourage the acting and gesticulations of common players; ecchoed their applauses of Nero with measured notes and symphony, and clapped in tune according to the rules of concert. You would have thought that they had really rejoiced, and it is probable their rejoicings were sincere, from an utter insensibility of public honour; or of the crying reproach which debased the Roman state.

But far different was the behaviour of such as dwelt in the municipal cities of Italy (for the countries of Italy as yet retained their primitive severity

and the sober manners of the ancients) as also of such as came from the remote Provinces, where they were unacquainted with the like wantonness and revellings, and attended then at Rome upon embassies, or their own private affairs; neither of these could bear this dishonourable spectacle, or were capable of discharging a task so unmanly; so that while, with irregular and aukward efforts in clapping, they marred the feats of the disciplined clappers, they were frequently bastinadoed by the soldiers, who stood in several clusters amongst the crowd, to watch that not a moment should pass either in unequal and ill-concerted acclamations, or in cold and lifeless silence. Certain it is, that many Roman Knights while they strove to retire, were through the straightness of the crammed passages, and the weight of the multitude, pressed to death; and that others, by never stirring night and day from their seats, were there seized with mortal maladies: for they dreaded even more than maladies the deadly consequence of their absence from this Imperial revel; since, besides the several concealed spies, there were a number of observers, who publicly noted names and faces, and all the symptoms of pleasure or melancholy in every particular of the assembly. Hence it was that, upon the vulgar and ignoble, instant pains were inflicted; towards those of illustrious quality his hate was for the present smothered, but soon after discharged in deadly vengeance. It was reported, 'That Vespasian was by
' Phœbus, Nero's freedman, bitterly reproached
' and even charged as a criminal, for having nod-
' ded, and hardly found protection even by the
' prayers and mediation of worthy and honourable
' friends: that perdition still hung over him; and
' he only escaped it by the grandeur of his ensu-
' ing destiny.'

The

The diversions of the Theatre were followed by the death of Poppæa, occasioned by a casual fit of passion in her husband, who killed her with a blow of his foot upon her pregnant womb; for to poison I cannot ascribe it, as some writers have done, rather through antipathy to Nero, than love of truth; seeing he vehemently coveted children, and was governed by a passionate fondness for his wife. Her corps was not consumed to ashes, according to the rites of the Romans, but after the manner of foreign Monarchs embowelled, and replete with spices, reposited in the sepulchre of the Julian family. Her obsequies, however, were publicly celebrated, and from the public Rostrum her panegyric was delivered by the Emperor, who magnified ‘ her beauty and happy lot, to have been the mo- ‘ ther of an infant, now enrolled amongst the Dei- ‘ ties,’ with many other blind endowments of fortune, which he enumerated as so many virtues. The death of Poppæa begat in Rome every appearance of sadness and mourning, but secretly instilled much joy into the hearts of all who remembered her lewdness and cruelty; and besides the reproach of this murder, Nero earned fresh detestation by forbidding Caius Cassius from assisting at her funeral, the first signal of his impending doom, nor was his doom long postponed. In the same fate Silanus too was involved, and each of them consigned to destruction, without guilt or offence in either; only that both were men of high and signal distinction; Cassius for his hereditary opulence and the exemplary gravity of his manners, Silanus for the ancient splendor of his race, and the popularity and eminent modesty of his youth. Nero therefore sent to the Senate a speech in writing, and in it argued for ‘ the necessity of removing both from any ‘ share in the administration of the state.’ To Cassius particularly he objected, ‘ That amongst ‘ the

'the Images of his ancestors, he preserved in high
'reverence that of Caius Cassius, thus inscribed,
'*The leader of the party*, for that he too was me-
'ditating the scheme of a civil war, and a revolt
'from the family of the Cæsars; but since in his
'design of exciting insurrections, he would not em-
'ploy only the influence of a name so obnoxious,
'he had engaged Lucius Silanus, a youth splendid
'in descent, of a tempestuous spirit, and one whom
'he set as a stale to produce and animate a public
'revolution.'

He fell afterwards directly upon Silanus himself, with great bitterness, urging against him the very same imputations which he had formerly objected to his uncle Torquatus, 'That already he assumed the 'port of a Prince, in his house had established offi- 'cers of Imperial state, and raised his freedmen to 'several dignities, some to be Auditors of the Re- 'venues, some to be Masters of Requests, others 'to be principal Secretaries;' ridiculous imputations, and as false as ridiculous! For dread of the pre- vailing tyranny kept Silanus under more awe and precaution, and from the late bloody doom of his uncle he had learnt a terrible lesson of circumspec- tion. Nero next prompted certain persons to assume the name of voluntary informers and forge an accu- sation against Lepida the wife of Cassius, aunt to Silanus, 'That with her nephew she had been 'guilty of incest, and in sacrifice had practised ma- 'gical rites of direful tendency.' As accomplices were seized and arraigned Vulcatius Tullinus and Marcellus Cornelius, two Senators, with Calpurni- us Fabatus a Roman Knight, men who, by appealing to Cæsar, did thence divert their instant condemna- tion; and as Nero was thenceforth intent upon more exalted atchievements in cruelty, they whom he con- sidered as smaller delinquents, entirely escaped his rage.

The Senate then proceeded to pronounce againſt Caſſins and Silanus ſentence of perpetual baniſhment; but to the judgment of Cæſar referred the puniſhment of Lepida. Caſſius was tranſported into Sardinia, and in regard of his great age, the ſhort remains of his life were ſpared. Silanus, under colour of ſending him away to the iſle of Naxos, was removed to Oſtia, and afterwards confined in Barium, a city of Apulia; while there, with the ſpirit of a wiſe man he ſupported a lot moſt unworthy of his virtue and innocence, a Centurion commiſſioned for the aſſaſſination laid hold on him, and adviſed him to cut his veins; he anſwered, ' That to die was the firm purpoſe of his ſoul, ' but upon an executioner he would not confer the ' glory of fulfilling that purpoſe.' Yet the Centurion perceiving him a man of great ſtrength, and though deſtitute of arms, reſolute and daring, and more diſpoſed to acts of wrath than thoſe of diſmay, ordered his ſoldiers to ſecure him: nor did Silanus fail to make vigorous reſiſtance, and to diſtribute blows with as much energy as by naked hands could be exerted, till at laſt he fell by the ſword of the Centurion, but under a multitude of wounds all received before, like thoſe of a brave man who falls facing the enemy in the day of battle.

Nor with leſs diſpatch and intrepidity did Lucius Vetus and his mother-in-law Sextia, with Pollutia his daughter, undergo their bloody doom. Towards them the Prince had long borne much vindictive rancour and hate, as thoſe whoſe lives were ſo many ſtanding reproaches upon him, for the murder of Rubellius Plautus, ſon-in law to Lucius Vetus. But the firſt handle for manifeſting this his hatred and cruelty was adminiſtered by a freedman of Vetus, his name Fortunatus, who having abuſed his truſt and defrauded his Lord, added malice to robbery, and became his accuſer. Into a partnerſhip

ship in this traiterons plot he assumed Claudius Demianus, one who for his villainies in Asia was by Vetus, then Proconsul there, sent in bonds to Rome, but now by Nero, in recompence of this his accusation, released. The accused, when he was apprized of this combination, and that against the credit of his freedman his life was staked, retired to a seat of his own in the neighbourhood of Formiæ, whither a Guard of Soldiers followed, and there secretly beset him; with him too was his daughter. She, besides the agonies which she felt from the present awakening peril, had a soul before sorely imbittered by a long course of sorrow, ever since she had first beheld the assassins sent to butcher Plautus her husband; and as she had passionately hugged his bleeding neck, she still preserved the garments stained by his blood, still persevered a widow, devoted to unrelenting grief and wailings, and a stranger to all nourishment, except what just saved her from the grave. Upon this occasion, at the request of her father, she travelled to Naples, and since she was denied access to Nero, she besieged his gates, and watched his coming forth, imploring him ‘ to hear the defence of an innocent ‘ man, nor to a traiterous freedman sacrifice one ‘ who had been once his colleague in the Consul- ‘ ship.’ And this her petition she continued to urge importunately, sometimes with the lamenting moanings of a woman, sometimes with a spirit surpassing her sex, and an accent vehement and imperious, till the implacable Emperor by his behaviour convinced her, that he was no more to be softened by distress and supplications than moved by the apprehensions of public odium.

Hence she reported to her father, ‘ That he must ‘ banish all hope, and meet a fate which he could ‘ not fly.’ Tidings at the same time arrived, ‘ That ‘ the Senate was hastening his trial and proceeding 'to a sentence terrible and merciless.' Nor were there wanting some who persuaded him to bequeath to Nero the bulk of his fortune, as the best expedient ' to secure the remainder to his grand-children,' a proposal by him rejected, nor would he stain the whole course of his life, spent almost in the fulness of liberty, by closing it with an act of servitude, but amongst his domestics distributed whatever sums of money were then in his possession, with orders, ' to appropriate to themselves and remove away whatever they found portable, leaving only three couches for the use of their corses.' Then all three opened their veins, in one and the same chamber with one and the same steel, and each covered for decency with a siugie rayment, were with dispatch conveyed into warm baths; the father's eyes intent upon his daughter, those of the old lady upon her grand-daughter, and hers upon both; all praying with emulation for a speedy issue of fleeting life, each wishing to expire first, wishing to leave behind such dear relations still alive, though hastening to die. Fortune observed the order of seniority and nature, the oldest first expired, and the youngest last. After they were buried they were accused, and voted to ' capital punishment according to the precedent of antiquity;' but against this Nero interposed, and would needs indulge them to die without prescription of form. Such were the instances of derision added to slaughters already perpetrated! Publius Gallus a Roman Knight, who had been intimate with Fenius Rufus, and not unacceptable to Vetus, was for such offence prohibited fire and water. To the freedman and accuser, in recompence of the meritorious pains and service, a place in the Theatre was assigned amongst the officers belonging to the Tribunes. And as the name of *April* was changed into that of Nero, so was *May* into that of Claudius, and *June* into that of Germanicus.

Germanicus. Cornelius Orfitus, from whose motion these alterations proceeded, declared, 'That he had therefore proposed abolishing the name of *June*, for that too of the Junii Torquati already executed for treason, had thence rendered that name abominable.'

This year, one stained with so many accumulated acts of tyranny and blood, was by the Gods too branded with devouring tempests and mortality. By the violence of whirl-winds, the country of Campania was ravaged, villages were overturned, the plantations torn up, the fruits of the earth scattered, and the extensive devastation carried as far as the neighbourhood of Rome; where, at the same time a fierce pestilence was, without any discernible malignity in the air, sweeping away all conditions of men. Full of corses were the houses, full of funerals the streets; nor sex nor age was spared by the impartial malady; to the same swift destruction yielded the bondmen and free, amidst the tears and wailings of their wives and children, who, whilst they were yet attending and lamenting their expiring parents and husbands, were themselves snatched away, and frequently burnt in the same funeral pile with those they lamented. As fast as the rest, perished illustrious Roman Knights and Senators, but less bewailed, since by a deadly contagion common to all, they escaped falling by the cruelty of the Prince. The same year recruits were raised in Narbon Gaul, and through Africa and Asia, for supplying the Legions in Illyrium, from whence had been discharged all such as were enfeebled by infirmity or age. To the inhabitants of Lyons, as a relief for their late calamity by fire, the Emperor presented a hundred thousand crowns, to repair the damages of their city, a sum once presented voluntarily by the Community of Lyons to Rome, during a time when she was under public distractions and embarrassment.

In the consulship of Caius Suetonius and Lucius Telesinus; Antistius Sosianus, one doomed, as I have above related, to perpetual exile for certain virulent verses by him composed against Nero, becoming afterwards apprized of the honour and distinction paid to informers, and of the Emperor's propensity to acts of rage and blood; being withal a man of a restless spirit, and no wise slack to embrace occasions of advantage, courted the friendship of Pammenes, and through the similitude of their lot obtained it. For Pammenes too was an exile of the same place, one celebrated for his science in the mysteries of Astrology, and thence engaged in numerous friendships. He judged, that without some important purpose so many messengers and so many quærists to consult him, could not be thus daily arriving, and learnt withal that from Publius Anteius a yearly stipend was allowed him; nor was it any secret to Sosianus that Anteius, for his zeal and attachment to Agrippina, was exposed to the malice and jealousy of Nero; that his opulence was sufficiently signal to stimulate that rapacious Prince, and that from this source only multitudes had suffered their deadly bane. With this view he intercepted letters from Antelus, and even stole the papers containing the calculations of his nativity, and the future events of his life, which were secretly kept in the custody of Pammenes. He besides found the scheme by him drawn concerning the birth and fortune of Ostorius Scapula, and then wrote forthwith to the Emperor, ' That might he obtain a short respite
' from banishment, he had mighty discoveries to
' communicate, such as were highly conducing to
' the personal safety of the Prince; for that An-
' teius and Ostorius were meditating some sudden
' attempt upon the state, and diving solicitously
' into their own destiny and that of Cæsar.' Immediately

mediately light pinnaces, were difpatched away, and Sofianus tranfported with expedition to Rome, where, upon the firft divulging of his difcovery, Anteius and Oftorius were by all men confidered rather already under the fentence of death, than fuch as were to be tried for their lives; infomuch that none dared appear to witnefs the execution of Anteius his will, till Tigellinus authorized it, having firft giving him warning, ' to lofe no time, but ' forthwith execute his laft teftament.' He then fwallowed a draught of poifon, but growing tired and impatient of its flow operation, accelerated his death by opening his veins.

Oftorius was then abiding at an eftate of his in a remote quarter of Italy, upon the borders of Liguria, and thither a Centurion was fent with orders to flay him with all difpatch. The motive for fuch precipitation, fprung from this fource; Oftorius was a man of a high military renown, diftinguifhed in Britain with a Civic Crown, of prodigious bodily ftrength, and from his experience in war eminently qualified for feats of arms: Hence Nero, who ever lived under continual dread, and fince the difcovery of the late confpiracy in the utmoft difmay and affright, was fcared, left that brave officer fhould take up arms and fall upon him. The Centurion, when he had befet with Guards every iffue from the villa, to prevent all efcape, acquainted Oftorius with his orders from the Emperor: Oftorius, without delay, upon his own perfon turned the edge of that bravery which he had fo often exerted with applaufe againft the foe; and feeing that from his veins, though largely opened, there flowed but little blood, he difpatched himfelf by a poynard, ufing fo far the help of one of his flaves, as to make him hold up the weapon fteadily; then grafping and ftrengthening the flave's hand with his own, he run his throat upon the fatal fteel.

Were I even recounting the rage of foreign wars and a series of deaths undergone for the Commonweal, in a detail of events and disasters, all like the above, resembling one another, I should doubtless succumb under the weary talk, and propose no other than to surfeit my readers, justly loathing a recital of the fall of citizens, however honourable, yet tragical and without end: Yet more irksome is the present work, in which such a deluge of blood tyrannically spilt at home, and the general and slavish passiveness under the Tyrant, are considerations that gnaw the soul and oppress it under anguish and sorrow. By such therefore as shall peruse this History, I desire it may be remembered (and it is the only apology I claim) that from no hatred of mine, but the duty of an Historian, I mention those who thus tamely submitted to perish: They perished, in truth, to satiate the vengeance of the Gods against the Roman State, which vengeance falling upon particulars, in a continued course of slaughters, its operations cannot justly be displayen in one general description, like the slaughter of armies or the storming and subduing of cities. To the posterity of illustrious Men let this occasional compliment be paid, that as they are not buried, like the common herd, but their obsequies distinguished from the promiscuous sepulture of the vulgar; so, by recounting the circumstances of their dying, they may receive and ever retain peculiar marks of remembrance.

For within the compass of a few days, Annæus Mella, Cerialis Anicius, Rufius Crispinus, and Caius Petronius, suffered, as it were all in a band, the violence of their fate. Mella and Crispinus were Roman Knights, in figure and estimation considerable as Senators; the latter particularly had been once Captain of the Prætorian Guards and distinguished with the ornaments of the Consulship,
but

but lately banished, as an accomplice in the conspiracy, into Sardinia, where, upon notice received that he was doomed to die, he slew himself. Mella, who was brother to Gallio and Seneca, forbore suing for the great offices of State, from a wayward ambition, that a Roman Knight might be seen to vie in authority with Senators of Consular dignity: He likewise judged that acting as Comptroller to the Prince, in the ministration of his private revenues, was a quicker road to wealth. Add, that he was the father of Lucan, a circumstance from whence accrued a vast accession to his fame and splendor; but after the untimely fate of his son, while with special sharpness and ardor he was recovering his effects, against himself he excited an accuser, Fabius Romanus, one of Lucan's intimate friends. He feigned, ' That in the conspiracy, the
' father and son were equally confederate;' and having counterfeited Letters, to this purpose, in the hand of Lucan, presented them to Nero, who after perusal ordered them to be carried to the accused, after whose riches he ravenously hunted. Mella anticipated his sentence by a passage to death, in those days, as the quickest, most frequently chosen, and broached his veins, when by will he had bequeathed to Tegellinus and his son-in-law Cossutianus Capito, an immense legacy in money, in order to secure the remainder. It is added, that in his will he inserted complaints concerning the rigour and iniquity of his doom, ' That he died guiltless
' of every crime deserving death, whilst Rufius.
' Crispinus and Anicius Cerialis, men virulently
' disaffected to the Prince, were suffered to live."
But all this was believed to have been a fiction, purposely framed to justify the execution of these two; for Crispinus was already slain, and over Cerialis the same bloody fate was impending: Nor indeed was it long ere he became his own executioner;

but fell with less commiseration then the rest, for that by him, it was remembered, had been disclosed to Caligula a plot concerted to destroy that Tyrant.

Concerning Caius Petronius some few particulars are to be recapitulated. He was one who in sleep wasted the day, and to the civil offices and gay delights of life devoted the night: As others by a course of pains and vigilance had acquired a name and character, Petronius was by signal idleness and indolence raised to notice and renown; nor yet was he esteemed either a prodigal of his fortune or a slave to his grosser appetites, like many who thus brutally lavish and devour their estates. Petronius was curious and refined in his luxury; and since his actions and sayings were frank and unrestrained, all accompanied with an air of negligence, the more so they were, the more pleasing they were, as bearing thence the impression of pure simplicity and artless nature. However, while he exercised the Proconsular Government of Bithynia, and presently after the Consulship itself, he manifested himself a man of spirit and vigour, and equal to great affairs; then relapsing into a habit of sensuality and vice, or affecting to appear vicious and sensual, he was by Nero associated with the select few, who composed his fraternity of intimates, and established master of elegance; insomuch that to the Emperor, in the midst of all his affluent enjoyments, nothing appeared delicious and ravishing, if it came not recommended by the taste and appobation of Petronius. Hence the hate and envy of Tigellinus towards one, in credit his rival, in the science of pleasures his superior. He had therefore recourse to the cruelty of the Prince, a passion to which all his other depraved appetites ever gave place. Against Petronius he objected an intimacy with the conspirator Scevinus, corrupted one of his slaves to accuse his master, precluded him from all

de-

defence, and to sudden bonds committed most of his domestics.

Nero happened at that time to be upon the road to Campania, and Petronius having accompanied him as far as Cuma, was there by order put under durance; nor would he longer bear to protract his fate, by humouring the impulse of hopes or fears; nor yet did he hastily throw away life, but ordering his veins to be cut, directed them again to be closed and bound, then to be opened by intervals, just as his fancy moved him, discoursing the while with his friends, but upon no subject serious or profound, nor in strains and sentences whence he could aim at the renown of magnanimity in braving of death. To them too he attended while they recited, no solemn sayings concerning the Immortality of the Soul, nor the Systems of Philosophers, but gay Sonnets, with Verses musical and flowing. With bounties he rewarded some of his slaves, with chastisements others: He even diverted himself with walking out, nay, refreshed himself with sleep, on design that his death, though in reality doomed, might appear like one altogether casual. Neither followed he in his last Will the example and stile of most, who perished like himself under the tyranny. Petronius flattered neither Nero, nor Tigellinus, nor any of the Partizans of power, but under the names of lewd women and pathics described all the secret abominations of the Emperor, with every practice of impurity by him used and admired as singular and new. To Nero he transmitted this picture of himself, carefully sealed, then broke his signet, that after his death it might not be perfidiously used and become a snare to the innocent.

While Nero was doubting and recollecting, by what means could be divulged all the various devices of lubricity in which he consumed the night,

N. 6 his

his fufpicion fixed upon Silia, one the better known for having married a Senator; one too by the Prince aſſociated into all the eſſays and diverſity of his pollutions, and thoroughly intimate with Petronius. On pretence therefore that ſhe had not concealed what ſhe had there ſeen and undergone, ſhe was doomed to baniſhment; a ſacrifice in effect to his own perſonal hate. To that of Tigellinus he made another, and to his vengeance ſurrendered Numicius Thermus, once Prætor, for that a freedman belonged to Thermes had uttered certain criminal imputations upon Tigellinus, an offence which the ſpeaker expiated under exquiſite torments, and his innocent Lord by a bloody doom.

After the ſlaughter of ſo many men ſignal in name and quality, Nero, at length, became poſſeſſed with a paſſion to hew down virtue itſelf, by devoting to butchery Thraſea Fætus and Bareas Soranus, both, long ſince, the objects of his hate: But againſt Thraſea he was incenſed from ſeparate cauſes, for that he had withdrawn from the Senate when the affair of Agrippina and the merits of her death came under debate there, as above I have remembered: In the ſolemnizing too of the preludes intitled *Juvenales*, he had manifeſted a behaviour far from courtly or acceptable; an indignity which pierced the Prince the deeper, for that Thraſea himſelf had, at Padua, the place of his nativity, chanted in the habit of a Tragedian, during the celebration of the Ceſtic Games, inſtituted there by the founder, Antenor from Troy. Moreover, when Antiſtius the Prætor was about to have been by the Senate condemned to execution, for a virulent Satire by him compoſed againſt Nero, Thraſea propoſed a mitigation of the ſentence, and carried it. Add, that when celeſtial honours were decreed to Poppæa, he was purpoſely abſent, nor afterwards attended her funeral: Offences which by Capito

Cossutianus were carefully saved from falling under oblivion: Besides the native bent of his spirit, abandoned to all feats of villainy, he bore special rancour towards Thrasea, since it was he who had supported the deputies from Cilicia in their charge upon Capito for extortion there, and by his credit obtained judgment against him.

To all these crimes of Thrasea's he added many more: 'He had avoided the solemnity of renewing
'at the beginning of the year the annual oath
'then taken to the Emperor; he had forborn to
'assist at the susception of yearly vows for the pre-
'servation and prosperity of the Prince, though he
'were at the same time invested with the Quinde-
'cemviral Priesthood: He had never made obla-
'tions for the safety of the Prince, nor for his voice
'divine. He who had been formerly so assidu-
'ous in attending, so indefatigable in affairs; he
'who was wont to interest himself in every decree,
'as a promoter or opponent of the most trivial and
'common, had not now in three years once en-
'tered the Senate. In an instance so recent as that
'of Silanus and Vetus, when the fathers assembled
'with such warmth and rapidity, to obviate and
'punish two men so dangerous, he only attended
'to the personal affairs of his clients. What else
'was all this but an open revolt, a party declared
'against the administration? and, if in many par-
'ticulars the same daring insolence were once found,
'what but a public war could ensue? As of old
'(pursued Capito) this city, one ever addicted to
'divisions and strife, was wont to discourse of Cæ-
'sar and Cato, as her two great chiefs and compe-
'titors then; so now with the same factious spirit
'it is discoursed of thee, Nero, and of Thrasea.
'Nay, he has his professed followers and partizans,
'or rather a body of champions at arms; men
'who in truth are not yet arrived to his boldness
'and

'and contumacy in counsel and speeches, but study
'an exact conformity to his mien and manners,
'to a behaviour rigid and melancholy, on purpose
'to upbraid thee for a life of gaiety and voluptu-
'ousness. To this man only is thy imperial life
'of no concernment; with him alone all thy ac-
'complishments pass unregarded: The events of
'thy reign the most prosperous, are by him treated
'with scorn; and is it not equally true, that with
'thy misfortunes and sorrows he is not satiated?
'Such is the contumacy of his spirit, that he would
'not believe Poppæa to be a Deity; and from the
'same spirit it proceeds that he would not swear
'to the validity and observance of all the public
'Acts of Julius Cæsar and of Augustus, Princes
'promoted to deification. It is thus he contemns
'the Worship of the Deities, thus cancels the
'Laws of the State. Through the Provinces and
'amongst the several Armies, the Journals of the
'Roman people are perused with the greater curi-
'osity and care, that thence may be learnt what
'transactions there are which bear not the name
'and sanction of Thrasea. In short, let us either
'embrace these institutions and politics, if they
'excel our own, or from a turbulent faction thirst-
'ing after innovations, let their Oracle and Lea-
'der be snatched away. Pupils and champions
'formed by the same sect were the Tuberones and
'Favonii formerly, names grating and grievous
'even to the ancient Commonwealth. It is only
'to subvert the Empire, that they use the fair sound
'and pretence of Liberty; if their evil purposes
'succeed, Liberty itself will be the next object of
'their violence. In vain hast thou banished Cassius
'from the State, if afterwards thou dost suffer a
'party, which emulate the Brutus's, to gather
'strength and numbers in it. For the rest, to the
'Senate and our management leave the judgment
'and fate of Thrasea, nor to that assembly do thou
'write

'wright aught about him.' Naturally furious was the soul of Coffucianus, and now further stimulated by Nero, who to him joined as his assistant in the accusation Marcellus Eprius, an Orator of great acrimony and vehemence.

The talk of accusing Bareas Soranus was already bespoke and undertaken by Ostorius Sabinus a Roman Knight, who arraigned his conduct in the administration of Asia, where he had governed as Proconsul with such signal vigilance and justice as thence to incur fresh jealousy and rancour from the Emperor. As another offence too, he had bestowed much pains about a popular work, that of opening the Port of Ephesus, and had besides left unpunished the Citizens of Pergamos for having resolutely opposed Acratus, one of Nero's freedmen, when he would have robbed their City of her pictures and statnes. These were his real crimes; those openly imputed were, ' his friendship with ' Plautus, and his intrigues to ingratiate himself ' with the Asiatics, in order to engage them in ' novel designs.' A particular juncture was chosen for awarding them their doom, that of the arrival of Tiridates to receive the Crown of Armenia; perhaps with design that, while the public attention and rumour were engaged in concernments from abroad, domestic iniquity and bloodshed might pass in quietness and obscurity; or perhaps Nero meant on this occasion to display the might and terrors of Imperial power, and the slaughter of illustrious men, as a feat of Majesty Royal.

Now while the whole City thronged out to receive the Emperor, and to behold a foreign King, Thrasea had orders to forbear attending the entry, yet was no wise cast down; but composed a Memorial to Nero: In it he besought to know ' the al- ' legations against him, and averred that he would ' vindicate himself, were he but apprized of the ' crimes, and had opportunity of clearing his inno-
' cence,'

‘ cence.' Nero received the Memorial greedily, as he hoped that Thrasea, under the influence of terror, might have written somewhat tending to magnify the grandeur and glory of the Prince, and to stain his own renown; but finding himself disappointed, and dreading withal the countenance, the spirit, and free speech of that great man, he ordered the Senate to be summoned. Thrasea then consulted with his friends and kindred, whether he should attempt a defence, or be silent. Their advices varied: They who counselled his repairing to the Senate, said ' That they were assured of his
' magnanimity there, and nothing would escape
' him, but what would procure him fresh glory.
' To the timorous only and the sluggard it belonged
' to hide the meanness of their end in shade and ob-
' scurity. It was fit the people should behold such
' a man going forth boldly to encounter death; it
' was fit the Senate should hear his words more
' than human, pronounced as it were by the mouth
' of some Deity, a miracle which might possibly
' soften even the heart of Nero. But though he
' should persevere in barbarity; yet surely in dif-
' ferent esteem with posterity would be the me-
' mory of a demise so worthy and distinguished,
' from that of such as chose stupidly to perish in
' passive silence.'

Those who gave different counsel, and were for his waiting the issue at home, acknowledged the same things of the behaviour and merit of Thrasea;
' but, if he went, over him was impending much
' cruel mockery, and many bitter contumelies;
' it behoved him to avoid having his ears assailed
' with invectives and the lashes of reproach. It
' was not Cossutianus only, nor Eprius that were
' prompt to outrages; there were others besides,
' who, perhaps, would assault him with violent
' hands and blows, to humour the savage brutality

' of the Emperor, and the precedent begun by the
' violent and bad, might, through dread, be fol-
' lowed even by the merciful and upright. He
' ought therefore to with-hold from that venerable
' body, which he had so long adorned, an occasion
' of so transcendent a wickedness and reproach,
' and to leave it to uncertainty and conjecture,
' what would have been the spirit and decree of
' the Senate, upon the seeing of Thrasea defend
' himself before them as a criminal arraigned. To
' hope that ever Nero would be moved to a sense
' of shame for his crying enormities, was rash and
' vain: Much more to be dreaded was his flying
' into fresh rage, and his discharging the same upon
' the wife and houshold of Thrasea, and upon
' every other object of his tenderness and care.
' Upon the whole; he ought to measure the glory
' of his latter end by that of the worthies, by whose
' steps and studies he had squared his life, and die
' in the strength of his integrity, in the fulness of
' fame.' In the consultation there assisted Rusticus
Arulenus, a young man of great spirit and fervour.
From this temper and a passion for fame, he offered to thwart the Decree of Senate, by interposing against it; for he was Tribune of the people.
Thrasea restrained his temerity, and cautioned him
against attempting ' methods in themselves wild,
' to the person accused unavailing; and to the per-
' son attempting them certainly fatal: For him-
' self, he had finished his course, and from the
' rule of life which for so many years he had with-
' out varying observed, he must not now depart.
' Into public offices Arulenus had but just entered,
' and upon his own choice it rested, how far to
' engage in transactions future: But it much im-
' ported him to weigh well before hand what path
' he ought to pursue, when during such times he
' engaged in offices of State.' For the rest, to the

result

result of his own meditation he left it, whether it were proper for him to appear in the Senate.

On the day following two Cohorts of the Prætorian Guards under arms environed the Temple of Venus the Prolific; a number of men dressed in the city robe, but armed with swords no wise concealed, had beset the entrance of the Senate; and in the great Squares, and several Temples, were every where posted bands of Soldiers in array. Through the midst of this scene of terror, and under the awe of objects so formidable and even menacing, the Senators passed to their assembly. There he, who was the Emperor's Quæstor, recited a speech by him sent, in which, without descending to name particulars, he upbraided the fathers, ‘ That they deserted the functions of the State, and ‘ from their example the Roman Knights too were ‘ lapsed into sloth and inaction. Hence what marvel, that Senators from the remote Provinces ‘ failed to attend, when many who had arrived at ‘ the Consulship, and been distinguished with Sacerdotal dignities, chose to withdraw from the ‘ publick, and rather to devote themselves to solitude ‘ and pleasant amusements in their Gardens?

This speech was as it were a weapon presented to the accusers, and greedily they snatched it. Cossutianus having begun the charge, it was by Marcellus pursued with greater acrimony and vehemence: ‘ The Commonwealth, the Commonwealth, he fiercely cried, was here concerned in ‘ her tenderest and most essential part: Such ‘ were the frowardness and contumacy of inferiors, ‘ that thence the gentleness and clemency of him, ‘ who bore rule, were checked and diminished: ‘ Over-mild and acquiescing had, to that day, been ‘ the temper of the Fathers, who could thus suffer ‘ so many capital criminals to evade chastisement, ‘ could suffer Thrasea so long revolted from public
‘ obe-

' obedience, suffer his son-in-law Helvidius' Priscus
' immersed in the same rebellious measures, Paco-
' nius Agrippinus too, one who possessed from his
' father an hereditary rancour towards the Empe-
' rors, with Curtius Montanus, employed in com-
' posing abominable Poems replete with treason.
' For himself, he wanted to behold Thrasea, him
' who had been Consul, now filling his place in
' the Senate; him who was a Pontiff, assisting at
' the solemnity where public vows were made; him
' who was a fellow-citizen renewing with the rest
' the oath of fidelity; unless he had already re-
' nounced every institution of our ancestors, civil
' and sacred, openly acted the Traitor, and now
' declared himself a public enemy. In a word,
' as he was wont to perform the part of an active
' Senator, wont to defend and protect such as had
' lampooned and defamed the Prince, let him re-
' sume his place, let him offer his sentiments, what
' he wished to have corrected, and what to have
' changed: Much more easily would they bear
' him carping at every particular transaction, than
' condemning by his sullen silence the whole admi-
' nistration at once. What was it that grieved him?
' Was it the profound peace established over the whole
' earth, or the public victories gained by our ar-
' mies without the loss of men? Far be it from
' the Senate to suffer such a man to gratify an am-
' bitiou so malignant and depraved, a man who sor-
' rowed for the felicities of the State, one to whom
' the public Places, the Theatres and the Temples,
' appeared so many desarts, wild and strange, and
' one who was continually threatening to relinquish
' his country and roam an exile. With him our
' Decrees here passed for none, our Magistrates for
' none; with him this Metropolis was no longer
' Rome. He ought therefore to cease to live in
' that City, since he had long since divested him-
' self

' felf of all tendernefs for her, and now could not
' bear her fight.'

As in thefe and the like flights of fury, Marcellus, even in his perfon horrid and grim, was raging againſt Thrafea, with eyes, voice, and vifage all on fire, the Senate no longer manifeſted that uſual air of fadneſs, which from the frequency of returning dread and peril, was become cuſtomary there: A terror altogether new, more deep and alarming poffeffed them, while to their light were prefented fuch a number of foldiers, their arms, and feparate bands. Their imaginations were alfo filled with the tragical lot of the perfon accufed, the venerable perfon of Thrafea: And there were who commiferated that of Helvidius, ' who muſt be doomed to
' puniſhment, merely for an alliance with a man
' void of blame. Againſt Agrippinus too what elfe
' was charged but the tragical fate of his father, a
' man who, in truth, had fallen himfelf an inno-
' cent victim to the cruelty of Tiberius. Nay,
' baniſhment muſt be the doom of Montanus, a
' young man and virtuous, for no Libel by him
' written, but purely becaufe by his Writings he
' had fignalized his genius and parts.'

In the mean while entered Oſtorius Sabinus, the accufer of Soranus, and againſt him urged ' the
' friendſhip between him and Rubellius Plautus;
' and that in his Proconfular adminiſtration of Afia,
' he had rather confulted his own popularity and
' luſtre than the public good and utility, by nou-
' riſhing animofity and tumults in the provincial Ci-
' ties:' Stale imputations, and long fince prepared by the accufer. But now he offered a recent charge, and in the crimes and peril of the father involved the daughter, ' That ſhe had with large fums feed
' the Magicians:' A tranfaction refulting purely from the paffionate tendernefs of Servilia (for this was the young Lady's name) towards her father, as
well

well as from the unwariness of her youth: Yet the whole of her consultation was; 'only upon the con-servation of her house, whether the wrath of Nero might not come to be appeased, and whether no tragical judgment would follow the cognizance of the Senate.' For this she was brought into the Senate; and before the Tribunal of the two Consuls, but at opposite sides, stood the father and daughter, he full of years, she under twenty, and, since the late banishment of Annius Pollio her husband, in a state of widowhood, solitary and sad. Her father's face upon this occasion she could not bear to behold, since she, as it seemed, had wofully heightened his danger and sufferings.

The accuser now questioned her, ' whether she had not turned into money her bridal Ornaments, and even stript from her neck her collar of jewels, in order to defray the expence of magic Rites and Sacrifices?' At first she cast herself down, and lay along upon the floor, then after a flood of tears, after long sobbing and silence, she rose, and embracing the Altars, particularly that of Venus; 'No mischievous Divinities,' said she, ' have I invoked; no incantations have I tried, nor was aught else the burden of my rash and disastrous supplications, than that thou Cæsar, and you Fathers of the Senate, would to this my dear and indulgent parent, beset with terrors and affliction, graciously afforded protection and safety. With this view I presented my jewels, my precious rayment, and other decorations peculiar to my quality; as I would have presented my blood and life, had my blood and life been required. To these Foretellers, men till now utterly unknown to me, it belongs to declare whose ministers they are, and what mysteries they use: By myself the Prince's name was not once pronounced otherwise than with those of the Deities.
' Yet

'Yet to all this proceeding of mine, whatever it 'were, my unfortunate father was an utter stranger; ' and if it is a crime, I alone am the delinquent.' These words alarmed Soranus, and while she was yet uttering them, he interrupted her; he cried out with earnestness, ' That his daughter went not with ' him to the Province, such too was her tender age, ' that she could have no possible acquaintance with ' Plautus: In the crimes of her husband she was ' no wife engaged; her only blame was that of ' filial piety over-strained: Let her cause be there- ' fore disjoined from his; his own fate, whatever ' it should prove, he was ready to undergo.' This said, he was hastening to embrace his daughter, who flew to meet him, but the Consular Lictors stepped between and prevented them.

To the witnesses next in immediate hearing was given, and however high the barbarous spirit of the accuser had already raised common compassion for the accused, equally high was the indignation excited by the appearing of Publius Egnatius as an evidence; a client and follower of Soranus, now bought with a price to overwhelm his patron and his friend. As he professed the rigid Sect of the Stoics, his testimony was from this circumstance to derive weight and consideration; for into such solemnity he had framed his countenance and whole exteriour, as to display the semblance of a man worthily disposed and virtuously employed, but possessed a foul traiterous and ensnaring, replete with avarice and every depraved appetite, all artfully concealed. But now the force of money, more prevalent than art, having laid open so much hypocrisy and imposture, furnished an instructive example, that as we guard against such as are branded for notorious frauds and contaminated with open villainies, so with no less care ought we to guard against men, who, under the fair guise of righteous life

life and acquirements, hide hollow hearts, alike prompt to profess and to betray friendships. On that same day, however, was exhibited a different and honourable example by Cassius Asclepiodotus, a man, for his signal opulence, of the foremost rank in Bithynia; yet without regarding what risk he incurred, the same devotion and reverence with which he had courted Soranus during the sunshine of his fortune, he ceased not to pay him, though now sinking under malignant fate. Hence he was despoiled of his whole fortune, and doomed to exile. Such was the lukewarmness and indifference of the Deities, alike unmoved by patterns of righteousness and those of iniquity. To Thrasea, to Soranus, and Servilia, was granted the choice of their own deaths: Helvidius and Paconius were to be banished from Italy: Montanus, for the sake of his father, had his pardon, with an exception annexed, 'That he should never be admitted to any 'Office in the State.' To Eprius, one of the accusers, was decreed a reward of more than thirty thousand pounds, to Cossutianus another, the like sum; and to Ostorius the third, as many thousand crowns, besides another recompence, that of the ornaments of the Quæstorship.

The Quæstor attending the Consul was, now in the close of the day, dispatched to Thrasea, then in his gardens. He was at that instant frequented by a numerous assembly of men and women, illustrious for their quality, but was chiefly attentive to Demetrius, a professor of the Cynic School: With this Philosopher, as far as could be conjectured by the intenseness of his looks, and by certain words, which, when they happened to raise their voices, were over-heard, he was reasoning and inquiring about the nature of the Soul, and concerning its departure from the body, till he was interrupted by the arrival of Domitius Cæcilianus. This was

one

one of his moſt intimate friends, and related to him what the Senate had decreed. As upon theſe ſad tidings the company melted into plaints and tears, Thraſea preſſed them 'forthwith to retire, 'nor to tempt danger by involving themſelves in 'the fate of a perſon condemned:' And as Arria his wife was earneſt to emulate the example of her mother, and to ſhare with her buſband in his laſt lot, he beſought her, ' to preſerve her life, nor ' deprive their common daughter of her only re- ' maining refuge.'

He then went forth into a gallery, and there the Quæſtor from the Senate found him, filled rather with cheerfulneſs than with any oppoſite paſſion, ſince he had learnt that againſt Helvidius his ſon-in-law, nothing worſe was decreed than his baniſhment from Italy. Having now had delivered to him in form the ſentence of the Senate, he took Helvidius and Demetrius into his chamber, and extending both his arms, the veins of both were cut: As the blood ſprang, he called the Quæſtor nigher, and with it beſprinkling the floor; 'Let us, ſaid he ' to him, make this libation to Jove the Deliverer. ' Look here, young man, and conſider; may Hea-' ven too grant there be no Omen in my words: ' But into ſuch times thy birth and age have thrown ' thee, as may juſtly require thee to fortify thy ' ſpirit by examples of magnanimity.' After this, as from the ſlow approaches of death grievous torments were enſuing, he turned towards Demetrius * * * *

The reſt of this Annal is loſt.

END of the SECOND VOLUME.

7256

University of California
SOUTHERN REGIONAL LIBRARY FACILITY
Return this material to the library
from which it was borrowed.

REC'D LD-URL

APR 1 9 1990